Acid House
THE TRUE STORY

Luke Bainbridge

OMNIBUS PRESS
London / New York / Paris / Sydney / Copenhagen / Berlin / Madrid / Tokyo

Exclusive Distributors
Music Sales Limited,
14/15 Berners Street,
London, W1T 3LJ.

Music Sales Corporation
180 Madison Avenue, 24th Floor,
New York,
NY 10016,
USA.

Macmillan Distribution Services
56 Parkwest Drive
Derrimut, Vic 3030,
Australia.

Every effort has been made to trace the copyright holders of the photographs in this book but one or
two were unreachable. We would be grateful if the photographers concerned would contact us.

Typeset by Phoenix Photosetting, Chatham, Kent
Printed in the EU

A catalogue record for this book is available from the British Library.

Visit Omnibus Press on the web at www.omnibuspress.com

Contents

Cast Of Characters

In order of appearance:

Terry Farley, DJ and founding member of *Boy's Own* (which became the in-house magazine of acid house)

Trevor Fung, DJ and promoter of The Project Club and others

Paul Oakenfold, DJ and recording artist, founder of The Project Club, Spectrum, Future and Perfecto Records. Remixed everyone from Happy Mondays to U2

Andrew Weatherall, DJ and producer. Founding member of *Boy's Own* and producer of Primal Scream's classic 1991 album *Screamadelica*

Boy George, singer with Culture Club and later house DJ

Greg Wilson, first specialist dance-music DJ employed by The Haçienda

Mark Moore, DJ, resident at Heaven and other clubs, and the man behind S'Express

Robin King, Delirium promoter and DJ

Noel Watson, resident DJ at Battlebridge Road and Delirium with brother Maurice

David Dorrell, DJ and member of M/A/R/R/S, who had a 1987 number one with 'Pump Up The Volume'

Nicky Holloway, DJ and promoter at Special Branch, Doo At The Zoo, The Trip, Milk Bar and others

Cymon Eckel, promoter and founding member of *Boy's Own*

Eddie 'Evil' Richards, DJ at Camden Palace, RIP and others

Tony Wilson, co-founder and director of Factory Records, TV presenter and impresario

Shaun Ryder, lead singer with Happy Mondays and Black Grape, reality TV star; his autobiography, *Twisting My Melon*, is out now

Mike Pickering, DJ and booker at The Haçienda, founding member of Quando Quango, T-Coy and M People

Bill Brewster, DJ, co-editor of DJ History website and co-author (alongside Frank Broughton) of the book *Last Night A DJ Saved My Life: 100 Years Of The Disc Jockey*

Jazzy M, DJ, radio presenter, record shop and record label owner

Winston Hazel, DJ at Jive Turkey

Justin Robertson, DJ at Spice, Most Excellent and others, and founding member of British big-beat group Lionrock

Mike Knowler, DJ at The State

Danny Rampling, DJ and founder of Shoom

Carl Cox, DJ and sound system owner, now has his own stage at Ultra Music Festival, Tomorrowland and Electric Daisy Carnival

Steve Hall, *Boy's Own* member

Mr. C (Richard West), DJ and rapper with The Shamen

Steve Adg, Stone Roses tour manager and co-founder of Blackmail Records

Graeme Park, DJ at The Garage and The Haçienda

Judge Jules, DJ, ex-BBC Radio 1 DJ and part-time entertainment lawyer

Andrew Barker, DJ, member of Spinmasters, Hit Squad Manchester and 808 State

Darren Partington, DJ, member of Spinmasters, Hit Squad Manchester and 808 State

Graham Massey, musician and member of Biting Tongues, Hit Squad Manchester, 808 State and Toolshed

Arthur Baker, legendary New York producer and DJ

Rene Gelston, founder of Black Market Records

Jon DaSilva, resident DJ at The Haçienda and musician

Damian Harris, DJ and founder of Skint Records

'Kid' (Lawrence) Batchelor, DJ at Hedonism, member of Bang The Party

Eric Barker, early rave promoter and manager of K-Klass

Alfredo, legendary Ibiza DJ

Johnny Walker, DJ and promoter

Richard Norris, DJ and musician, founding member of electronic dance group The Grid

Chris Butler, Shoom/Trip regular, now manages Underworld, X-Press2 and Steve Mason

Timna Rose, Shoom regular

Anthony Donnelly, rave organiser and co-founder of Gio-Goi fashion label

Chris Donnelly, rave organiser and co-founder of Gio-Goi fashion label

Dave Haslam, journalist and DJ at The Haçienda

Sasha, DJ and artist, "The world's first DJ pin-up" (*Mixmag*)

Wayne Anthony, promoter of Genesis raves

Anton Le Pirate, clubbing face and promoter

Des Penney, manager of Flowered Up

Russell Morgan, DJ and founding member of K-Klass

Paul Roberts, DJ and founding member of K-Klass

Fabio, BBC Radio 1 DJ

Paul Cons, Haçienda promoter

Paul Mason, Haçienda manager

Fiona Allen, Haçienda staff member, writer and star of comedy sketch show *Smack The Pony*

John McCready, Haçienda DJ and journalist for *The Face*

Billy Caldwell, Haçienda regular and later DJ

Karl Brockbank, Haçienda regular

Chris Jam, DJ, one half of The Jam MCs and licensee of Konspiracy

Darren Greene, DJ and member of the group MVITA ("Manchester Vibes In The Area")

Chris Goodwin, Haçienda regular and member of Manchester rock group The High

A Guy Called Gerald (Gerald Simpson) DJ, member of Hit Squad Manchester and 808 State before going solo

Sarah Champion, journalist and author of *And God Created Manchester*

Leo Stanley, founder of Identity clothing, Manchester

Charlie Colston-Hayter, sister of Tony Colston-Hayter, promoter of Apocalypse Now and Sunrise

Steve Redhead, academic and author

Moonboots (Richard Bithell), DJ and Haçienda regular

Suddi Raval, founding member of rave group Together

Jeremy Taylor, co-promoter of the Biology raves

Andy Spiro, co-founder of Sankeys Soap nightclub, later joined Bugged Out club night

Drew Hemment, DJ at The Twilight Zone and academic

Steve Proctor, DJ at Promised Land, Shoom and many of the early raves

Quentin Chambers, co-promoter of the Biology raves

Paul Rutherford, member of pop group Frankie Goes To Hollywood, then solo artist, releasing acid-house cult classic 'Get Real' in 1988

Ken Tappenden, head of the police's Pay Party Unit

Bobby Gillespie, founding member and lead singer of rock group Primal Scream

Greg Fenton, DJ at Spice and Most Excellent

Mekon (John Gosling), DJ at The Tunnels and musician

Luke Howard, DJ at Horse Meat Disco and others

Johnno, DJ and co-founder of *Jockey Slut* magazine

Fred (pseudonym), promoter and small-time drug dealer

Irvine Welsh, author and scriptwriter whose books include *Trainspotting* and *Ecstasy*

Peter Hook, founding member of Joy Division and New Order, part-owner of The Haçienda

Martin Fry, founding member of New Romantic pop group ABC

Introduction:
The Second Summer Of Love

The summer of 2013 marked the 25th anniversary of the zenith of Britain's last youth culture revolution – the explosion of acid house, which became christened the second Summer of Love. A quarter of a century on it is clearer than ever that acid house was the UK's greatest music revolution since the birth of rock'n'roll – a seismic, explosive movement which changed the face of music and youth culture irrevocably. The arrival of a new music and a new drug fuelled the biggest youth revolution since the Sixties, and altered the cultural landscape forever. Forget punk. Forget grunge. Forget everything. Acid house was the most spectacular and dramatic youth movement, and had an infinitely bigger, more devastating and far-reaching impact. Unlike punk, acid house transcended class, race, geographical and cultural divides – strangers and soul mates, black and white, straights and gays, girls and boys, north and south, football hooligans and doctors, cops and robbers, students and scallies. Acid house was truly egalitarian. It was also one of those moments of paralysis that happen perhaps once a generation, where barriers seem to fall.

Within little more than six months, the scene had gone from a few pockets of clued-up clubbers to a nationwide explosion and warehouse parties holding 20,000 ravers. For a while, the weak became heroes and everybody felt love. Every generation is desperate for something to call their own, something their parents don't understand. Acid house was *so* new your older brother didn't understand it, let alone your parents. The established industry had no idea what it was dealing with and those who couldn't keep pace with the rapidly changing times looked and sounded like dinosaurs. "It's the closest thing to mass organised zombie-dom," frowned BBC Radio 1 DJ Peter Powell, the 'nation's favourite station's' dance-trend arbiter and roadshow veteran. "I really don't think it should go any further."

Powell couldn't have been more mistaken. The acid house revolution, which started in basements, warehouses, under railway arches and outdoors in fields (and in one case, in a subterranean fitness gym), had gone much, much further than even the most evangelical early devotees could have imagined. It changed the social and cultural habits of a generation and every following generation, and the fundamental notion of a night out in this country. It challenged authority, prompting Parliament to pass new laws aimed at curbing the revolution, and the police to establish a new unit dedicated to stopping unlicensed parties. Acid house was the perfect storm. The shattering collision of new technology (samplers, drum machines and mobile phones) and a new drug (ecstasy) combining to produce a new musical and evangelical youth movement which swept aside everything that had gone before.

On the 25th anniversary of 1988's 'Second Summer of Love', the time felt right to ask the key protagonists who led the revolution to tell the true story of how it all unfolded and how they view it a quarter of a century on. From the DJs and musicians in the limelight to the promoters and more nefarious elements in the shadows, to those on the dance floor who fuelled the revolution, this is their story.

But as well as telling the true story of the birth of acid house in this country, I wanted to ask them about its legacy and lasting impact. Why has the free party scene never really been replicated, despite new technology heralding greater capacity to organise events and disseminate information? How did the change in drugs, away from ecstasy towards other, harder drugs, affect the music and the party scene? Has there been any lasting effect of such an explosion in drug use? Who were the real winners and casualties in the story? How do the biggest DJs today view that time 25 years on, now that acid house has been assimilated into mainstream culture?

warehouse parties in London and there were about 500 people there and it was really fantastic, although I suspect we ourselves were pretty shit as we were hardly technically proficient and hardly anyone was mixing back then. But we ended up playing a few of those Demob parties.

NOEL WATSON: We then started the Battle Bridge Road parties with two guys called Julian Woolley and Sean Oliver, who was in Rip Rig + Panic with Neneh Cherry. Battle Bridge Road was a squat in Kings Cross in a disused school and we did a party there every week for about a year. Sean's brother, Andrew, and Neneh Cherry would do the bar for us. We'd give them £500 on a Friday and they'd go to a cheap Indian store in Acton and get all the booze and set it all up. There were no real lights because it was an illegal venue. We were charging £9 to get in so we were making quite a lot of money, but that caused us a lot of problems as well because there were quite a lot of people involved who were all taking money out, so there was a bit of friction.

[DJ] Nellee Hooper and the Wild Bunch* boys would also come down to Battle Bridge, and Jazzie B from Soul II Soul and his lot. Joe Strummer was there all the time and even John Lydon would come down occasionally. The music was cutting edge because we had our own decks set up by then so we were cutting breaks properly, and Maurice was a brilliant cutter, mixer and scratcher.

By this stage we were properly crate digging and searching out records. Malcolm McLaren would come down and give us cassette tapes of Zulu Nation playing on the New York radio station Kiss FM, and we would listen to them and try and track down the tunes that DJs like Red Alert and Afrika Islam were playing. That's also how we first started hearing house records, on those cassettes, because the Kiss FM DJs on just before Zulu Nation were Tony Humphries and Merlin Bob, and they would be playing stuff like D-Train and O'Jays but cutting them and extending them, and they would blend them with early house

---

* Wild Bunch were a DJ collective from Bristol, who included the future members of Massive Attack.

records, which was the first time we heard it. Maurice became obsessed with this music and he ended up shooting off to New York to find out more about it.

There was no ecstasy at the Battle Bridge Road parties. There was a bit of amphetamines and dope and a wee bit of cocaine as well, but the big drug there was heroin, which became an issue. The real problem we had was dealers dealing heroin in the girl's toilets – that was one of the reasons we had to curtail things a bit at Battle Bridge, and why the police started to come down on us heavily.

DAVID DORRELL, DJ/MEMBER OF M/A/R/R/S:* I grew up in Bloomsbury in central London, so everything was a five-minute walk for me. When I was young, the Blitz club was happening in Soho and that was a five-minute walk from my door. Then when I started DJing we used to throw parties at the famous squat on Battle Bridge Road, five minutes in the other direction. There were quite a few great warehouse parties around; there were also the Demob parties in a basement off Rosebery Avenue, which were run by Chris Brick with Noel and Maurice. The Dirtbox parties were also around then and I got to meet Rob Milton and Phil Dirtbox. They were doing their illegal parties in various holes around London and they also had a legal club night on Oxford Street, which was on a Thursday. I DJ'd for them at various parties, including one in a disused power station near Battersea Bridge. Jay Strongman was a big DJ back then, as was Norman Jay with his Shake'n'Fingerpop night, and Steve Lewis at Le Beat Route.

NICKY HOLLOWAY, DJ: I first started DJing in the late Seventies at home. I would wait until my mum went to work and then sneak back in the house when I was supposed to be at school. She had one of those old box record players where the record drops down, and I had one the

---

* M/A/R/R/S had a number one hit in many countries with their only single, 'Pump Up The Volume', widely recognised as being an influential and significant milestone in acid house music.

same, so I would get them and put them next to each other and practise playing two records.

I saw an advert in *Record Mirror* that said, "DJs wanted, beginners considered," so I replied and got a couple of interviews with a guy called Mervin Thomas who ran an agency called Rainbow – I think he still runs a strip bar on Shoreditch High Street under the same name. It took me three interviews before he gave me my first job. In those days no one was interested in whether or not you could mix; they just wanted to hear if you could give it all "Here we go, ladies and gentleman!" and put on a good Tony Blackburn-type voice. I used to get £6 a night, which wasn't bad money then, and sometimes I could earn as much as £12.

By the early Eighties, a lot of local villains in south London were spending their ill-gotten cash doing up shitty pubs into cocktail lounges and getting 2a.m. licences. I worked quite a lot of those and it was a learning curve, as I didn't quite realise the sort of people I was working with at first. I even ended up DJing at the Krays' associate 'Mad' Frankie Fraser's coming out [of prison] party.

But I was more of a soul boy, and I managed to start to build myself up in the soul scene, which was dominated by people like Chris Hill and Robbie Vincent and the Caister Soul Weekenders. I became a bit of a thorn in their side because I started something called Special Branch in 1983, which sort of fused the two worlds existing at that time – the trendy West End boys and the suburban soul boys; Special Branch was somewhere between the two and it worked. I would take DJs from the trendy West End clubs, like Jay Strongman, Rob Milton, Jonathan Moore and Dave Dorrell, and the young DJs from the soul scene, like Pete Tong and Gilles Peterson.

Special Branch started at the Royal Oak on Tooley Street [on the southern bank of the Thames in Bermondsey], which was just desolate then: it was a No Man's Land, just dead. We opened until 2a.m. because there were no neighbours. The resident DJs were me and Pete Tong downstairs, who would play rare groove, funk and soul, then later we would start to play early house records, and Gilles Peterson upstairs, playing more jazzy stuff. We had a really cool crowd, all in their mid twenties.

As it got better we started doing parties at London Zoo, which were called Doo At The Zoo, and also some great big parties at places like the Natural History Museum. We also did a couple of Special Branch holidays to Ibiza, long before acid house hit. We were doing parties in Café del Mar before anyone else knew it existed – back then, it was where the Spanish went to get away from the British in San Antonio.

TREVOR FUNG: Paul Oakenfold and I started a club night in 1983 at a place called Ziggy's on Streatham High Street on a Friday. We had a guy called Carl Cox as our warm-up DJ – he ended up being with us for nine years – and guests like Gilles Peterson. The club changed its name at various times to The Funhouse (after The Funhouse in New York which we'd been to when we were over there) and, later on, The Project.

I was working for a guy called Felix who owned Fred & Ginger's on Old Burlington Street, and out of the blue he came in one day and told me he'd bought the club Amnesia in Ibiza, and said, "Do you want to go and work in Ibiza?" So I went out there in the summer of 1983 as the resident DJ, but it was dead and in the end he said, "I'm going to close it." I then starting working at Star Club, which was opposite [club] Es Paradis. I spent all summer out there and got to know lots of people in the bars and clubs. Then I came home for the winter and would go back to the soul circuit, and began playing things like Nicky Holloway's Special Branch.

★

In the North of England, the musical climate was very different. The 'rare groove' scene that had a stranglehold on London hardly made a dent beyond the capital city, while much of the North's soul music came from a more rhythmic, four-to-the-floor northern soul background. On top of this, the arrival of electro had a bigger influence on the underground dance scene in the North than it did in London and the South.

GREG WILSON: The rare groove scene was a London scene. It was very important, that whole scene, particularly the pre-acid house warehouse scene which was going on down there, but that wasn't what was happening in the North and Midlands. There may have been the odd rare groove night, but what happened there was a direct continuum from electro into house and techno.

It annoys me a bit when people think there's a straight link from northern soul to acid house in the North, the argument being northern soul equals dance all night, fast music and drugs and acid house equals dance all night, fast music and drugs. But there was a seven-year gap between Wigan Casino shutting and acid house taking off, so you're missing a seven-year chunk of musical history, and what you're missing out is the influence of the black music crowd in laying the foundations for acid house in the North. Black kids were never really into northern soul – check out any of those videos of Wigan Casino and you'll only see a few black kids there.

I started out DJing in Liverpool, but it was hard to play black music there in the early Eighties after the Toxteth riots because club owners were wary about attracting that sort of crowd. So I spent a couple of years DJing abroad before coming back to the UK and getting a gig at Wigan Pier, which was a hugely important club then. We had a huge crowd from all over the North coming to listen to electro.

Then I moved to Legends in Manchester, which was an incredible club. There was a little 17-year-old sharp-arsed kid called Kermit, who was a great dancer, a jazz dancer, and a face on the scene even then. Kermit came up to me in Legends and told me he'd got a breakdance crew together called Broken Glass who were dancing in Piccadilly Gardens. So I got involved with them and organised what I called a 'Street Tour' of the Northwest. We'd go to shopping centres in Widnes, Liverpool, Birkenhead or Blackpool. We'd just turn up with a ghetto blaster, the crew of about 12, and they'd start dancing, but I would ring up the local newspaper before and say, "There's this new thing happening in New York and we're bringing it to Birkenhead." It just developed from that. They got more organised and we started getting club bookings and then TV. The first thing we did was *Granada Reports*, which was late '83. Then by '84 I had moved to [Manchester club] The Haçienda, and we did *The Tube*, on the same show as Madonna making

13

her UK TV debut, and then we did the Haçienda Revue, which was myself, Quando Quango* and Broken Glass.

★

At the time, the drug of choice for many young clubbers was acid. One West London circle of friends including Andrew Weatherall and Cymon Eckel, who together would later launch acid house fanzine *Boy's Own*, and their mate Phil Goss, who went on to run Evisu jeans, developed a ritual of dropping acid simultaneously at 9p.m. on a Friday night. It became known as 'The Nine O'Clock Drop'. The friends would listen to a mixtape Weatherall had made, a precursor to the Balearic mix that would later play at key acid house clubs like Shoom. Nearly two decades later, Weatherall re-created the mixtape and released it as the compilation album *Nine O'Clock Drop*.

ANDREW WEATHERALL: The very first time I took acid in the early Eighties, I thought, "Right, this is not to be fucked with," and I went to the library and took out every book on acid I could – psychology, physiology – and read up on it. Well, not when I was on acid, obviously, but a few days later. Unfortunately for me, when acid house came along it became known that I knew about acid. So I could be on the dance floor at half four in the morning and someone would come and find me and say, "Oh, Splodger's having a bad trip, can you come and sort him out?" and I'd have to go and see Splodger, or Bodger or Todger, or whatever he was called – some nefarious ne'er-do-well – and talk him down from his bad trip. That was how me and Nina [Walsh, fellow musician] first got together. I'd known her for a while, but that's how we became an item because we spent five hours in a car together, with me talking her down from a bad trip.

---

* Quando Quango was formed by Mike Pickering, Hillegonda Rietveld and Reinier Rietveld, and signed to Factory Records. They are best known for their track 'Love Tempo', which reached number four on the US *Billboard* Dance Chart and was a big record at the Paradise Garage in New York City, where they were asked to perform it live.

Myself, Cymon Eckel and Phil Goss, an old schoolfriend of mine, would drop a tab of acid at nine o'clock even if we weren't together because we knew we'd end up meeting later and Cymon would drive into town. The test of whether the acid was working was when we drove past Heston Services [on the M4 motorway in the London Borough of Hounslow]. There was a kiddies, playground there that had a slide which looked like a tree with a face on it. If we drove past and the tree was talking to us, we knew the acid was working.

Acid is quite hairy. I don't do it anymore because I'm more aware of my own mortality, but in my late teens and early twenties I wasn't so aware. We got a puncture on the M4 once and we were all tripping and I was literally wandering around in the fast lane of the motorway and Phil Goss, in a moment of clarity, pulled me out of the way of a car and I literally felt it swish past my face. I also nearly jumped off a balcony once; I've done all the classic acid casualty things. But you're not so aware of your own mortality then, so you don't mind throwing the dice of chance. As you get older you think, "I've thrown the dice so many times, I'm going to get snake eyes any minute."

I had about 20 acid tabs on me once and we were driving the wrong way up a one-way street near Piccadilly, past the Ritz. All of a sudden a police car came screaming into view and stopped us. I thought, "What's that? Twenty trips, first offence? That's got to be at least two years." I'd resigned myself to time at Her Majesty's but, luckily enough, he got a call on his radio to an urgent incident and he just looked at us and said, "You're the luckiest three cunts in London tonight... we've got better things to do."

If you drop acid every Friday for a year like we did your memory is going to be hazy, but I remember going to Nicky Holloway's Special Branch in Tooley Street and various parties in railway arches. The music then was an eclectic mix – you'd have two or three rooms at a warehouse party and you would have people playing rare groove, electro. It was only a bit later in the West End when it started to get a bit more specialised, and that's when I started to lose interest.

CYMON ECKEL, PROMOTER/*BOY'S OWN* **CO-FOUNDER:**
No matter where you were you at nine o'clock on a Friday night you

had to drop a tab of acid, even if we weren't together. The best one, or the worst one, was my 21st birthday party. Andrew and Phil didn't turn up until about 11 o'clock but I dropped my tab at nine, 'cause that was the rule. So there I was, on my own, surrounded by my working-class family and my grandfather, who was an ex-Grenadier Guard, and I'm tripping my tits off trying to keep it together. Then Andrew and Phil bounded in the room at about 11, with the biggest smiles on their face. Needless to say we only lasted about another 15 minutes.

★

Some of the West End crowd began to frequent the Camden Palace Theatre when it was relaunched as a glamorous new club called Camden Palace. Based on the leading clubs in New York – Studio 54 and Paradise Garage – the club was hosted by Steve Strange and Rusty Egan, who had made their names at the Blitz club, and they brought a trendy crowd with them. The resident DJs were Colin Faver and a then unknown DJ from Milton Keynes, Eddie Richards.

EDDIE 'EVIL' RICHARDS, DJ: I started DJing with a friend of mine when we were teenagers. We bought one turntable, then another and then sent off for an amplifier, which we had to build ourselves. We wanted to be a mobile disco so we built this big coffin out of chipboard to house it all and covered it in orange Fablon – we christened it 'Ministry Of Sound', which we had in writing across the front. I've still got some of our 'Ministry Of Sound' business cards left at home somewhere. So it made me laugh when the club Ministry Of Sound* came up with the same name years later.

My dad used to drive us in his Morris Traveller to our gigs. Then when I learned to drive, I replied to an advert in *Melody Maker* for DJs wanted and got the job. I had a Transit van and had to drive all over the country playing big roadshows – Penzance one day, Norfolk the next.

---

* Ministry Of Sound was one of the first breed of superclubs that opened in the early Nineties, after the initial explosion of acid house. It was the first club in the UK to have a 24-hour licence.

Then I decided to go to polytechnic in London and I got a job DJing in strip-clubs at lunchtime around Elephant & Castle.

My first DJ gig in a club was a place called Poppers in Milton Keynes. Because Milton Keynes was a new town then, you had a weird mix of people who'd been thrown together, from gays to bikers. A couple of gays that came into the club said to me, "You should go to this club in London called Heaven." So I went to check it out and I'd literally never seen anything like it. I felt like I'd found what I was looking for, even though I hadn't known I was looking for anything. I just thought, "This is what I want to do with my life, play this sort of music." I got the attention of the DJ, who turned out to be Colin Faver, and we started talking and he told me about the music he was playing and where he got it from and gave me some tips. I invited him to come up and play at my club in Milton Keynes, and he turned up at the train station with his records in a black bin liner over his shoulder, which looked really weird. Not long after, he phoned me up and said, "There's a new club starting in London called the Camden Palace, do you want to come for an audition?" I guess he liked what I was playing at the time, which was across the board: a bit of gay disco, a bit of New Romantic stuff. They liked it and I got the job, which launched me into a completely different world.

From knowing nothing about the scene a few months previously, I was now at the forefront of it. The owners of the Palace had basically been to New York and copied all the best ideas from Paradise Garage and Studio 54. They tried to get Richard Long, the guy who designed the Paradise Garage system, to design the sound, although they couldn't get him. We had three Technics decks, a reel-to-reel tape machine and reverb units, and everything was high-end. Steve Strange and Rusty Egan brought in all their West End crowd from the Blitz club; Wham! were there all the time, Spandau Ballet, Boy George and Duran Duran – it was just full of stars. It was amazing and it was voted Best Club In The World by *Record Mirror*. I started getting offered quite a few extra jobs because I was playing there and ended up DJing for Duran Duran at their club, the Rum Runner, in Birmingham.

★

In Manchester, Factory Records had also opened a nightclub inspired by clubs in New York City like Danceteria, The Funhouse and Paradise Garage, which New Order, A Certain Ratio and Quando Quango had experienced and played at during trips to the United States. Located in an old yacht showroom, and designed by Ben Kelly, The Haçienda was unlike any other nightclub the UK had seen before. But although it was inspired by New York discotheques, it was predominantly used as a gig venue in its early years. The club's name was taken from a line in Ivan Chtcheglov's situationist text *Formulary For A New Urbanism*: "You'll never see the Haçienda, it doesn't exist. The Haçienda must be built." Unfortunately, the Factory directors hadn't fully thought through exactly for *whom* it would be built.

TONY WILSON, FACTORY RECORDS/HAÇIENDA FOUNDER: Someone asked about two weeks before The Haçienda opened, "Who the fuck have you built this for?" and we went, "Well, the kids." And they went, "Have you seen the kids recently? They're wearing long raincoats, you dick – you've built them a New York discothèque." And we all went, "Ooh yeah, sorry." And in fact they were completely right, 'cause it was empty for the first five years, completely empty.

SHAUN RYDER, HAPPY MONDAYS/BLACK GRAPE: There wasn't anyone in The Haçienda for the first five years. It was dead. But it always felt like an important place, like a space where you knew things could happen.

MIKE PICKERING, DJ/M PEOPLE: I didn't DJ for the first few years of The Haçienda; I was the booker and used to book all the bands. But I eventually got pissed off with the DJs because none of them were what I'd seen in New York at places like Paradise Garage and The Danceteria; they all wanted a microphone! Hewan Clarke was a great DJ but he wasn't very electro. I couldn't find a DJ that was right so in the end I thought, "Fuck it, I'll do it myself!", which is very Mancunian.

In October 1984, we started Nude on Friday nights. At first I DJed with Andrew Berry, one of the Haçienda hairdressers*. I was playing electro and the precursor of what would become house and he'd play a bit more northern soul and indie.

We'd also moved the DJ booth by this time, to the balcony overlooking the dance floor. When The Haçienda first opened, the DJ booth was below the stage and you just had this little window slot above your head where all you could see was people's ankles – it was fucking ridiculous! Hewan used to have a stool down there and just sit and read magazines while he was DJing!

Nude got a crowd almost instantly, within about two or three weeks. It was only £1 to get in and if you were on the dole it was free. That's when we decided to reverse the door policy: I just went, "Look, most of the people following Factory are scallies or Perry Boys** but they can't get in The Haçienda, but a thug wearing a tie can." The crowd at Nude was very black at first, probably about 60 per cent black, and we'd get various dance crews like Foot Patrol and The Jazz Defektors coming down and doing their formation dancing. Everyone smoked weed. We never needed a smoke machine in there because there was that much weed being smoked.

★

Across the Pennines, in Leeds, another New York-inspired club called The Warehouse had opened. Greg James, an American DJ who was now based in London, was employed to advise on the installation of the sound system.

BILL BREWSTER, DJ/DJ HISTORY EDITOR: The Warehouse was fucking amazing. It was the first place I'd heard a DJ mixing and it

---

* Berry became a hairdresser in 1978, later setting up his salon, Swing, at The Haçienda and cutting hair for Morrissey, Johnny Marr and Bernard Sumner, among others. He was early to the scene and one of the first resident DJs at the Manchester club.

**Perry Boys were a late Seventies and early Eighties fashion subculture, emanating from Manchester and Salford and the terraces at Old Trafford. Members favoured Fred Perry shirts and wedge haircuts with a flick.

was a great room because it was basically just a box, painted black, with a great sound system and a sprung dance floor. It was super basic but it just felt super cool. I didn't realise it was so ahead at the time; I just thought it was brilliant. Ian Dewhirst would be playing stuff like Peech Boys, The SOS Band's 'Just Be Good To Me' and The Clash but all mixed together very well. It wasn't super underground; it had crossover appeal but it was just done really, really well.

★

Nightclubs weren't the only thing bands and DJs travelling to New York City in the early Eighties had discovered. Groups like New Order, A Certain Ratio and Soft Cell also came across a new drug called MDMA, also known on the street as 'ecstasy'. New Order included the track 'Ecstasy' on their second studio album, *Power, Corruption & Lies*, released on the Factory Records label in May 1983. Soft Cell's first album, 1981's *Non-Stop Erotic Cabaret*, was recorded in New York on ecstasy, and the clubber they met in Studio 54 who supplied them with the drug, Cindy Ecstasy, even rapped on the record.

NOEL WATSON: The first time I took ecstasy was in New York when my brother Maurice gave it to me in the back of a limo. He was DJing at Area and we went there with Ramalzee [performance and hip hop artist] and another dude. Maurice was spending more time out there and I would be going back and forward from New York because my girlfriend at the time, Bunty, was a ballerina and danced with Bill T. Jones'/Arnie Zane's company. When I was out there I would play at The World, Area and MK. Bunty was the maître d' at MK on certain nights, which was a huge über club attracting people like Spike Lee, George Clinton and Prince.

MIKE PICKERING: We had come across ecstasy in America when I was out there in the early Eighties with Quando Quango and New Order, but it was slightly different then. Quando Quango did a live PA at Paradise Garage because 'Love Tempo' was a big track there. It's now an underground cult classic in the UK, but at the time everyone fucking hated it here. *Everyone*. But it was big in Chicago and New York. We were supporting Chaka Khan who actually collapsed halfway through her set. I think she was having problems at the time.

★

By late 1984, there was a small clique of people taking ecstasy in London's Soho, but only when they could get it back from New York. Although ecstasy would later fuel the acid house revolution, it wasn't necessarily seen as a drug that got you dancing... yet.

DAVID DORRELL: Soft Cell had been over to New York and met Cindy Ecstasy, which is a really important part of the story because it predates the myth ecstasy arrived with acid house by four years. But it's not as if there were big bags of pills coming back. Someone might bring back 30 pills. But it was definitely beginning to surface in little pockets here and there by the end of 1984.

EDDIE 'EVIL' RICHARDS: Soft Cell used to come to Camden Palace and obviously they'd met Cindy Ecstasy in New York. Colin knew them so they would come and have a chat and they might have ecstasy on them, so I think we tried it pretty much before anyone else, because unless you were going to New York, you couldn't get it in the UK. The drugs back then were strong and really pure, but whatever we had was just shared around, so I probably didn't have enough at that time for it to have a proper effect on me or the music. I didn't really start taking drugs until I was playing at RIP later on, when pretty much everyone was taking them... you needed everyone to take them, really.

★

The famously decadent club Taboo, launched by performance artist, fashion designer and club doyen Leigh Bowery* in 1985, is considered by many to be the first place ecstasy took hold in London. A club that made Oscar Wilde's proclamation "Nothing succeeds like excess" its mantra, Tattoo

---

* Leigh Bowery was a famous performance artist, designer and celebrated face of London nightlife. He died in 1994, aged 33.

21

attracted the likes of fashion designers John Galliano and John Richmond, ballet dancer Michael Clark, film director Derek Jarman, and pop stars Boy George, Frankie Goes To Hollywood, Paul Young and Wham!

MARK MOORE: The first place I came across ecstasy was at Taboo. Lots of my friends were talking about this new drug and how they gave it out to married couples that weren't getting on, so you could get it on prescription. Tony Gordon (not to be confused with Fat Tony), who ran Taboo with Leigh Bowery, would come back from New York with some. In those days it was either really expensive – £30 or £40 for one – or it would be free, as someone might give them out willy-nilly and everyone would be on ecstasy. Although I think they called it 'X' then. It was very euphoric but it hadn't translated into that 'loved up' acid house thing yet; it was more "I'm off my face and I'm going to fall on the floor and hug this person here." It was more "Let's get completely out of our fucking heads and it doesn't matter what we look like, or what we do." Everyone would be dancing and sniffing poppers, and then one person would fall on the floor and everyone would just fall on them in a mass bundle and they'd all start writhing around. It was very Bacchanalian – it was *great*.

Jeffrey Hinton was Taboo's DJ and he was playing these Italo and Hi-NRG records*, which I then went and bought. If you heard them by themselves they were actually really boring but they might have a good bit lasting for 30 seconds, and what Jeffrey would do was make his own tapes by looping that good bit over and over, and putting sound effects on it, and they were really tripped out. He made it into drug music. I always thought Jeffrey was underrated for years, but recently people are starting to talk about him and he's now playing trendy places like Dalston Superstore. Unfortunately he's lost or given away all those original tapes, so we're trying to track them down.

---

* Italo is a genre of electro-dance music originating in Italy. Hi-NRG is uptempo dance music, which originated in the States and the UK in the late Seventies.

TERRY FARLEY: The first time I ever heard of people taking ecstasy was at Taboo in 1986. I never used to go there because I didn't like the music and it was very St Martins. The door policy was such that I don't think they would have let me in anyway, I would have looked far too straight. My missus used to go, and girls seemed to be fine getting in. But a lot of people took ecstasy there.

People have also told me stories about ecstasy being around long before then, at places like The Wag Club, but they would take it and sit down. There was no connection with ecstasy making you dance, in fact the total opposite: you took it and you didn't dance. I suppose with any drug, half of the effect will be what you are told to expect that it is going to do to you. But you also need to get enough people doing it first, you need a group effect – even a small group, particularly with ecstasy.

ANDREW WEATHERALL: We first discovered ecstasy in 1986. We were living in Cymon Eckel's dad's flat on this estate called Ward Royal in Windsor and my flatmate, Simon Alder, was seeing a lady who I'm not going to name, because she's a very successful businesswoman now. She was very wealthy then and she's even more wealthy now. She went off to New York one time and when she came back she said, "They've got this new thing over there called ecstasy." She had five of them and they looked like Refreshers sweets – they were wrapped in silver foil and were quite big. So we all took them.

A bit later that night this drunken guy was walking home through the estate and when he passed our front door he could see there was a party going on, so he knocked on it and tried to come in. We wouldn't let him, so being drunk he punched the old lady's window through who lived next door. So I went outside and said, "Look, sorry mate, you've got to go," and ended up fighting with him. So obviously my first experience of ecstasy didn't really work because that's not the buzz you get from ecstasy. You shouldn't end up punching someone on your first ecstasy, no matter what they've done. It took me a couple of years to try it again.

CHAPTER 2

Building Blocks

"It was so raw. It was like a punk version of disco. I just thought, 'Oh my god, the energy in this music is just ridiculous!'"

Jazzy M

By 1985, the first house records from Chicago had started to reach the UK. The term 'house' originated from a club called The Warehouse in Chicago, where the music was first played. Regulars to the club would go into the record shop Imports Etc, where most of the radio and club DJs in the Windy City shopped, asking for music they had heard in The Warehouse. The music quickly became known as 'Warehouse music', which was then shortened to 'House music'.

A few independent record shops and buyers were key to spreading the word about this new music genre in the UK. As well as DJing at The Embassy club, the American DJ Greg James had set up a record shop in Croydon, which he called Spin Offs because it was a 'spin off' from his main job. James' links back to America would prove hugely influential in introducing one of his staff, an aspiring DJ, to this new music from Chicago.

JAZZY M, DJ/RECORD STORE OWNER/FIRST PERSON TO PLAY HOUSE ON THE RADIO IN THE UK: I started as a Saturday boy in a record shop in Putney called Shady Deals in about 1977. That was when I first got interested in dance music, funk, soul and then electro. I got a show on a pirate radio station called Radio Fulham where I was just known as DJ Mick, which was a bit boring. I didn't even like being called Mick, I preferred being called Michael. We started doing parties in a function room at a Kensington hotel and we could get up to 700 or 800 people at times. I was playing jazz funk, disco and fusion, and later electro – basically anything electronic.

My big break as Jazzy M came when I joined London Wide Radio (LWR) in 1984. I had moved to work in a record shop called Spin Offs, which I ended up running. It was owned by two guys, Greg James and his partner David, whose surname I can't remember. Zac, who ran LWR, used to come in and I found out he was running a pirate station and being the cheeky young upstart that I was, I just said, "Give me a slot!", and he did. I started on the graveyard shift at 2a.m. playing jazz funk and fast Latin music, which is where the Jazzy name came from. I've always been into upbeat music, which is why house was such an easy transition for me when I heard it.

Greg James was a *hugely important* link in the arrival of house in the UK, and he always gets forgotten about. Greg was a DJ and was originally brought over here from the gay scene in the States by the Embassy club, so Greg himself was an import. But the crucial thing is he had the all-important direct links with the US. Every other record shop would have to go through a distributor and a middleman, but through Greg, Spin Offs had direct contact. Being in the right place at the right time plays a big part in this. I'm a little bit OCD, so I like everything to be right, and I hate reading accounts of what happened and thinking, "Nah, that's not what happened, that's a load of old crap!" I always like to see people given the right respect and props.

The first house record that came into the shop was 'On And On' by Jesse Saunders, which pretty much *is* the first house record. There was 'On And On' and then another track called '(I Like To Do It In) Fast

Cars', which was horrendous. Jesse went under the name of Zee Factor on his own label called Jez Say – as in Jesse – which was a sister label to the whole Trax Records empire.* There was also Precision Records, which was pre-Trax, which had early tracks by Jamie Principle and Vince Lawrence. Jesse has never been given his real props, and Vince is another unsung hero of Chicago house. It's weird that the people who come first are never really given their props. I know how they feel. I'm not bitter, but I predate most of the acid house scene in the UK and I'm not given the props. It didn't used to bother me but it seems to matter more and more.

When I first heard those very early Chicago records I thought they were weird and underproduced, but they had a raw quality and I loved the energy of them. I've always loved music that is different and goes against the grain and is not commercial. Greg himself was a proper disco queen, a real purist, and he hated this new house sound. I remember his exact words: "Oh my gawd! That's so *underproduced*, that's just *disgusting!* It will *never* catch on!", which made me have a little snigger to myself.

We started to get in stuff like J.M. Silk's 'Music Is The Key' and Adonis's 'No Way Back' and I just thought, "Oh my fucking god, the energy in this music is just ridiculous!" It was so raw. It was like a punk version of disco, much rougher and rawer, with more energy. So I very quickly started up a 'Chicago house' section in the shop. I can't remember exactly when I first heard the term 'house' used to describe this new music but it must have been from one of the distributors in America, and obviously the term derives from the Warehouse club in Chicago.

That direct contact with America was so important then. The suppliers would test you each time they sent you an order. They would put a couple of extra records in there for you, and if you liked it you could go back and order it. I also started playing those first records on

---

* Trax Records was a hugely important Chicago record label, started by Larry Sherman and 'Screamin'' Rachael Cain in 1984. Trax would put out a lot of the first house records, although they also attracted criticism, both for exploiting young and naïve artists and the poor quality of the record pressings.

my radio show on LWR, in a dedicated section of the show called The Jacking Zone, after one of those early records that came through called The Jacking Zone by Risqué Rhythm Team. I loved *The Twilight Zone*, so when I heard Risqué Rhythm Team had based a house record on it I was like, "This is fucking cool!" and I adopted it as the signature tune to that part of my show.

DAVID DORRELL: By 1985, I had started hanging around with Oliver Peyton [now a renowned restaurateur and judge on the BBC's *Great British Menu*] and he wanted to start a new club and found the space that became RAW. Oliver had an amazing capacity to tramp the streets of London and discover hidden gems of space. He got talking to a guy called Mike who ran a gym space four floors below the YMCA on Tottenham Court Road – the same way he found the space which later became the Atlantic; he just nipped into a hotel off Piccadilly for a piss and started snooping around, opening various doors, and found this huge, mothballed Grade II listed ballroom. I don't even know if anyone at the YMCA actually knew this guy Mike was hiring out the space to us as a club, but it worked. We used the back entrance and people would tramp down four floors to this subterranean basement, which was a phenomenal club for its time. Oliver said to me "Right, you'll be the DJ," and I said, "Great, but I need someone else as well," so I got Rob Milton from Dirtbox in.

I got a lot of records free through my work at the *New Musical Express* but I was also travelling a lot for them, so was able to pick up records in New York or Europe that other people weren't getting, which really helped me put together an interesting record box. We'd play everything from vaguely northern disco stompers to electro; we could get away with anything at RAW. I got my first house record after RAW had been running for a while, which was Farley Funkin Keith's 'Funkin With The Drums', but it didn't seem to quite fit in with anything else at first.

EDDIE 'EVIL' RICHARDS: I first heard house music either late in 1985 or early in 1986. I was buying my music from a record shop called

Smithers and Leigh in Oxford Street. A guy called Dave Lee [who would later become a DJ and an acid house star in his own right, recording under the name Joey Negro] was the buyer for their dance department and really knew his shit, so he used to get some really good music in there and it was the only place I could find selling house music.

The first house record I got was 'I've Lost Control' by Sleezy D on Trax. Those early records were really early stripped-down tracks because the guys making it didn't have much money, so they would just go to the store and buy the cheapest equipment, which happened to be a 303* and drum machine. People were saying, "Why are you playing this stuff? It's just drum machines." They were famously terrible pressings as well.

BOY GEORGE: The first time I heard house music was in 1986 at the Paradise Garage, and that was purely by accident. I was recording the last Culture Club album, *From Luxury To Heartache*, with Arif Mardin, and it was really, *really* overproduced. I was in New York and I went out clubbing and someone dragged me to the Paradise Garage, which I'd never heard of. I remember arriving and there were metal detectors on the door to make sure people weren't carrying guns and I thought, "Oh my god, is this place safe?" But we went in and they played 'Set It Off' by Strafe. That was the first real house record I'd ever heard and I remember thinking, "Oh my god, we've got it *so wrong!* We've got it *so, so wrong*. Oh no! This is *so genius!* What *is* this music?? It's so empty and spacious." It sounded kind of out of tune but it really fucking worked. I just thought, "We've really missed the mark."

That was the beginning for me, hearing that music at Paradise Garage and seeing people dance in a different way. I then got to meet Larry Levan and got quite friendly with him, but it was a little while later before I really got into the music.

---

* The Roland TB-303 was a bass synthesizer with built-in sequencer manufactured by the Japanese company Roland from 1982–1984. The 303 sound was hugely influential in the development of acid house.

WINSTON HAZEL, DJ: The first house record I heard was 'Set It Off' by Strafe, which I think I got off the import van in Newton-le-Willows, in Merseyside. That's the one I remember standing out as completely different to everything else I was playing then. It was syncopated, monotonous and hypnotic. It was recognisably electro but different enough that it would make people leave the dance floor, so I tried it with loads of different tracks because there wasn't enough house music around, so it wasn't that easy to integrate it at first. But we started to get a reputation for it at Jive Turkey* because a lot of other DJs had stopped pushing the boat out. It was a transition period in a way, so a lot of DJs stuck to what they knew. But we only got a reputation among people we knew; we never sung from the rooftops about Jive Turkey because that wasn't Sheffield style.

MIKE PICKERING: In late 1985 and early 1986, we started getting early proto-house records like J.M. Silk's 'Music Is The Key', Dhar Braxton's 'Jump Back (Set Me Free)' and Colonel Abrams' 'Trapped'. They were precursors to house because they had that four-to-the-floor beat and when I was playing those records, you would get people doing old northern soul dancing. Then one night at The Haçienda this kid from Moss Side came in and said, "Check this out, Mike," and gave me a copy of Adonis' 'No Way Back'. I don't know where the fuck he had got it from. I listened to it on the headphones and went, "Fuck me, this is *amazing!*" so I stuck it on and people came up banging on the DJ booth, asking what it was. Straight away I thought, "I've got to track down everything on this label", which was Trax. Then I found out about the sister label DJ International as well. Kenny at Spin Inn record shop in Manchester was brilliant at that stage, really brilliant at getting those records in.

GREG WILSON: A misconception of The Haçienda is that house music exploded there in 1988, but Mike Pickering had been playing

---

* From the mid Eighties, Jive Turkey was a hugely influential and seminal Sheffield club, and one of the first to play acid house on a regular basis. The resident DJs were Winston Hazel and DJ Parrot.

some house records at his Nude night since 1986, alongside hip hop and street soul – it was a black music night and had quite a black crowd. To their credit, The Haçienda really believed in their approach and stuck with it, and it eventually paid dividends.

JUSTIN ROBERTSON, DJ/LIONROCK: I moved to Manchester in 1986, to study philosophy at university. Even though I lived quite near London growing up, I didn't go in there much. I hated living in the suburbs and romanticised Manchester because of the music and I liked the radical and political history of the place. Especially as Labour used to put candidates out in my hometown for a laugh really, they hadn't a hope of getting elected and would lose their deposit.

I'd played guitar in bands at school and our first band was a space-rock band called The Amazing Wobbly Jelly Band. I was a massive fan of The Fall and obviously a big fan of the whole Joy Division, New Order and Factory thing, like everyone else. The other attraction of Manchester for me was that I wanted to get as far away from home as possible really.

I found it hugely exciting when I arrived. There wasn't much there compared to now but there were all these cool little clubs and just a real creative buzz in the air. It was high on pretension as well, which I kind of liked. The Cornerhouse art house cinema had just opened up, and I loved being away from home and just absorbing all this stuff. We were all really into *The Face* and *i-D* at the time. I said recently to my friend Richard Hector-Jones (who is younger and came to Manchester a year later) that for the first year after I arrived in Manchester I must have been a complete wanker. My life changed completely overnight and friends from back home would come up to visit me and I'd be walking round in a beret with a flower in my pocket quoting this, that or the other, thinking, "You don't understand, my life is art," like an absolute knob.

I used to go to [DJ] Dave Haslam's The Temperance Club because I was a bit of an indie kid, then a friend of mine called Eddie, who was a year older and from Leeds and had been going to The Warehouse, played me a lot of early house records he'd heard there. To suddenly change from this quiet town life to vibrant city life was a revelation. I had friends introducing me to electronic music and hip hop, and there was a real change in what I was listening to.

MIKE KNOWLER, DJ: I first started DJing in 1969. By the early Eighties I was DJing at The State with Steve Proctor and then Andy Carroll, where we were playing alternative dance, everything from New Order to Fad Gadget. The State also had a sister club called Kirklands which had a black crowd, and the owners of the two clubs wanted to make sure they had two separate audiences so they didn't really want us to play black music, although we did play a bit of hip hop.

I remember the exact day I first came across house music. In July 1986, I went to New York for the first time, well it's still actually the only time I've been to New York. I was there on holiday for three weeks with my ex-wife, visiting friends of hers in Queens, but I knew the New Music Seminar* was on in Manhattan at the same time so I asked my wife if she'd mind if I took three days out of the trip to go. I met quite a few people there, including Paul Oakenfold, who was a plugger more than a DJ then, but we didn't discuss house music. I also met a guy called General B from Chicago, who described himself as a dub poet, and when I told him I was a DJ at a club in Liverpool called The State, he said, "Do you play house music in The State?" I said, "I don't know what house music is." He explained, "Well, it's from Chicago and originated in a club called The Warehouse, and it's kind of a cross between New Order and Philly Soul." That's how he described it, which sounded interesting, so I asked him if he'd give me some song titles and he wrote down a list of house tracks which he considered essential listening. So I went to a record store called Downstairs Records and I bought some of these records he recommended, including 'Jack Your Body' by Steve 'Silk' Hurley.

While I was at the seminar I also went to one of the club nights where there was a performance by LL Cool J and Joyce Sims, and the DJ was playing house. I'm not sure who the DJ was, but that was the first time

---

* The New Music Seminar was a music conference and festival held annually in New York City from 1980–1994. It was relaunched in 2009.

I'd heard someone playing house music in the mix and it just sounded like the future. I knew straight away that was it.

When I came back from New York I played these house records to my co-DJ, Andy Carroll, and we started to try and play a bit of it; we could play a bit of acid house at the start of the night at 10a.m., but when it got to the peak time it wasn't what most of our crowd wanted at that stage.

JAZZY M: When I started the Jacking Zone segment of my show it was only 15 minutes or so because there were hardly any records, but it just grew and grew until it eventually became a Top 100 rundown. I compiled this myself and used to run down the Top 100 on the show every week, and then they began to publish it in both *Black Echoes* and *Soul Underground* magazines. I'd change the chart every week with records going up and down, and new entries, depending on how stuff was selling in Spin Offs and the responses on the radio. So it was pretty accurate, although only based on the sales from one shop. But there weren't any other shops selling this music at the time.

The response to The Jacking Zone was mental. The only way for people to get in contact with us was via post because there were no mobile phones and obviously we couldn't have a landline, since it was a pirate radio station and would be traceable, so we used to get loads of letters.

We would broadcast LWR from everywhere and anywhere – from butcher's shops, the backrooms of houses of ill repute, the top floor of blocks of flats. We'd often broadcast from somewhere on the North Peckham estate, which was a notorious estate back then and nicknamed 'Crack City'. It was a no-go zone for the police, making it an ideal place for a pirate radio station. Unfortunately, it wasn't quite as ideal trying to get in and out with all my records. Because the estate was so rough, I developed this system of transporting my records in my mum's old shopping trolley. I'd have the records at the bottom of the trolley then a pair of nunchukas and two scythes (I did martial arts back then), in case anyone tried to mug me. Then I put a towel at the top of the trolley to hide everything. Fortunately, I never had to use them. I had one nasty scare where I was chased down a set of stairs by a gang of four or five youths, but I managed to get the shopping trolley on my back and run, so I never had to resort to anything. One night I was stopped by a police car who said, "What the fuck are you doing here?" and I said, "Er..." and he went, "Go on, fuck off." So I did, because I obviously didn't want to be searched, although I was more bothered about losing my records than them finding my weapons of mass destruction.

The shop really did well out of The Jacking Zone, and the shop I went on to manage after – Mi Price in West Croydon – did even better. I was there from 1985 to 1988 and in that time it went from being your average CD and record shop to the leading house music shop, and everyone came because Jazzy M from The Jacking Zone was working there.

NOEL WATSON: The most important shops in London then were Trax, Groove, Black Market and Jazzy M's shop. My collection of records started at Groove in Greek Street, almost opposite Le Beat Route. Every Friday afternoon we'd go down there and wait for the latest imports to come in. The shop was run by a family, and there was an old woman who would just sit in there doing her knitting. Greg Edwards would be in there, and Robbie Vincent and Steve Lewis would be down there on a Friday afternoon.

BILL BREWSTER: The first time I heard house music was actually on John Peel's radio show [on BBC Radio 1], but I only realised it years later. I used to tape every show, and then once a month I would edit them down to an hour and a half, a 90-minute tape of all my favourite stuff he'd played that month, and I would write out the track listing. I've kept all those tapes and a few years ago I went back and digitised them all and realised there's several house records on there. They were actually quite obscure ones as well. I've no idea where Peel was getting those records from because he wouldn't have been sent them.

The first house record I ever bought was 'Hey Rocky!' by Boris Badenough, which came out on Trax Records in 1986, which was kind of a novelty record really. So I was listening to house without knowing it. A lot of people say, "As soon as I heard this, I knew it was the new sound," but I didn't feel that way. For me it felt like a continuation of all the other things I'd been getting into in 1985 and 1986, like Mantronix*, who I was hugely into, John Robie productions**, Tricky Tee's 'Johnny The Fox', 'My Adidas' by Run-DMC. I didn't see a lot of difference between those records, personally. For me those early house records were just one strand of what was going on in clubs in the mid Eighties, rather than this thing that was obviously going to crush everything else. It was only really when ecstasy was added to the mix that everything changed. Prior to that, it just felt like another interesting thing rather than something all-pervasive.

MARK MOORE: The first time I remember hearing a house record was when I was hanging out with Colin Faver when he was playing at The Jungle at Busby's on a Monday night. It was a mainly gay, black crowd, soul music for the most part, but he played 'Music Is The Key' and I remember saying, "Wow, what's this?" and he showed me the cover and I went and bought a copy. At that stage I shopped in Bluebird Records on Edgware Road and Groove on Greek Street. I remember being in Bluebird and they were having a discussion about what they were going to call this new music and I think they decided on 'basement music'. Groove had a little house section but they didn't know what it was either. I also went to Record Shack, which was a gay shop, and any early house records in there would end up in the bargain bin because none of the only Hi-NRG gay DJs who shopped in there would touch it with a barge pole.

★

---

* Mantronix were an influential 1980s hip hop and electro-funk music group founded by DJ Kurtis Mantronik (Kurtis el Khaleel) and rapper MC Tee (Touré Embden). Kurtis also worked in A&R for Sleeping Bag records, with artists such as KRS-One and T La Rock.

**John Robie is an American musician and record producer who played on many seminal early electro records. He is best known for his work with the legendary New York record producer Arthur Baker on tracks like 'Planet Rock' and 'Play At Your Own Risk'.

Rooting through the bargain box on one of his trips to Record Shack, Moore found a copy of a record he had never heard of. It would become the first house record to break in the UK.

MARK MOORE: I remember finding a record in there called 'Love Can't Turn Around' and playing it and going, "Oh my god, this is *FUCKING AMAZING!* I can't believe this is in the bargain bin!" I played it at The Mud Club that night and everyone went crazy, and then about an hour later I played the dub mix and they went crazy again. Then I played it at Heaven and they went *even more crazy*. Jay Strongman said to me, "Wow, what's this?" and I said, "I just got it from the bargain bin in Record Shack, there might be another one – go and have a look." We were just caning that song for ages.

★

Shortly after, London Records signed the track by Farley 'Jackmaster' Funk featuring Darryl Pandy. It was released in September 1986 and reached number 10. The same week, a new club called Delirium opened at the London Astoria on Charing Cross Road, promoted by Robin King and Nick Truelock with Noel and Maurice Watson as the residents.

ROBIN KING: I first met Nick Truelock when he used to come to my St Martins parties; by that point he had run a couple of nights at the Embassy club. Then he rang me one day and said, "I've got the keys to the Astoria, do you want to run a night there?" I've had a few phone calls like that, which you know could change your life, and I said, "Yes!" straight away. At that time the Astoria had a crazy licence because it was a theatre and it was allowed to stay open until 6a.m. I'd first met Maurice and Noel Watson at their Battle Bridge Road parties, which were great parties, so we approached them to see if they would come to the Astoria.

NOEL WATSON: When Maurice came back from New York he had an amazing collection of records. We started playing at The Wag and were also doing a Tuesday at The Limelight, which probably held around 350. We put on Fingers, Inc., Kym Mazelle and Darryl Pandy, but no one really knew who they were at that time, apart from some of the gay kids. Nick Truelock and Robin King then came down to see us and asked if we would do Delirium.

When we started Delirium it was quite hip hop and we would have people like the Beastie Boys and Run-DMC come down when they were in town. We tried to blend in house music but Maurice could clear the floor if he started playing just house and disco, and then I'd have to jump back in and play beats'n'breaks. It would split the crowd, as the hip hop guys really didn't like it. Even the Beastie Boys said to me, "You're barking up the wrong tree with that stuff, it's *shit!*" But I was like, "No, it's *not* shit!" But it was Maurice who was really determined; he would be like, "Listen, they're *going* to fucking listen to this because this is the *future* of music." He also wanted more gay people coming to the club. Maurice loved going to the gay clubs in New York, he loved that scene. More than me, I have to be honest.

★

There was a period of 18 months from 1986 until late 1987, before ecstasy became more freely available, when house music really polarised opinion in London. The Watson brothers even had to have cages built around the DJ booth at The Astoria to protect them from the people yet to fall under house music's spell.

NOEL WATSON: The crowd were throwing cans and bottles at us when we were playing house. We were getting a lot of abuse. Guys would come up to us and say, "Don't play that gay music or we'll come in there and beat you up!" The thing is, if you're looking back at that period a lot of the people who say they were there at the beginning of house music in London were still actually anti-house at this stage. Almost all of that crew were still playing rare groove. The only other DJs playing house and disco then, for my money, were Mark Moore, and Colin Faver and Eddie Richards at the Camden Palace. Maurice and I would go to the Palace and listen to them, as they were two of the only other DJs we could stomach. Colin and Eddie could both mix and made an effort to put on a good show, so we respected them, but a lot of the other DJs in London Maurice and I had no fucking respect for because none of them could mix. They were all basically just getting gigs because of who they knew.

EDDIE 'EVIL' RICHARDS: Noel and Maurice were really early on house music, but no one else was – it was really difficult trying to play it. I think we were lucky at the Camden Palace because we were mixing, and everything we played had a beat and most of it came from disco, so house music kind of fitted in. If you were playing rare groove it would be much harder to try and blend in house music. We were the most upfront club in London. I didn't know of any club playing house before us. Jay Strongman was doing Dirtbox but that was more soul and rare groove. I went to play one night at The Astoria and Norman Jay got on the mic in between DJs and started having a go at those of us playing house music, saying, "We shouldn't be playing this house music." Pete Tong and Jeff Young both worked at Polydor Records and they refused to get into this new music. They actually had this thing for a short while called LADS, which stood for League Against Disco Shit, which meant against house music because they wanted everything to be rare groove. Within six months Pete Tong was putting together the *Future Sound Of House* compilations. What a change.

TERRY FARLEY: The story written in the stars is that London didn't like house music at first, but if you look a bit deeper you'll find out that wasn't the case. Frankie Knuckles was guest resident at Delirium in the summer of 1987. To be honest with you, that wouldn't have meant fuck all at the time because hardly anyone in London knew who he was. But I remember seeing Darryl Pandy at The Limelight doing 'Love Can't Turn Around' and there was a huge crowd in there. Noel and Liz Torres, and Frankie Knuckles* at Delirium. Back then it was just seen as another black American music, the same as go-go, the same as rare groove; people didn't differentiate between them, or think one was going to be bigger than the other. In London at that time DJs mixed in a hip hop style, they cut records, and you could cut 'Love Won't Turn Around' into Eric B [American rapper]. In the North of England, DJs like Mike Pickering, Graeme Park, Winston [Hazel] and DJ Parrot had already made the decision to play mostly house all night, so their mixing was more based on bpm [beats per minute].

CARL COX, DJ: I was bit outside of the loop at first because I was living in Brighton in 1986. I had my own sound system and I was playing funk and soul music of around 98 bpm. The very first acid house record I bought and started to play out was Chip E.'s 'Time To Jack'.** When I first started playing it, everyone around me thought it was the most queer, stupidest, monotonous record. People thought it was terrible – they thought it was worst record I'd ever played. Which was a statement and a half. I thought to myself, "If I keep playing this half of my fan base are not going to go to my parties anymore." But I loved it, so I did start playing those early Trax records at some of the parties I played in late 1986 going into 1987, and what happened was I *did* lose half my crowd, who just weren't interested, but the other part of my crowd were like "Whoa, this is the future man, I'm really into this," which led me to go and buy more records like that.

★

* Frankie Knuckles is regarded by many as 'the Godfather of house'. He started DJing at New York City's Continental Baths with Larry Levan, then moved to the legendary Warehouse club in Chicago that gave house music its name. He worked with Jamie Principle on the seminal 'Your Love' and has remixed everyone from Michael Jackson to Whitney Houston, won a Grammy and been inducted into the Dance Music Hall Of Fame.
**Chip E. was one of the key early producers of Chicago house music and his seminal 'Time To Jack' was a landmark release.

Since 1985, Terry Farley, Andrew Weatherall and their friends had talked about the idea of launching a fanzine, inspired initially by the fact nothing currently in print spoke to them, and then by a fanzine from Liverpool that Farley had picked up called *The End*, which was edited by Peter Hooton, singer with Liverpool band The Farm. They chose the name *Boy's Own* and, though they didn't know it at the time, it was to become the in-house magazine of acid house.

CYMON ECKEL: I think Terry and Steve Mayes had the idea, "How about doing a fanzine?" and Andrew was up for it. I remember the first meeting when they came round to our flat in Ward Royal and said, "Let's have a chat about it." So we did, over a nice cup of tea and some chocolate bourbons.

It wasn't born out of angst or anything. The idea was first muted back in 1985 but the first issue didn't actually come out until 1986. Terry and Maisy would have come across *The End* because they were going to football and myself and Andrew weren't. But Andrew was very aware of things like that so he might have picked up on it, and I think it had been mentioned in *The Face*. Myself and Andrew had grown up with style, music, fashion, imagery, art through our own leanings, while Terry and Steve had grown up the other route, where they picked up on fashion and music by integrating with other football firms. If you read the first copy of *Boy's Own* it's all about the chap sitting on the terraces one minute, reading Brendan Behan, then bouncing around the Wag club the next, which was quite a new and refreshing attitude. The whole world had become money-obsessed, possession-obsessed and very materialistic. We were still young and fresh faced; we weren't married and didn't have children or properties. We thought we could reflect our attitude through this fanzine. All the other magazines and periodicals were talking about 'lifestyle', which to us was an obnoxious thing. It's now the *lingua franca* of most magazines but back then we thought it was supposed to be more about the music, the clothes and the meaning.

STEVEN HALL, *BOY'S OWN* CO-FOUNDER: It was Terry's idea to start a fanzine really. He was more involved in football than the rest of us, so he was aware of the banter developing between different clubs, and music and clothes started to become more important. He'd also seen *The End*, which was a direct influence. The vague idea was to be a more clubby version of *The End*. Terry's ideas were more the silly stuff, the lists and stuff, and Andrew would do all the interviews, since he wanted to be a journalist.

TERRY FARLEY: I just thought there was nothing out there for us. I used to buy loads of magazines like *Blues & Soul* or *NME* but there was just nothing speaking to me. I first read about *The End* in the *NME* I think, and sent off for a copy. Then I just copied all the best ideas from it straight away, because as far as I was concerned no one else had ever seen *The End* in London! But they'd copied most of their best ideas from somewhere else as well. I never thought anyone would be interested in *Boy's Own* anyway, and we only ever really sold about 1,500 copies. That's the most we ever printed. I certainly didn't think people would be talking about it 25 years later, obviously.

MR. C (RICHARD WEST), RAPPER/DJ/THE SHAMEN: I first started going out as a teenager and I would go to see DJs like Steve Walsh at The Lyceum and Chris Hill at Busby's. I was a big fan of Jazzy M and his Jacking Zone show on LWR radio, and also Jasper The Vinyl Junkie and Ron Tom [real name Ronald Tomlinson], who were also on LWR. I used to rap for Jasper The Vinyl Junkie and did all the jingles for him and Ron Tom. I became the MC for the LWR Soul Syndicate, so I had a real crossover: I rapped over hip hop, rare groove and funk before I switched completely to house.

The first DJ I heard playing house was my old school chum from Holloway, Kid Batchelor, who started playing with Soul II Soul. Around the same time Jazzy Q was also playing house for Soul II Soul, and Jasper The Vinyl Junkie and Jazzy M were also playing house out.

Colin Faver and Eddie Richards were a big influence on me. In early 1986, I made a decision to switch to just rapping over house and started rapping about jacking the body and things like that. Colin and Eddie had introduced house music at Camden Palace and I thought, "I'm going to see if they'll let me on the mic." So I went up to Colin Faver and said, "Hey mate, I'm a rapper, can I rap?" and he said, "You're a proper rapper?" and I said, "Yes," and rapped a little bit for him and he said, "OK, let me get some hip hop beats on." But I said, "Nah, I prefer to rap over *house*," and he said, "Rap over house? *Really??*" I said, "What about 'Nitro Deluxe'?" and he said, "OK," and threw it on. I got on the mic and the whole place went absolutely bonkers. I was there every week after that and became Colin and Eddie's rapper.

EDDIE 'EVIL' RICHARDS: When Richard first came down he was too young to get in, so he used to break in sometimes through the roof. He used to have this *Clockwork Orange* look, complete with the bowler hat and everything. He told us he was a rapper and we let him rap a bit over the mic, and he was pretty good. Through Richard I then met his friend Kid Batchelor, who wasn't really DJing that much. I used to live near him in King's Cross and I used to go round his flat and hang out for a couple of hours before I went up to play at Camden Palace, and got to know him like that.

MR. C: Later in 1986, I went into the studio with Eddie Richards to make a track. We were originally going to do a hip-house number but Eddie had this really deep house track that was about 118 bpm, which I really liked. I said, "I've got a real deep interest in meditation, positive thinking and synchronicity and what can be achieved with all that stuff, so can I do a spoken word track about meditation?" and he said, "Yeah, sure." We recorded it at the end of 1986 but it didn't come out until August 1987. If we had done a hip-house number it would have been the first hip-house record in the world because the first hip-house record I heard was 'It's Percussion' by Steve 'Silk' Hurley featuring M. Doc, so I would have beaten that. But it wasn't what I wanted to do; I thought there was something more important.

Adonis also wanted to a track with me in 1986. Jasper The Vinyl Junkie used to do a party on Sundays at The Cricketers in Chertsey, which was amazing, in this big barn-like room at the back of the pub that held about 500 people. Jasper knew Adonis was in London so he invited him down to do a PA. Adonis heard me rapping over house music and he was blown away and said, "We need to get this on record!" but because he was in Chicago and I was in London it never ended up happening.

★

Up north there was also a nascent warehouse scene in Manchester, as well as plenty of shebeens and parties in Hulme and Moss Side. The first warehouse party in Manchester was on 20 July, 1985, organised by the colourful Steve Adg of Blackmail Records, tour manager of a then little-known band called The Stone Roses. Taking place behind Piccadilly Station, on Fairfield Street, the location was kept secret and punters were told to ring Spirit Studios on the night of the party to find out the location.

STEVE ADG, BLACKMAIL RECORDS/STONE ROSES TOUR MANAGER: We called the first party The Flower Show because we planned to do a different one each month with a different name. Because it was Blackmail Records, we made the poster up with letters cut out of the paper, like people make blackmail letters. We kept the location secret and it sold out in advance. No one had seen anything like it in Manchester before. We didn't get any hassle; the police had no idea at all. They turned up in the morning when we were cleaning up and said, "What's been going on here then?"

"Oh we've just been filming a music video."

"A music video?"

"Yeah, we had that Tony Wilson down here."

"Tony Wilson from the telly? *Really?*"

That seemed to impress them, and that was it – they just fucked off.

★

One of those at The Flower Show was intrigued local journalist Auss Parsons, who then wrote about the night in Dave Haslam's fanzine *Debris* under the headline 'What Is A Warehouse Party?'

> It's an idea generally thought to have first seen the light of the night in London... for those unfamiliar with the term, a Warehouse Party is literally a party in a warehouse, organised secretively and strictly by ticket and word-of-mouth only. On the bill was Manchester band The Stone Roses and in between, disc jockeys played music throughout the night and early morning. There was well over the 200 I had been told to expect. When I spoke to some of those attending, the general feeling was they thought it different and enjoyable. The Stone Roses took to the 'stage' at 1.30a.m. The set they played was full of power and the audience obviously appreciated them, somehow seeming to suit the surroundings with their gutsy music. One person I spoke to remarked that it had been a long time since he had seen so many people together enjoying themselves and certainly a rarity in local nightclubs.

Steve and Mark would put on several proto-warehouse parties, including Junction Box featuring Mike Pickering's band Quando Quango, The Men They Couldn't Hang, The Mighty Lemon Drops and The Stone Roses. Adg would go on to tour manage The Stone Roses and is still their tour manager now, 25 years later.

There were also a number of early house nights happening in Moss Side, at the youth centre. Nights featuring DJ crews like Mastermind and Foot Patrol were frequented by, among others, a young Gerald Simpson, who would go on to be A Guy Called Gerald and start 808 State [*see* page 49]. At The Haçienda, Mike Pickering had now been joined by Martin Prendergast in the DJ booth, and the two would DJ as MP2. More and more house music was beginning to seep into their sets: Marshall Jefferson's 'Love Can't Turn Around', Mr Fingers' 'Can You Feel It' and Steve 'Silk' Hurley's 'Jack Your Body'.

JUSTIN ROBERTSON: Because my mate Eddie was into house, we started to go to Nude night to hear Mike Pickering and Martin Prendergast and it was just a revelation. I remember walking in there and hearing Rhythim Is Rhythim's [aka Derrick May] 'The Dance'. All those records sounded so alien. They were really long and completely un-arranged, in the traditional song sense; it was just relentless trance machine music, particularly in The Haçienda, which really was key to me. Hearing those records in that environment made a huge difference. I'd be thinking, "What the fuck is this music? It's absolutely insane!"

The crowd at Nude was still pretty black at the time and when Foot Patrol came on they would clear the dance floor, and people would make way for them. Ecstasy hadn't arrived, but arguably the energy was as intense as it was when it did because everyone was really going for it. We used to spend most of the night on the dance floor at Nude night and I'm sure there was some pretty bad dancing going down. But we were going for it. It wasn't what became rave dancing, when you would just wave your hands in the air – we were kicking our feet up and going for it, and everyone was really dressed up.

In Manchester, house music was *the* black music, not swingbeat or R&B, it was house. All the DJs that used to go into The Spin Inn were buying house.

There was also a party called Trash that Andy Madhatter did, which was big with students and moved around different venues. They did one at The Tropicana with Coldcut, and the best one was at The Boardwalk. He was playing rare groove and soul that no one else was playing then in Manchester. So I went there to hear it because the rare groove thing in Manchester was completely non-existent, it was a London thing. From about 1986 the real sound of the underbelly of Manchester was house music.

★

Meanwhile, at The Garage in Nottingham, a young DJ called Graeme Park had also started to try and push the embryonic house sound on to his audience.

GRAEME PARK, DJ: I had played saxophone in bands as a teenager and then I got a job at Selectadisc, which was an amazing record shop – well, two amazing shops because there were two of them in Nottingham. After a while I became one of the buyers. One day the guy who owned it, Brian Selby, came in and announced he's bought the local Rasta club and, "I'm going to relaunch it as The Garage because Nottingham needs a club like that." We all raised our eyebrows and said, "When?" and he said, "Tonight, and you're the DJ." I was like, "Me?!"

I started out playing alternative music, then I started buying more hip hop and electro, which Brian wasn't that keen on. Then one day in 1986, one of the reps from the distributors came in with his new releases and at the end he said, "Just one last thing; we've got these really weird 12-inches from Chicago on this label called Trax and there's another label called DJ International."

"What do you mean, weird?"

"Well for a start they're really bad pressings, and they haven't got any picture covers and there's all these weird synth noises on them."

"Sounds good to me, I'll have one of each."

It was all those early records like J.M. Silk, Steve 'Silk' Hurley, Farley 'Jackmaster' Funk. I started playing them and was like, "Oh my god! This sounds amazing." Brian Selby came out of his office and said, "What the bloody hell is this? Get this off, I don't want this nonsense playing in my shop!"

"I'm just checking them out, Brian, it's this new music from Chicago."

"We're not selling it, are we?"

"I'll probably buy them myself, Brian."

"You're not going to be playing it at the club, are you?"

Over the next few weeks I'd get a few of these 12-inches seeping through, and then it started to snowball.

BILL BREWSTER: In the mid Eighties, one of my best mates from Grimsby was doing an engineering course in Nottingham and shared a flat with a guy called Mark Lyons, who was manager of a club called The Garage, so we used to get in for free. Graeme Park would be playing upstairs and a guy called Martin Nesbitt downstairs. The room upstairs where Graeme played was small but brilliant, and he played lots of hip hop, lots of Jonzun Crew*, stuff on Sleeping Bag Records, and then he started to play early house records. But to be honest, I didn't know they were house records – to me it was electronic music or electro, although I really didn't think it was anything different.

---

* Jonzun Crew was an early Eighties electro/hip hop group, led by Michael Jonzun and his brothers, Maurice Starr and Soni Jonzun.

CHAPTER 3

Everything Starts With An E

"That's when everything changed really. That's when life suddenly went from black and white to Technicolor. When I first had the E…"

Shaun Ryder

In January 1987, Steve 'Silk' Hurley had the first house smash hit with 'Jack Your Body', which went to number one, despite most of the UK still not having heard the term 'house music' or being aware that it was part of a new wave of music from Chicago. Shortly after, the first ecstasy seizures were reported in London. In their story, *The Times* called the drug a "sexual stimulant".

TERRY FARLEY: People forget we had 'Jack Your Body' – which is a really good, proper house record – at number one in the pop charts in 1987, a full year before most people realised what house was, and when that sound was kind of lumped in with pop music and Hazel Dean and all that Hi-NRG stuff. The early house records more likely to be played in London were the more soulful records, things like J.M. Silk and Darryl Pandy. The rawer, more stripped down records were seen more as Hi-NRG. It wasn't until acid house and ecstasy came together as a whole package that people said, "Ah, I get it now."

NICKY HOLLOWAY: Pete Tong was working in London and started licensing early house records. The two records that started to change things were 'Jack Your Body' and 'Love Can't Turn Around'. People don't mention 'Jack' so much because it became so popular it was then a bit naff. But we used to play it when it first came out, along with maybe two or three other house records in a night.

JUDGE JULES, DJ: I started DJing as a young teenager in north London, and by the time I was finishing school I was already putting on my own nights. The first night I put on was with a friend of mine called Rollo [Armstrong], who went on to be a founding member of [British electronica band] Faithless, and his little sister went on to be pop star Dido. We hired a function room above a local pub in Tufnell Park and sold tickets to our friends and that was the start really.

I then met Norman Jay quite early on, but I think it was inevitable we were going to meet as there were probably only around 20 people doing what we were doing in a city of seven million people, so inevitably you met all those people. He was doing similar events to us in west London but had a different crowd to our middle-class crowd, so we decided to pool our resources at our Family Funktion and Shake'n'Fingerpop events.

A school friend of mine had moved to New York in 1986 and was living in the West Village and going to Paradise Garage, so I could go out there for a month at a time and stay with him. It was quite oppressive for a white, middle-class, straight kid from Highgate to go to a sexually-charged, black, gay club in New York, but it was a huge influence. Norman also had a cousin called Terry in Brooklyn, so both of us were going to New York and buying records. In the UK, we started going to The Haçienda just to hear what was going on because they were playing house music up there before it caught on in London, although they would mix it in with other stuff like Factory records.

I think one of the reasons people remember our events is we were ahead of our times in terms of brand consciousness; the other events that weren't don't really have any lasting memory. I went to a few one-off warehouse parties around Old Street around 1987 but I can't remember the name of them.

★

In Manchester, a new collective of musicians, DJs and MCs had formed around the record shop Eastern Bloc. Originally opened in 1985 by a co-operative headed by Martin Price*, Eastern Bloc specialised in underground electronic and alternative music. It quickly attracted an assortment of loyal young followers, including a loose collective of a dozen or so members called Hit Squad Manchester, from which would emerge Manchester's first acid house stars Gerald Simpson and 808 State plus Ruthless Rap Assassins and MC Tunes. The line-ups were quite fluid on some of the early recordings and live shows. The first line-up of 808 State was Martin Price, Simpson and Graham Massey, although Simpson and Massey would sometimes play shows on their own. Among the most persistent of the regulars were two young DJs from Ancoats, Darren Partington and Andrew Barker, who called themselves The Spinmasters and would later become part of the second lineup of acid house pioneers 808 State (*see* page 161). Simpson had always also worked on solo material as A Guy Called Gerald, and would leave 808 State to concentrate on his solo material around the time of their second release, *Quadrastate*.

ANDREW BARKER, DJ/808 STATE: We first started DJing in around 1984 at the Salvation Army in Ardwick, near us. The only reason we started there is because we couldn't afford decks, and they had decks. It was an all-in-one system with decks and lights built in and it didn't even have faders or sliders, it had knobs you had to turn.

DARREN PARTINGTON, DJ/808 STATE: We started out playing electro and hip-hop and that street soul sound. I think our families

---

* Martin Price was the co-founder and owner of the Eastern Bloc record shop and founder of independent record label Creed. He formed hip-hop collective Hit Squad Manchester with a group of customers from the shop, including Graham Massey and Gerald Simpson. The three soon shifted to an acid house sound and became known as 808 State.

thought we were weird; round our way, if you don't want to go out and just get pissed up all the time and get off with a girl or get into a fight, you're a bit weird. So I'm sure they all thought we were weird just sitting in Andrew's bedroom playing music, like, "What's up with those two weirdos? Are they gay or something?"

We then set up a breakdance crew and we all had matching tracksuits. There's a picture of us from Andrew's sister's birthday around that time and we've got our matching tracksuits on and these tiny little headphones. We called ourselves The Spinmasters and our crew was Turntable Rockers. We would set up sound-system challenges with [A Guy Called] Gerald who had a crew called Scratchbeat Masters, based in Longsight, and other crews around Manchester. We'd set up in a school hall and one sound system would play one record, then the other would respond, like a Jamaican sound-system clash but with electro and hip-hop in Manchester. We started going into the record shop Spin Inn and we would just sit there for four or five hours at a time. Eventually they accepted us and we got to know them. They were selling a lot of Hi-NRG records to the gay clubs in Manchester then, but a lot of what they were calling 'Hi-NRG' was actually early acid house. They might be quite gay tunes but they had a little bit of a 303 in them.

ANDREW BARKER: Spin Inn had a slight attitude and if you weren't a big-name DJ it took you a while to get accepted. Then we started going into Eastern Bloc and there were a few small groups and crews like us that used to hang out there and they would share cassettes of their own music they had made, saying, "Here y'are, have a listen to this, see what you reckon." Gradually we came together as Hit Squad Manchester.

Eastern Bloc had a basement with an entrance just off this little alley called 'Pisser's Alley', because all the pissheads used to just nip in there for a piss. Half of the basement was used for stock and after a while Martin Price said we could use the other half for rehearsing, so me and Daz did all the building work and turned it into a little rehearsal studio for us.

DARREN PARTINGTON: That basement became somewhere to culture the sound, this new sound, because the shop was like a magnet for all the freaks into left-of-field electronic music and dance music. Eastern Bloc didn't attract the purists back then, it attracted people open-minded; you could find kindred spirits in that shop. We were the musical misfits of Manchester and Eastern Bloc was the catalyst that brought us all together and kept us together.

Martin Price got to know Graham Massey [soon-to-be 808 State member] because he was working in the butty shop across the road, and Martin used to go in for a butty at lunchtime and got talking to him. Graham was on a recording course at Spirit Studio around the corner and he got free studio time, so Martin said, "Well why don't we get a load of these lot together in the studio, to experiment a bit?" So that's how we first came together as Hit Squad Manchester.

GRAHAM MASSEY, DJ/808 STATE: I was in a band called Biting Tongues and we were signed to Factory, so I got a free pass to The Haçienda and used to go on Fridays quite a bit, so I'd hear Mike Pickering playing acid house. We'd get there early on a Friday, get on the dance floor and dance all night. But what really helped establish house music in Manchester was Stu Allan's show* on Piccadilly Radio on Sunday nights, which everyone used to tape. It was something about the alien sound of house music that captured the imagination. Previous to that I'd been into stuff on ON-U Sound Records and [industrial hip-hop group] Tackhead.

I was doing a recording course at Spirit Studio and working in a café opposite Eastern Bloc, so I got to know Martin Price. Lots of kids were coming into the shop and giving him tapes and generally hanging around doing hip-hop things, like standing there in bubble jackets, and gradually we all started working together. We all had little bits of equipment and we were influenced by those early house records, so we started experimenting and trying to create our own version of it.

★

---

* Stu Allan's radio show was hugely influential in and around Manchester. It was the northern equivalent to Jazzy M's The Jacking Zone, and was the first place you could regularly hear acid house on the radio in the North of England.

Meanwhile, across Manchester, plans were coming together for a new music project which would result in the first British house record. Mike Pickering had been making post-punk new wave dance music with his Quando Quango project since 1982 but, increasingly influenced by the sounds of Chicago and in particular the releases on Trax Records, Pickering and Quando Quango percussionist Simon Topping, along with pianist Ritchie Close, formed T-Coy (which stood for 'take care of yourself', according to Topping) and recorded the Latin-influenced track 'Carino'. The hand-folded and printed sleeve of the record described it as "Latin house" and it is now widely recognised as the first British house record.

MIKE PICKERING: I'd done Quando Quango with Gonnie [Hillegonda Rietveld] and Simon Topping, then Simon had gone off and lived in New York for a year, doing a course in percussion at the Harlem School of the Arts. When I was out in New York we used to go record shopping at the Latin record shops on the Lower East Side, then go out to Latin clubs on Upper Broadway and Harlem. We went to the most amazing Latin clubs, with people from the age of 21 right up to 70 dancing, really amazing clubs. That was a huge influence on us, along with the early house records from Chicago, so we decided, "Let's make a Latin house record." So we just went into an eight-track studio in Didsbury and recorded it quite quickly, onto cassette. We gave it to Stu Allan, who had a show on in Piccadilly on Sunday nights and he went, "Fucking hell, this is amazing!" and started playing it every Sunday night.

Down in London, the Coldcut crew got hold of it on cassette and loved it and started playing it, and I think Norman Jay played it as well. I remember coming down to do a show on Kiss, which was still a pirate station back then broadcasting from the top of a tower block in east London, and they were playing it. But no one wanted to put the record out. Everyone just went, "What the fuck *is this?* It's just a 10-minute long groove." I took it to Factory but they weren't interested. It was all friendly and we didn't fall out about it; I think Rob Gretton knew dance music was going to happen, but Tony Wilson just said to me, "Dance music will never happen because there's no stars." So in the end my management, Keith Blackhurst and Pete Hadfield, just said, "Let's start a record label and put it out ourselves," so we started Deconstruction Records. We only pressed up 1,000 copies of 'Carino', and to be honest it was hard getting rid of them. There were only the pirate stations and Stu Allan and a few other DJs who showed interest at first.

DAVID DORRELL: I was super lucky to get a white label of 'Carino', which was a breakthrough record for me. It became a huge record at RAW. That is the start of British house music to me. Graeme Park was also doing stuff out of Nottingham and I've still got some of his early adventures into the form, although they were perhaps slightly less successful than Mike Pickering's. By the time 'Carino' dropped I was already playing house records, I just don't think anyone was calling it 'house' just yet... apart from Noel and Maurice Watson, and a handful of people in Manchester.

I'd met Mike when I went up to review The March Violets and some other goth band for the *NME* and Happy Mondays were third on the bill. I was absolutely blown away by The Haçienda, I thought it was phenomenal. There was nowhere like that in London then. But it wasn't busy.

★

'Carino' was to prove hugely influential to a generation of British bedroom DJs and musicians, demonstrating house was no longer a sound only imported from America. Simon Reynolds, writing in the *Melody Maker* at the time, was one of the few journalists to recognise how important the record was: "Wave after wave of Latinate percussion rises up from the depths of the mix, making you sprout new limbs to dance in unprecedented ways."

Dave Dorrell also then made the jump from DJing to production when he got involved with a recording that started out as a collaboration between two indie artists on the 4AD record label, and ended up becoming the first British acid house hit.

DAVID DORRELL: Around late May, this guy came down to RAW and doorstepped me at the end of the evening. We got talking and he said he worked for MTV and offered me money to go into the studio to create some idents for them. So I went with Martyn Young from the band Colourbox, a friend of mine, and came up with the bones of something, but it never saw the light of day.

A few weeks later, Ivo Watts-Russell at 4AD had the idea he could have a hit if he got his two biggest acts – Colourbox and A.R. Kane – working together, so he roped in Martyn to work with Kane on the project. By day two Martyn was hating it, so he called me and said I think I've got the bones of something here but I can't work with A.R. Kane anymore, so I went into the studio with him. I had started managing a band called Nasty Rox Inc., with Nellee Hooper on percussion and decks, who was then replaced by CJ Mackintosh, MC Kinky on percussion and Dan Fox, which I think were the first group to use turntablism in their act. We got signed to ZTT and the idea was Trevor Horn was going to produce us and we were going to be the next Frankie Goes To Hollywood. But then Trevor Horn [who signed and produced Frankie] got dragged into court by the existing Frankie Goes To Hollywood. So we had access to Trevor Horn's studio, SARM, because we were recording there with Nasty Rox Inc. I called up CJ to get him involved because he was technically better than me; he could transform, for instance, and I couldn't. He was UK scratch champion and had a vast archive of music. His brother, Lawrence, was a huge record collector and at one stage the floor of his bedroom actually collapsed from the weight of records.

ARTHUR BAKER, NEW YORK PRODUCER: I met Dave Dorrell at the New Music Seminar in New York in July 1987, before 'Pump Up The Volume' came out. I was putting out a record called 'Put The Needle On The Record'. He came to my studio and played me this instrumental track, and I said, "Oh that's really great, but why don't you add some samples like I've done on my track?" and I played him 'Put The Needle On The Record'. I gave him a copy and he went away and, unbeknown to me, ended up sampling it.

A while later I called up Pete Edge at Chrysalis, who had put out 'Put The Needle On The Record' in the UK and said, "How's the record going?" and he said, "Yeah, it's going well but there's this other record that has the same sample on," which was 'Pump Up The Volume', so it stole my thunder a little bit.

When I was in London, I went down to check out Dave's night at RAW – I was probably going to kick his arse for sampling me! It was a dark, dingy basement, with a crappy sound system and Dave DJing on this makeshift set-up. It was all pretty rudimentary, but it was great.

DAVID DORRELL: The first version was almost all instrumental, it just had 'Pump Up The Volume' which I sampled from 'I Know You Got Soul' by Eric B. & Rakim, which I'd only bought that day. We then went back into the studio and built it up. I played it on a test pressing at RAW and I thought, "This sounds OK." I remember playing it out of 'Carino', and there's a similar feeling at the beginning of both tracks, which was a tip to Mike Pickering. Rob Milton had left by this time, and Ben and Andy, The Boilerhouse Boys, were now my DJ partners. They said, "This is great. What is it?" and I said, "This is the track I said I was doing with Martyn in the studio."

NOEL WATSON: Dave was at Delirium a lot. We had John 'Jellybean' Benitez over from New York one week and Dave brought us in an early copy of 'Pump Up The Volume' and Jellybean played it three times in his set that night, he loved it so much.

DAVID DORRELL: We were all surprised when 'Pump Up The Volume' took off. It had been Ivo's cunning act to pool two of his most successful acts so he could have a hit, and it worked, just not in the way he originally envisaged. It just captured people's imaginations and suddenly it was all over the radio. It went up to something like number 22 in the charts, and then it was on the verge of going Top 10, and then before we knew it we were at number two, only held off the top spot by Rick Astley's 'Never Gonna Give You Up', which had been number one for something like 14 weeks. We eventually knocked Rick off the top spot, and even managed to hold off Michael Jackson.

RENE GELSTON, BLACK MARKET RECORDS: I was living in New York when the Paradise Garage closed in September 1987, and for me New York was done then – it felt like the end of an era. So I decided to come back to London.

Our club night, Black Market, was still running at The Wag but the DJs were still playing rare groove. All the time I was in New York, I'd been buying a lot of early house records and sending them back to our DJs in London, hoping they would play them. I've still got a handwritten list of the records I was sending back from 1986, including 'Love Can't Turn Around', Chip E.'s 'Time To Jack' and all those early house records. But when I spoke to my wife, Vivienne, she said, "They won't play them!" When I got back they said, "Rene, this house isn't going to happen." But having seen house in New York, I wasn't having it. Steve Jervier and Horace were the residents by then, and I simply sat them down and said, "Look, we've done Black Market for four or five years and it's been great but we've got to move on, and house is the way forward." That was a big statement to make at the time because Black Market was the club that had founded rare groove and it was still one of the most popular and cool nights in London. So it was sending out a big message: rare groove was over and house was the future. Steve Jervier said he knew a young kid in London who was playing house music called Frankie Foncett, so I got Frankie in with Noel Watson downstairs, and Norman Jay was playing upstairs.

JON DASILVA, DJ: I'm from Preston originally, and when I first started to go clubbing there was quite a strong jazz funk scene there. Then I went to the University of Kent in Canterbury, which I found really boring, so I just started messing around with record decks to amuse myself. We started a little DJ crew called The Lucky Bag Crew, which was myself, my ex-girlfriend Francesca Iliffe and Damian Harris, who was a 16-year-old kid from Whitstable who worked in the local record shop then, and later went on to create Skint Records. We were playing everything from Prince to Velvet Underground, to early house to disco. It was, dare I say it, Balearic. Our first gig was at the Labour Club in Whitstable; we charged 50p to get in and Alan Davies, the stand-up comedian, who was a drama student in the year above me, told banana jokes at half-time.

DAMIAN HARRIS, DJ/SKINT RECORDS FOUNDER: I met Jon when he lived in Whitstable where I grew up and we DJ'd together for a while. He was called Jonathan Hibbert then, but he moved to London and then back home and then a few years later I started reading about this DJ called Jon DaSilva, and then I saw a picture of him in a magazine and I was like, "Bloody hell, it's Jon!"

I think the first place I heard house music was on John Peel. At first I was just reading about house music in places like *Record Mirror*, and then you might go to London on a Saturday and manage to buy one record on import from Groove.

JON DASILVA: I moved to London after university to try and make it as a DJ, but it was still the rare groove period and everyone was stood about in floppy caps listening to early Seventies James Brown and The J.B.'s and stuff. There wasn't much happening there in the way of house but up north it was starting to happen, so I moved back home.

One day, on the train back to Preston, I bought a fanzine edited by Sheryl Garrett (who went on to edit *The Face*) at Birmingham train station and there was an article by Steve Harvey about the New York scene; he'd interviewed the main faces, including François Kervorkian, Shep Pettibone and Larry Levan, and that article just completely inspired me. I'd never been to New York, and in fact I didn't until 1994 – almost 10 years later – by which time it was nothing like the scene I had read about. But it was that article and reading about the New York scene and those DJs' techniques and imagining what those clubs were like which inspired me. Most DJs back then had never seen anyone mixing so they had no idea how to do it – they were just guessing – but in 1987 in Preston I was fortunate enough to see a guy called Mike Knowler (see page 31), and he was correcting the vinyl and the pitch on the varispeed – the basic nuts and bolts of mixing. He was way ahead of his time.

★

In London, Mark Moore, Colin Faver and Eddie 'Evil' Richards were introducing more and more house music to their sets, but they were still quite out on their own.

MARK MOORE: Pyramid at Heaven was me, Colin Faver and Eddie Richards originally, although Eddie left later. The crowd at Heaven was amazing. It was meant to be a gay night but because a lot of straight people were still into dressing up flamboyantly at that point, they would come down there because they knew they wouldn't get hassled or beaten up for being a man and wearing eyeliner or looking weird. I'd say it was about 65 per cent gay but the good thing was there was a lot of gay black men, so they really got into the house music when we started to play it.

At first we didn't really know it was house music, we'd just be like, "Oh, here's another one from Chicago…" Eventually the term 'house music' came into use, but at that stage we were still mixing house in with other electronic music like Janet Jackson's 'Control', Soft Cell, Vicious Pink Phenomena's 'Can't You See', Yello, Yellow Magic Orchestra, Liaisons Dangereuses, 'Los Niños Del Parque', Klein + M.B.O.'s 'Dirty Talk', which was a huge record, plus some cheesy Italo. But gradually, house began to take over more and more of the set.

★

Towards the end of the summer of 1987, the promoter Nicky Trax decided to launch a new night called Planet Love at The Fridge in Brixton and installed Mark Moore as resident. By this stage, Moore had made the decision he was going to be more militant and, unlike other DJs in the capital, he was *only* going to play house music.

MARK MOORE: I did adopt a kind of 'take no prisoners' attitude when it came to Planet Love. I had just become so frustrated; I was like, "I don't *care* if you don't like it, *this is great*. You're just *stupid* if you don't realise how good it is. How come no one likes this? This is *ridiculous!*"

I'd read about how some of the DJs were playing house music up north, but I think their crowds were used to a faster tempo, so they could slot it in easier and keep the dancefloor. It was harder in the straight clubs in London at first; it was fine in the gay clubs but the straight clubs just wanted you to keep playing rare groove and hip hop. So when I started Planet Love, which I did with Ian B from Eon, we even put a warning sign outside the club that said, 'WE PLAY HOUSE MUSIC – IF YOU DO NOT LIKE THIS PLEASE DON'T COME IN' as we thought that might stop us being shot by someone.

BILL BREWSTER: When I moved back down [from Nottingham to London], a friend of a friend of mine called Adrian was doing the warm-up slot for Mark Moore at The Fridge in Brixton and we went down to see him, and he was playing what a lot of people were in London – just a mixture of stuff. Then Mark Moore came on and basically declared war. I know that sounds ridiculous but that's what it felt like: as if he was on an absolute mission, and I hated it because it was so extreme. I'd never been in a club where they'd played only one type of music, and those early house music records were so raw. That was the first time I knew what I was hearing was house music and I decided I didn't like it.

Part of it was age I think. When punk happened I was 17 or 18 so it felt like my thing, but by the time house happened I was 28 and it just felt like a threat to everything I knew, which is why it took me much longer to be converted. I didn't avoid it like the plague, but for the next year I went to rare groove parties, squat parties and Soul II Soul at The Africa Centre.* London was quite vibrant just before acid house; it wasn't as if it was crying out for something to come and save it, so that's maybe why house took a while to take off.

★

Promoter Graham Ball started running a night called Enter The Dragon at The Park in west London, playing some house music. More importantly, he ran one-off parties called Westworld at venues like Brixton Academy. Westworld parties were a big step up production-wise from early warehouse parties like Battle Bridge Road, and with fairground rides

---

* Soul II Soul's pre-acid house warehouse parties were hugely influential, but their best-known parties were held at The Africa Centre in Covent Garden.

and the like they were almost a precursor of the huge raves that would come with the explosion of acid house.

NOEL WATSON: Westworld events at Brixton Academy were huge. Graham Ball was the first one to take on big venues and have the vision to bring an element of circus or theatre to it – he would instal a carousel and put on bands and have people dressing up.

TERRY FARLEY: Those Westworld parties Graham Ball did were great and were really almost like a blueprint for the later outdoor raves, with dodgem cars and fairground rides.

★

However, despite the efforts of DJs like Maurice and Noel at Delirium, house music still wasn't gaining wider acceptance. When Mike Pickering came down from Manchester and played the same records that were rocking The Haçienda, he found himself booed off stage.

NOEL WATSON: In the end the owners of The Astoria asked us to move, partly because we had too many black people in the club for their liking because they thought the black kids didn't drink enough. By this stage ecstasy had started to drift in.

JAZZY M: House music still wasn't accepted in London. When we did LWR parties I had glasses and bottles thrown at me and I was threatened. It was tarnished in some people's eyes as being gay music, which just seems fucking ridiculous now, looking back. Some people would refer to it as "batty man music" and I even got abuse in my own record shop if I put house music on. Lads that had come in to buy hip-hop would start shouting at me.

MIKE PICKERING: I started going to London more once we started Deconstruction. After 'Carino' came out I got offered a couple of shows on Kiss and a few DJ gigs, but it was all still very much rare groove and hip hop down there. I did a swap with a guy called Simon Gough at

Fever towards the end of 1987 and I actually got booed off. There were quite a lot of black kids in the house and they were booing the shit out of me, and one of them passed me a note saying, 'Why are you playing this homo music when you could be playing the real groove?' So, being a Manc, I just went, "Right, Fuck you!" and stuck a Derrick May [aka Rhythim Is Rhythim] track on and just upped the tempo.

The funny thing was, six months later I came back to play the first night of Nicky Holloway's night The Trip [*see* page 118] at the same venue, and this time they're all in smiley T-shirts and bandanas, and they all now *love* house music. I was like, "Fucking cockneys! Always six months behind!"

TERRY FARLEY: Mike Pickering may have been passed a note saying, 'Why are you playing this homo music?' but he was playing at The Astoria, which was predominantly a hip-hop club with a hip-hop crowd.

MARK MOORE: I don't think the reaction against house was blatantly homophobic to the extent that they were going to beat you up for playing house, it was more a case of just pure ignorance. A lot of people would just dismiss it as 'fag music' while other people were saying house music was 'just not right for London'. I remember saying for house to take off what was really needed was for the drugs to change, because weed was still the drug of choice, and people just laughed at me. But people were still smoking and into a stoner vibe. I knew if straight people changed the drugs they were taking, the music would really take off. Up north they weren't just stoners, and they had the northern soul influence of speed, which I'm sure helped.

The other club I did was Transatlantic at The Wag Club. That was another of the very first nights on the London scene to concentrate on just playing dance music. I remember playing 'Acid Trax' there when it came out. By that stage there was a core of people, a few key faces, who were first onto house in London, which included Bang The Party – Kid Batchelor, Keith Franklin and Leslie Lawrence – and also people like Trevor Jackson, who turned up at Transatlantic. That's how I met him and asked him to do the sleeve for the first S'Express single. Harvey and other DJs also used to come down to The Mud Club.

I was still mixing it up at The Mud Club at this stage: I'd start the night off with hip hop and build it up to house, then go into Hi-NRG. Because I was playing hip hop, some of the well-known hip hop kids, like Flash and Magic, who used to breakdance in Leicester Square, started coming down to Heaven. I remember the first night they came they were a bit terrified because it was a gay club, worried something might happen to them, but after a little while they were like, "This is fine, they're just normal people!" So they told all their friends, who started coming down, and then one night LL Cool J was in town and someone told him to come. It was incredible to have LL Cool J in Heaven, but he was fine – he wasn't uptight either.

'KID' (LAWRENCE) BATCHELOR, DJ: I grew up on Caledonian Road and went to Copenhagen Primary School and then Holloway Boys school. I was at Holloways Boys with Richard [West, Mr. C] but we weren't particularly close at first, until we found a connection through music.

I started DJing when I was about 15 in about 1983. That's where I got my name from; I was the youngest in my family so I was always the kid, and because I started DJing so young people used to call me 'the kid Batchelor'. My family still call me 'the baby' now – I'm six feet tall and when I walk through the door they say, "Here's the baby."

I started out with Soul II Soul, as Jazzie B was another school friend of mine, and he was responsible for spotting my talent, if I had any. We used to play shebeens all over east London. Then we started doing warehouse parties and then the rare groove scene exploded and we started doing warehouse parties in collaboration with some of the white trendy crowd. Then came Soul II Soul at The Africa Centre. From there I developed an interest in electronica and this new fresh sound coming from Chicago, which was really disco in the raw to me; minimalist DIY music they were making in their bedrooms. You forget how revolutionary it was because everyone is making music in their bedrooms now, but house was really the first instance. I first heard that music through DJs/producers I used to follow and I would see their names next to records, people like Boyd Jarvis, Timmy Regisford, Tom Moulton* and Larry Levan.

In London I only heard house music in the gay clubs at first. People like Mark Moore and Colin Faver were playing it. I used to go to a black gay club called Stallions, which was next to Busby's in Tottenham Court Road. Stallions was very black and very gay, and they were playing house very early on. Because I was so into the music, that was the club I had to go to.

I then got together with Keith Franklin and Leslie Lawrence and started Bang The Party dance group. We were based at 389 Harrow Road, which was the reggae studio used by the likes of Aswad and Lee 'Scratch' Perry. It was owned by a guy called Tony Addis, who I got quite friendly with. We kind of became the new generation of that studio, which was steeped in reggae and roots. We brought the electronic beats and fused them with the musical history of the studio. Soul II Soul would then use the studio after us. That multi-million-selling sound came from 389 Harrow Road; it all comes from the history of that studio. That's why there was a heavy bass to those Bang The Party records America loved – that heavy end just came through *that* desk.

GRAEME PARK: I was still plugging away on my own in Nottingham in the summer of 1987, and it still felt very underground. You wouldn't read about house anywhere. The first coverage I remember was when *Blues & Soul* magazine came up to The Garage and did a little feature on what I was playing. The only other time I heard anyone playing house was if I went to a funk and soul weekender and Simon 'Bassline' Smith, Trevor M, Jonathan Woodland and Colin Curtis would generally be playing soul and funk, but some of the house stuff could work in there. Then *i-D* decided to do a feature towards the end of 1987 on 'The New Breed Of DJ', who didn't use the mic and didn't play stuff in the

---

* Tom Moulton is an American dance music producer and pioneer of the remix and 12" vinyl.

charts. I was invited down to London to be part of it. That's when I met Nicky Holloway, Mark Moore, Jazzie B, Jazzy M, Judge Jules and Mike Pickering. I was already aware of Mike because of his Quando Quango releases on Factory and T-Coy's 'Carino' on Deconstruction, which was a record I played at The Garage. Mike and I were the only non-London DJs in the feature and we got chatting and realised we were both playing house. Most of London was still playing rare groove; Mark Moore will argue house music started in London but we all know it started in the North. If I met him now we'd still have a light-hearted but serious debate about it.

★

In late summer of 1987, the first ecstasy arrived in Manchester. Groups of lads from Manchester had been going to Europe since the late Seventies and early Eighties to watch football and 'graft' in Amsterdam. There they were introduced to ecstasy, before bringing it back to their fellow Mancunians.

SHAUN RYDER: The summer of 1987: that's when everything changed really. That's when life suddenly went from black and white to Technicolor. When I first had the E. It was Bez [soon-to-be fellow band member] who gave me my first one, predictably. The first ones we got were little white ones. They didn't have anything written on them. They came from a French guy in a gay club in Amsterdam. One of our lot used to buy some weed off him, and one night he gave my pal this pill to try. He was knocked off his feet and brought a few back to Manchester in a tube of toothpaste. I'm pretty sure they were the first Es to arrive in Manchester, in that tube of toothpaste. One tube of Colgate changed everything. People bang on about the Sex Pistols gig at the Free Trade Hall in Manchester in 1976, and how there were only 40 people there, but [the E] changed everything. When we first had the E, there couldn't have been more than about a dozen of us. There was me, our kid, Bez, Big Minny, Little Minny, Muzzer, Platty, our Matt and Pat, Cressa, Eric Barker and a couple of other kids. We were the only ones with the E at the time. No one else had a clue what was going on.

ERIC BARKER, GRAFTER/PROMOTER: The first time I came across ecstasy was in The Haçienda. Before that The Hac was just like trying to have a good time in big empty warehouses. Bez and Shaun and a few of the other lads, like Platty, got onto it first, and I just observed it initially; I didn't dive straight in, as I wasn't normally one for not being in control. I'd dabbled in bits and pieces of drugs before, mainly speed, but I wasn't really into drugs before ecstasy. Eventually I decided to try it and someone gave me half a California Sunrise and that was it. All bets were off, and I was up on a podium with my arms in the air. There must have been only about 15 of us at it at first, in our little corner of The Haçienda. God knows what the rest of the club thought. People must have wondered what the fuck we were on. It was like a zoo and we were the exhibits. If you walked into The Haçienda, everyone else would look kind of normal, and then you'd look to the left and see about 15 of our lot going bananas and dancing very weirdly, completely differently to everyone else in the club.

I've no idea where the dancing styles came from, but we all had our own little mad styles from the start. Platty used to have a mad little dance, and obviously Bez had his own unique style. I had always been a dancer anyway, since my sister taught me to dance to Motown when I was 10. By the time acid house arrived I'd been going out in Manchester for 10 years and I'd always been dancing, but never with my hands in the air. I mean, who *did* dance with their arms in the air before ecstasy? No one in Manchester, I'll tell you that. But when the E arrived, all of a sudden you felt your hands rising up in the air while you were dancing. You couldn't help it. A few of the lads were a bit shy about dancing because they'd never really danced before, which is why I ended up on the podium first. I was like, "You want to dance? I'll show you how to fucking dance!" and just got up there and started going for it.

Within a few months of first taking the E I was wearing silk pyjamas and a fez to The Haçienda. The pyjamas came about because your jeans would get soaked through with sweat; you got so hot everyone looked like they had been on fire when they walked out of the Haç at the end of the night, there was steam rising off them. So I started wearing silk pyjamas, which were a lot cooler and better for dancing. It seemed like a good idea at the time; admittedly, looking back now, I might have looked a bit 'off' walking through town.

SHAUN RYDER: The lads bringing the E back from Amsterdam got us involved, and after a few weeks we started to make a bit of money from the E, from introducing people to it, but it did take people a little while to get used to spending £25 on it; people weren't used to spending that amount of money on drugs, especially on one little pill.

MIKE PICKERING: As soon as they got hold of E, the whole place just went berserk. It was like a tidal wave across the club from their alcove. One of the first noticeable things to me was the dancefloor went a lot whiter. Ecstasy made the white kids dance. You could see the black kids who had been the main dancers getting moved over a bit because of all this rave dancing. People were going mad, so there wasn't much floor space. It was the best scene I've ever been involved in; there were people from all walks of life, all getting on, and it was so creative when it first started. It was new to everybody. There were some real characters about, and everyone had mad names, like 'Jeff The Chef'. Some of the things people got up to would make great films, although no one would believe it was based on real life.

Nude was the first big night for acid house at The Haçienda. It had started in 1986 and I gradually introduced some acid house. By 1988, we had about 1,600 people in there and when ecstasy hit it was like a Mexican wave that swept through the club over a three-week period. Suddenly everyone was on ecstasy. I could just stop a record and put my hands in the air, and the place would erupt. The whole club would explode.

ERIC BARKER: We were paying £20 for Es when they first arrived, which was a lot of money, so I very quickly moved on to shifting a few. I would buy 10 for £100 and then lay them on someone else for £15, and they would knock them out for £20. So everyone's making a fiver a piece and paying for their own drugs and getting on it. Which was fine, until everyone got so loved up they started giving them away. You'd lay some Es on for someone and then they'd come back and say, "Sorry, I've given them all away." But because you were loved up yourself, you just let them off and it just ended up with one big circle of everyone owing everyone else money, but no one gave a fuck. It wouldn't happen today; in fact, it only happened back then for a short while because after a little while the drugs changed slightly and everyone stopped being so loved up and got a bit more hard nosed about it.

★

In the first national coverage of the scene that would eventually become branded 'Madchester', the Mondays and their cohorts were featured in a short piece in *i-D* magazine in October 1987, which christened them 'the Baldricks', likening their haircuts and unkempt appearance to Tony Robinson's character Baldrick from the TV period sitcom *Blackadder*. But the nickname was never adopted up north.

SHAUN RYDER: No one in Manchester called themselves a 'Baldrick'. No one. In Manchester, the lads would have called themselves Perry Boys earlier on, then Pure Boys, but by that time they were probably just 'boys'.

★

Trevor Fung had moved back out to Ibiza at the start of 1987 to open a bar with his cousin Ian St Paul, which they called Project Bar. Their timing couldn't have been more perfect. It may have been lost on most of the Brits who visited in the early Eighties on Club 18-30 holidays, but Ibiza has been a sanctuary for hedonists and freedom-seekers for thousands of years. According to legend, Ibiza's Es Vedrà is where the Sirens lured sailors to their deaths in Homer's *Odyssey*. The seventh-century Carthaginians named the island after their god of dance, Bez (no relation to the Happy Mondays dancer), and in the Sixties the hippies descended on the isle, along with Pink Floyd and The Rolling Stones.

Originally a *finca*, Amnesia had been converted into a club in 1976 but wasn't an immediate success; Trevor Fung had DJed there in 1983 when it was dead. In 1984, Alfredo took over, having spent the previous two seasons building it up.

ALFREDO, DJ: I can pinpoint the exact night everything changed. We were all waiting around to get paid as usual. The club would close at 6a.m. but we would all have to hang around until the owner turned up at 7a.m. to pay us. I was only getting paid 5,000 pesetas a night, which is about 30 euros or £25. My girlfriend suggested I play some records for everyone while we waited. So I said OK and re-opened the DJ cabin. There was only a handful of people there; almost all of them were people who worked at the club or their girlfriends and boyfriends. But then a few people walking home from Ku Club heard the music and came over to investigate. They loved what I was doing because back then what I was playing was so different from the music in the other clubs. There were no more than 100 people that night, but they went home and told all their friends and brought them down the next night. So the next night we had 300 people, who in turn all went home and told their friends, and after a week the club was full. For the first time ever. So we then decided to open the club later; we had been open from 12 midnight to 9a.m. but after those initial few weeks when the club was full, we decided we wouldn't open until 3a.m. but stayed open until midday, which was the first time a club had done that in Ibiza.

Amnesia was the first after-hours club on the island – no one even used the phrase 'after-hours club' until quite a few years later, when it became more of a trend. We weren't really aware of what was happening off the island at that point, but I later found out it was probably the first after-hours club anywhere in the world.

Back then people weren't used to dancing all night, for hours on end, and finding themselves dancing as the sun came up. That for me was always a sign that I had played a good set, if people lost all sense of time and then suddenly they'd be like, "Wow, it's 9a.m. in the morning!" They felt the music had taken them somewhere else, into a trance almost, and it's only when their feet had come down to earth again they realised they'd been dancing all night.

These people were coming back because the club was different, the atmosphere was different, and the music was different to what was played in all the other clubs. I very quickly realised that in this unique open-air space, with a pretty diverse and open-minded crowd, I could play music which wasn't necessarily written for the dance floor. One of the first records I used to play regularly was [Art of Noise's] 'Moments In Love', which is certainly not a song written with the dancefloor in mind, but when I incorporated it into my set and people danced I began to realise it was possible for me to pick out records that weren't made for the dance floor and I could actually make them *work* on the dancefloor.

Some famous people came but they were cool famous people who wanted to be anonymous, not famous people who just wanted to be seen; they were the sort of famous people that heard about it by word of mouth and were just happy to be part of this wonderful organic atmosphere. There were no private areas or reserved seats. People came and they danced wherever they wanted and they stayed as long as they wanted. Grace Jones would dance next to some anonymous guy or girl from the street, a barman, whatever. If someone like Grace Jones or The Clash came down hardly anyone would realise anyway; no one made a fuss because it wouldn't even register with the sort of crowd we had in that club. We had so many famous people – musicians and artists, painters and actors, from Spain, England, Europe and all over the world – and I wouldn't even know they had been there until later. Sometimes I will read about someone famous saying, "Oh, I remember Alfredo at Amnesia," and think I don't ever remember seeing you. But many of the people who came down I didn't even see myself because I was playing records. I never saw Freddie Mercury when he came down because people weren't making a fuss.

★

In September 1987, it was Paul Oakenfold's 25th birthday. To celebrate, Oakenfold, Johnny Walker, Danny Rampling and Nicky Holloway went to Ibiza to visit Trevor Fung and Ian St Paul. They had also heard, through Fung and Paul, about what Alfredo was up to in Amnesia.

DANNY RAMPLING: The Ibiza chimps party. Nicky Holloway and Paul Oakenfold organised it. Nicky had already done a few parties in Ibiza, which must have been in '83, '84 or maybe '85, that I'd been to and enjoyed thoroughly. I'd also been there with a girlfriend in '81, but I knew nothing about the island then and we didn't really see a great deal of it. Even so, you could feel the energy of the island.

There was just the four of us who went, for a week. Nicky had hired a villa on the outskirts of San Antonio, near the bay, which was quite a flash thing to do but he was quite a Harry Enfield 'Loadsamoney' character back then. He'd also hired villas there previously. The place was quite lovely; we were only 24 years old in a villa probably costing £1,000 a week.

NICKY HOLLOWAY: We were only kids and thought it would be a cool, flash thing to do.

NICKY HOLLOWAY: I was quite anti-drugs. I was always worried about people smoking weed in my venues because you could lose your licence and it would be my neck on the block. In those days 'drugs' was a bad word. But we'd heard about ecstasy and Trevor was talking about it. I was the last one to take mine; it's only when I saw all the others having such a good time I went, "Fuck this, I'm in." Then we went to Amnesia and that was it. Our lives changed. You can draw a line in the sand right there. It was a different world – I know that sounds stupid, but it was. We were all walking round with these big fluffy heads thinking if they gave this [ecstasy] to everyone there'd be no more wars.

PAUL OAKENFOLD: Amnesia was an old farm, miles away, so we were like, "How are we going to get there?" In those days, we had just about enough money for a bread roll – Ibiza's expensive, always has been. But we went. It was the first night of our holiday and we'd heard it was something special.

DANNY RAMPLING: Amnesia was a complete revelation. Alfredo, as a DJ, blended texture and music in a way I would compare to a Miro painting. For me, he was the Larry Levan [legendary DJ from the Paradise Garage in New York in the late Seventies] of Europe. Interestingly, Alfredo was connected to an American who was part of the Paradise Garage group, who used to supply him with records. Dancing in the open air, surrounded by an incredible mix of sexy people, was mind-blowing.

PAUL OAKENFOLD: In England at that time, clubs only played one type of music, and London was full of attitude. But at Amnesia you had 7,000 people dancing to Cyndi Lauper. Total freedom.

ALFREDO: In the summer of 1987 I was playing Thrashing Doves' 'Jesus On The Payroll', Elkin and Nelson's 'Jibaro', Joao Gilberto, Talking Heads, Prince, Bob Marley, the Woodentops. Early in the evening I'd play Manuel Göttsching's 'E2-E4' or Art of Noise's 'Moments In Love'. I was playing music from South America, Europe, different places. It was the time of the Berlin Wall, glasnost, and there was a feeling of unity among Europeans that influenced the music.

NICKY HOLLOWAY: We all tried ecstasy for the first time together, and then the whole thing made sense. Alfredo was playing [Chicago house label imprints] Trax and DJ International next to Kate Bush and Queen, all the white English acts we'd turn our noses up at. But on E, it all made sense. Half an hour or so after you necked a pill you would suddenly feel this euphoric wave go through you, like Shooom! – hence the name of Danny's club – and you suddenly felt that everything in the world was all right.

JOHNNY WALKER, DJ: We were under the stars, in the warm summer air, hearing this amazing mixture Alfredo was playing. In the middle of the open-air dance floor was a mirrored pyramid, then around the edges were bars and chill-out areas with cushions and Mediterranean and tropical plants. It was high walled, like being in a tropical garden.

NICKY HOLLOWAY: The music was a strange mix. If we hadn't had the Es we would have thought it was shit. Alfredo was playing early house records on D.J. International*, but he was also playing Queen and 'Sledgehammer'. It was a mix of Europop and early house, which is now what we call Balearic, and it included bands from England we'd never heard of before, like Thrashing Doves.

DANNY RAMPLING: I'll bring something different to the table here. I discovered something recently, through my own research. In August 1987, there was an event called the Harmonic Convergence, a global shift in unity consciousness through dance rituals, which is part of the Mayan calendar teachings. I felt there was something deeper, spiritually, running through the whole experience.

NICKY HOLLOWAY: Afterwards, we went back to the villa and it was all a bit weird. We were all standing in the pool, holding hands listening to Art of Noise's 'Moments In Love', like a load of wallies, all chilled out and loved up, thinking it was going to change the world.

TERRY FARLEY: People say they went to Ibiza in 1987 and it changed their world. That's fine, but Ibiza hadn't always been that way. The first time I heard about Ibiza was when a kid from my estate, who was a hairdresser and in a band, was signed to Elton John's record label Rocket Records and they flew him out to a party at Ku in 1979. He came back and told everyone stories of gay waiters in jock straps walking round with trays of cocaine. We were like, "Yeah, fuck off!" We thought he was a bullshitter until years later when we read about those parties. Nicky Holloway had been doing stuff out there. But I think it only seemed to really change when Alfredo started the after-hours at Amnesia; that was when all the freaks on the island came together, and you had a critical mass of freaks to make something happen. Before then, there wasn't

---

* D.J. International was a pioneering Chicago label that released many of the early house records, including Steve 'Silk' Hurley's 'Jack Your Body' (which went to number one in the UK) and Farley 'Jackmaster' Funk's 'Love Can't Turn Around', which was also a huge UK hit.

enough people and probably not enough drugs in one place for it to explode, so he's no doubt responsible for that.

ALFREDO – Back then I knew people really liked what we were doing, that they loved the democracy on the dancefloor of Amnesia – the democracy of the music and of the people, and how open-minded the music was, compared to other clubs. But I was in a little bubble really. I knew what we were doing was unusual, and was not happening at other clubs, but I had no idea at first how big it was becoming, and certainly no idea that it would become known outside Ibiza and become famous.

I wanted to be successful at what I did, but by that I just meant playing a great set each night at Amnesia, creating the best party and giving people the best night out. I honestly didn't think any bigger than that. All I thought about was Amnesia and the next night. That was my focus, it was the only thing I thought about. I certainly wasn't thinking that I was creating this whole new thing called Balearic beat. That thought never entered my head. Which is good, because that wouldn't have been good for my ego... and a little later when I did begin to think a bit about how big this whole thing had got, it did mash my head a bit.

★

Although many of the emerging British DJs had found their way to house from the soul scene, pockets of musicians from very different musical backgrounds were discovering the new music from Chicago and attempting their own approximation of it.

RICHARD NORRIS, RECORD PRODUCER/MUSICIAN/ THE GRID: People came to acid house from very different backgrounds. A lot of people came from that soul boy background, from Nicky Holloway's Special Branch. But I very much came from the alternative background, from 23 Skidoo and stuff like that.

In the summer of 1987, I was working at this record label called Bam-Caruso and editing this magazine called *Strange Things* and I went to interview Genesis P-Orridge and he was fascinating; he just said to me,

"Have you heard acid house?" and he started wittering on about it. Turns out he hadn't really heard it either but we both loved the idea of this psychedelic dance music, so he suggested we go in the studio and I was like, "Great, why not?" He found this tiny studio in Chiswick, which was literally about 12 foot wide and we went in the next weekend. I brought a load of people from Bam-Caruso and he brought a load of his mates including Dave Ball from Soft Cell. We had an early Akai sampler and an ancient Atari computer with the music software Cubase on it, but we were really lucky to have a young, enthusiastic, great engineer called Richard Evans, who was phenomenally quick and went on to be Peter Gabriel's main engineer at Real World.

P-Orridge had already done a lot of that 'found' sound and there was *My Life In The Bush Of Ghosts* [a 1981 album by Brian Eno and David Byrne, named after Amos Tutuola's 1954 novel], Tackhead and stuff like Cabaret Voltaire*, so it didn't seem that much of a leap to purely sample-based music. We basically all turned up with a pile of records and films and fed all this stuff into a sampler, stuck it on a keyboard, made a noise with it and added drum loops. We used the sample from the film *Wild Angels* that Primal Scream later used on [1990's] 'Loaded', a bit of Tiny Tim and even a sample of Genesis and his wife shagging! Each song was written and recorded in an hour. Me and Dave Ball took an hour and a half on one track and Genesis was like, "Come on! What are you *doing*? This is taking *ages*!"

There was a real desire to do things quickly in that period, and time seemed to be very sped up. Those few months between the late summer of 1987 and spring of 1988 seemed to last about five minutes, and things were changing so quickly. Even what people wore was changing all the time; they started loosening their collars and then all of a sudden they were turning up in fluorescent Mambo T-shirts.

★

* Formed in 1973, Cabaret Voltaire was an influential experimental electronic music group from Sheffield.

On returning from Ibiza, Paul Oakenfold and Trevor Fung decided to hold an Ibiza reunion at The Project Club. One Friday, Oakenfold DJ'd at the normal hip-hop night until closing time at 2a.m. Those who had been tipped off then waited behind for half an hour, before the club re-opened for the Ibiza reunion party.

CARL COX: Oakenfold would have his hip-hop night from 8p.m. to 2a.m., where he'd play Def Jam records and Profile records. Then once that was finished he'd have an after-party and put up DayGlo banners and get a smoke machine and play acid house and Balearic beat until 6a.m. He'd end up getting guests like Pete Tong and even Alfredo from Amnesia to come and play, and I would basically warm up for them. That, for me, was where I began to make a name for myself really, by playing this music. I never really went to any of those early clubs to be inspired by any of those other DJs or anything; I created my complete own destiny when it came to playing this music.

STEVEN HALL: The first person to go down to The Project was Gary Haisman. Gary said, "You've got to come down this club, you'll love it, it's ludicrous – the music, the clothes, they even dance funny – you've got to come." A few of the people down there were ex-football heads, so Terry and Gary knew them from that.

CYMON ECKEL: I remember Gary Haisman, Rocca and Terry went to The Project at Ziggy's in Streatham. I think Rocca said he was cowering in the cloakroom because he couldn't believe the sort of people he was surrounded by because they all looked like proper hooligans. The rest of them were like, "Fuck me, this is crazy, the music is brilliant," and they really got into it.

DANNY RAMPLING: A lot of the old London crowd hadn't got it at first. When I played gigs in regular clubs people were like, "He's lost his mind! What's going on here? This is the work of the devil, I don't want anything to do with it!" So many people dissed it in the early stages, at the tail-end of 1987, and then all of a sudden people's enthusiasm for the whole experience just exploded in a matter of weeks. I can still see the faces of some of the people in those clubs; the look of bewilderment was just astonishing. It was like, "God, you don't know what we're experiencing here, you don't know what you're missing out on." Subsequently, a lot of those people joined the party, around the late summer of 1988, particularly a lot of the old rare groove and funky crowd. They weren't going to miss out on the greatest thing to come along in years.

★

House evangelist Mark Moore was the next DJ to try his hand in the studio, with the help of indie label Rhythm King Records, who were fresh from the success of the 1987 Bomb The Bass single 'Beat Dis'.

MARK MOORE: I started work on what would become S'Express in the autumn of 1987. Tim Simeon had got together with Pascal Gabriel as Bomb The Bass and produced 'Beat Dis', and Rhythm King just thought it was incredible. When I heard it I asked them if I could do a record.

I was kind of doing A&R for Rhythm King records in an unofficial capacity; I lived across from their offices on the Harrow Road so I would just go in and see if I could ponce a few imports on 12-inch. I'd started advising them what records to sign up and they got their first hit with Taffy's 'I Love My Radio', which used to be played at Taboo, then I got them The Beatmasters' 'Rok Da House' and Renegade Soundwave and Baby Ford. They said, "You haven't asked for anything in return – what do you want?" and I said, "Can you put me in the studio?" They just went, "Yes, amazing! Tim worked with Pascal, so why don't you go in with him?" I had all the ideas already and made a cassette with all the bits on, and I explained which bit went where and Pascal and I just went in and did 'Theme From S'Express', 'Superfly Guy' and the B-sides in the first sessions.

Pascal and I just hit it off really well and it didn't take long at all. But ['Theme From S'Express'] took a little while to come out, so it was on white label for ages. The first time I played it was off cassette at Heaven and the response was *amazing*, completely brilliant. Except for one thing: I had a Donna Summer sample on there at that stage, from 'Our Love', which is one of my favourite Donna Summer/ Giorgio Moroder tracks; there's a break where she comes in and goes, "Our love will last forever, our love…" and then a drumbeat comes in, which I'm pretty sure influenced New Order's 'Blue Monday'. This was around the time that Donna Summer was alleged to have said something along the lines of AIDS is "God's way of saying that gays are wrong," which I actually don't believe she said. But that night when I first played the track at Heaven, when the Donna Summer sample came in someone booed. Only one person, but I went home and took it out. If you listen to the 12" version now, there's a gap where Donna Summer should be. I've still got the Donna Summer version on cassette somewhere.

Danny Rampling, Paul Oakenfold, Johnny Walker and Pete Tong all used to come down to Heaven. Oakenfold had been coming down for a long time because he was running a record promotions service called Rush Release, and he would bring records down for us. After I started to play 'Theme From S'Express' at Heaven, Danny came up to me and said, "I've *got* to have a copy of that track of yours that goes, "I've got the house for you, I've got the house for you," and I laughed and said, "It's 'hots', Danny – 'hots'!" So I made a cassette of it for him, and we struck up a friendship and he invited me down to his new night called Shoom, and asked me to DJ. Danny had already got Colin Faver in to DJ at his new night, and it felt like everyone was starting to connect. Prior to Shoom, I suppose I was part of the West End trendy (although I hate that word) scene, which would be covered in *i-D* and *The Face*, and Danny and most of that lot were all part of the soul scene and Special Branch, which was a lot straighter, a lot more heterosexual, so I hadn't had much to do with it. I'd never been to Special Branch.

★

Danny and Jenni Rampling launched their new club on a Saturday night in November, in the unlikely location of a fitness centre in the equally unlikely location of Southwark in southeast London.

CARL COX: Danny used to come to Nicky Holloway's Special Branch and he'd also come down to The Project when I was doing that with Oakey and Trevor Fung. When I first knew him he was called Danny Rampo and he was playing funk and soul, not house music. Then he went to Ibiza and saw the light and he never looked back. He wanted something to define him, something that would make him. But at the beginning he knew he needed some kind of alliance, someone to help him do it: he knew I had the music; he knew I had the sound system; and he knew I would bring a certain amount of people to the party.

On the first night we played, half the people came down in afro wigs, flares and platform shoes, and the other half were in dungarees and DayGlo. But of course we weren't playing funk and soul, we were playing acid house, so those in the afro wigs and flares soon realised they were in the wrong place. It did take a little while to weed that element out, but within a few weeks Shoom had become a phenomenon.

DANNY RAMPLING: I picked up on the smiley face logo from a fashion designer called Barnsley. I ran into him one night when he was covered in these smiley face badges and I thought, "Wow! That's it! The smiley face completely signifies what this movement is all about - big smiles and positivity." I think we first used them on the flyer for the third Shoom, and everyone picked up on it.

CHRIS BUTLER (SHOOM/TRIP REGULAR): The first Shoom was in November 1987. I didn't go to that but Rocky from X-Press2, who I now manage, did, with Mark Jones from Wall of Sound. He's got a great story about driving through south London with this massive wooden 'X' in the back of the car, covered in Silver paper, that Danny would put in front of the decks. I went to the second Shoom, and then every one after that. I'd not really heard acid house before that. At the early Shooms, a lot of people were still wearing flares and a lot of the

78

rare groove gear. Everyone was on E apart from a guy called Wayne M. He was the only person in there who was straight. I can remember him stood there with a can of beer, horrified, like "What the fuck are you lot doing?" But even he went bananas on E later down the line. There were some great characters. A lovely black kid called Breeze, who later died unfortunately. Leonard the Dog, who always started barking when he was off it, even back at my house, he'd just stand in the corner of the room and start barking. Anton Le Pirate, who could drive you insane if you were stuck with him too long.

TIMNA ROSE (SHOOM REGULAR): A friend of ours, Gayle, knew Jenni, so she was our in really. She asked Jenni if it was OK to bring us and Jenni said yes, it was all very word of mouth at first. I turned up in these old dungarees with flowers all over them and yellow converse trainers. We dropped an E on the tube on the way there, so that by the time we got there we would be coming up. Jenni saw us in the queue and let us in. I can still remember vividly walking in to Shoom for the first time. I was coming up as we walked down the steps and you just felt this energy and buzz that was overwhelming. I turned to Lewis, my boyfriend at the time, and said, "This is it… this is what I've been waiting for all my life." I can remember that first night so clearly. I can remember being on the dancefloor and needing the loo, but the smoke was so thick I was completely disorientated. I had no idea which way was left or right or up or down. I think we went almost every week after that. There was no way we were going to miss one night of Shoom. The second night of Shoom I ran into this girl that I had filmed with called Lisa Grayley, who became my best friend for years, as we worked together and were part of this secret scene together, so we were real partners in crime. She passed away unfortunately, a few years ago.

NICKY HOLLOWAY: I had a massive fall-out with Danny around the time he launched Shoom. He was my mate, but the first I heard about Shoom was when I saw a flyer for it on the floor of my club. He had used my flyer guy, my security guy and the guy who used to supply my sound system, Carl Cox. It was just a bit weird because I didn't know about it until it was in print. I was like, "Oh, he's gone and done a gig behind my back and not told me about it." As far as I was concerned, Danny was my mate and my box carrier, and no one really took him seriously, and then all of a sudden he was catapulted to superstardom. I had my nose put out of joint, I really did.

JAZZY M: I was asked to DJ at Shoom before it even started. They wanted me to DJ with Danny and Colin Faver – I think this was before they decided to get Carl Cox involved. But I fell out with Jenni Rampling immediately. Literally. So I never ended up playing there. I can't even remember why I fell out with her to be honest. I have a bit of a reputation as a hothead, although I prefer to think of it as passion. I have learnt over the years to separate business from passion a bit more successfully. But I did go down to one of the first Shooms and it was just mental. It was great, just properly, properly mental. Bonkers.

MARK MOORE: Danny invited me down to Shoom, but when I first arrived everyone was just kind of moping about like zombies in clouds of dry ice, and I thought, "This isn't very good, what's the big deal?" Then about an hour later, as everyone came up on their Es and the energy started, it was incredible, madness – everyone hugging each other, lots of people asking your name, people coming up and trying to arrange your face into a smile. I just thought, "Oh my god, they're *all* on ecstasy! That's what it is." It was great.

The thing is they were all on drugs but because they were all so young and fresh faced, they still looked incredible. It was a different crowd to West End clubs like The Wag; these kids were less pretentious, they weren't fashion victims and they probably would have been turned away from The Wag Club to be honest. But they were lovely and it was so refreshing to be mixing with another crowd. I'd been to warehouse parties and stuff in south London but I'd found them quite straight.

★

Although Mike Pickering had already introduced house music at The Haçienda, for some there was another club that launched acid house in Manchester, a small gay club called Stuffed Olives which would play house music on a Sunday night. It had previously been called Bernard's Bar, and Morrissey had name-checked it only a year earlier in an interview with *Melody Maker*. "The gay scene in Manchester was always atrocious. Do you remember Bernard's Bar, now Stuffed Olives?... If one wanted peace and to sit without being called a parade of names then that was the only hope."

By late 1988, there was no hope of getting peace in Stuffed Olives – not on a Sunday night, anyway. Steven Patrick Morrissey would have been shocked by the shift in music policy and the young and tender hooligans the club was attracting to its packed Sunday nights.

JON DASILVA: Sunday nights at Stuffed Olives, or Stuffed Bums as some people used to call it, was really important early on in Manchester. The DJs were Dominic Montague and Andy Madhatter, and after 10.30p.m., when they were supposed to close, they used to put the rags over the beer pumps and the optics and they would only serve spirits and we continued partying. I managed to get my break there. It was one of the first places in Manchester to start playing house and I could mix – no one else was mixing at the time – so I managed to make a name for myself, and that's where it started for me really. It was Stuffed Olives that would get me the gig at The Haçienda.

ANTHONY DONNELLY, RAVE ORGANISER/GIO-GOI FASHION LABEL CO-FOUNDER: I know exactly where I first heard acid house and where I first experienced it, which are two separate things really. I'd ended up back at Bernard Sumner's new house one night in late 1987, with Keith Allen and a few others. I'd had cocaine that night but still hadn't had an E, and Bernard had a cassette of acid house which he stuck on this massive system he had, but it didn't really do anything for me.

I first properly *experienced* it a short while after, at Stuffed Olives on a Sunday night. I went to watch United at Old Trafford one week and I bumped into Eric Barker and he was wearing silk pyjamas. Silk fucking pyjamas! At the match! The rest of us were all in the latest clobber – top trainers and jackets, and Eric was stood there wearing silk pyjamas and a Moroccan beanie. I said, "What the *fuck* are you doing wearing wearing silk pyjamas at the match?!" He just looked at me like an Indian guru who had just got out of bed and said, "You *need* to get on the Es." I said, "What do you mean?" and he just repeated, "You *need* to get on the Es." So he made me meet him the following night and he took me down to Stuffed Olives.

When we got there, someone Eric knew gave me a pill and it just sent me fucking mental. Bananas. The dancefloor was slightly lower than the rest of the club and there was a railing round it, and I was just stood there gripping this railing. The smoke was really thick and I could smell and taste it because they used to put poppers in the smoke machine. I thought I was in a fucking spaceship. My whole body is rocking and I'm still gripping this railing, and Eric kept saying to me, "Let go of the bar... let go of the railing...", so I did and as soon as I did, fuck me, I just took off. That was it then. Honestly, all of a sudden it's like someone switched the lights on. There was no going back.

That very week there was a phone call to London to see if someone could get hold of any of these Es. Within a week, 200 Californian Sunrises arrived, and they were individually bubble-wrapped.

CHRIS DONNELLY, GIO-GOI CO-FOUNDER: Just before acid house broke I had long hair and was into smoking weed and listening to Frank Zappa, and then the week before I went to Stuffed Olives I had all my hair cut off. Then Anthony took me down there and I had the same experience as he had and one of my first thoughts was, "Oh no, why did I cut all my hair off?" and I started growing it again straight away.

It was mind-blowing. It actually was like a zoo in there. It was mostly gay but then there were a few football hooligans, us lot,

An early acid house convert at The Trip club night, The Astoria, London 1988. DAVID SWINDELLS/PYMCA

YO! B.U.M. RUSH

i-D magazine March, 1988.

DJ Danny Rampling at his original Shoom club night, at the fitness centre, Southwark, July 1988. The dancer in the background is well known acid house face Anton Le Pirate. DAVID SWINDELLS/PYMCA

Paul Oakenfold, Lisa Lashes and friends at Shoom, 1988. DAVID SWINDELLS/PYMCA

Terry Farley, DJ and co-founder of Boys Own fanzine, early acid house rave, 1988. DAVID SWINDELLS/PYMCA

Shaun and Bez and their entourage. We hadn't been in a gay club before but it didn't faze us; it probably freaked them out more to see scallies like us coming in their club to be honest. At first, it felt like you were going to war every week. As soon as you'd had your first experience, then you'd want to recruit your pal and take him into battle with you next week. That was the best thing about acid house at first – turning other people onto it and seeing them have the same reaction you'd had when you first saw the light. You'd tell them what the experience was like, and then watch them take their first pill, shitting their pants, then see them start to come up. Then you'd bump into them on the middle of the dancefloor an hour later and they'd have a huge grin and their arms and legs would be going in different directions.

They used to leave these little notes on the bar in Stuffed Olives which just said, "Ecstasy – one is all you need but is seldom enough," by which I presume they meant you only needed one to open the door but then you'll just want more.

ANTHONY DONNELLY: The Haçienda was great, like nothing else. But Stuffed Olives is where it first really happened in this town for me. You had to fight for your fucking life to get in there on a Sunday night. People would sell their mothers to get in there because by the time they'd arrived, they'd already dropped their pill and there was nowhere else to go, so if you didn't get into Stuffed Olives you were fucked. I remember the police being sat outside in a car looking at everyone trying to get in, all with eyes like 10-bob bits. They were scratching their heads going, "What the fuck is going on here? It's like a zoo," especially as they knew they didn't even serve booze in Stuffed Olives. They couldn't work out what the fuck was going on.

SHAUN RYDER: We used to go across to Stuffed Olives as well around that time, as that was one of the only other places that was playing acid house at that stage. There was still only a handful of us into it. We pretty much had the last few months of 1987 to ourselves really. There were still only a few pockets of people who had turned on to what was beginning to happen at the end of 1987. It wasn't until early 1988 that the E scene really started to kick off.

CHAPTER 4

Shoom Shoom

"They were almost like disciples of Danny's; I remember one girl telling me she could see his aura while he was DJing, and do you know, to a certain extent maybe you could."

Terry Farley

DAVE HASLAM, DJ: I clearly remember bumping into Tony Wilson on the street at the start of 1988, and I'd been record shopping and had a bag of records with me and he said, "What have you been buying?" and I said, "Acid house," and his eyes widened and he said, "Is it music that people take drugs to?" I would have said no then, but if he'd asked me a month or two later I would have said yes. That was a quintessential Tony moment for me. I was able to bring him up to speed with what the kids were listening to, but he immediately identified something in there which was far more interesting – straight away he realised it was about more than the music.

Shortly after, in February and March, ecstasy went from something a small group in The Haçienda were into to being absolutely everywhere in the club. The Haçienda was a big club but it only took ecstasy six weeks to take over the whole club. If you went to The Haçienda at the end of January 1988 and then came back in April, you simply wouldn't recognise the place; it was two completely different clubs.

Not long after I'd bumped into him that day on the street, Tony Wilson asked me to go on his Granada TV show, *The Other Side Of Midnight*, to talk about acid house. I was interviewed in the studio explaining what acid house was, not very well I must admit, and then Graeme Park was also interviewed in the DJ booth at The Haçienda. The problem was we still didn't really know what to talk about at that stage – we knew something really, *really* exciting was happening but we didn't know how to describe it yet, we didn't have the language. We just wanted to say to people, "Look, *something* is happening here and we're not exactly sure what it is yet, but it's *really exciting*."

SASHA, DJ: We hadn't been to The Haçienda for a few months, and when we walked back in at the start of 1988 all hell had broken loose, literally. It was full-on acid house and strobe lights and everyone was in DayGlo, doing this new crazy trance dance. It was absolutely fucking bonkers.

TERRY FARLEY: The first week in January 1988 was the FA Cup third round and Chelsea were drawn against Manchester United away, so we decided to go up on Friday so we could go to The Haçienda on Friday night. There was me, Gary Haisman and about half a dozen Chelsea fans and then half a dozen non-football fans including Johnny Rocca and Dirtbox Phil. We turned up all dressed a bit lairy, like really lairy – that Duffer of St George look, big hats with feathers in and leather trousers.

GRAEME PARK: At the start of 1988, Mike Pickering called me up and said I've had this idea to do a Northern House Revue at The Haçienda and invite the press up. The idea was we would get T-Coy to play live to promote Deconstruction, my band Groove to do some tracks to promote Transmission, and then we got another band in from Leicester called T-Cut. So we did it on the Nude night on Friday, February 26, which was the first night I played The Haçienda. I actually played live on the stage as Groove before I DJed. I was still only 24 and there I was, this massive Factory fan, miming keyboards on stage at The Haçienda. I just couldn't believe I was doing it: *"I'm performing on stage at The Haçienda, owned by Factory records and New Order!"* Then I DJ'd later that night and I thought, "This is great! Nice DJ booth looking down on the dance floor." It worked because *Record Mirror* did a big feature on this amazing new sound going off in the North, and a few other magazines covered it as well.

★

Rene Gelston had made a big statement by changing the music policy of his London club, The Wag, from rare groove to house when he returned from New York in late September 1987. He called it Trax, but it didn't quite have the impact he'd hoped for.

RENE GELSTON: It didn't work. It lasted three months – it was just too early. After five years of doing the Friday night and then three months of Trax, the owner sat me down and said, "Listen Rene, this ain't happening. It might happen in the future but it's not happening now."

★

Like Maurice and Noel Watson, Rene Gelston was just slightly premature, just a little too far ahead of his time. Although the early London warehouse parties like Battle Bridge Road, Dirtbox and Demob had been hugely influential, a new warehouse party, launched in February 1988, ushered in a real turning point for acid house in London.

MARK MOORE: Hedonism is where the penny dropped for a lot of people. Every DJ in London that counted was there, and every promoter in London that counted was there. I could see they had finally caught on.

KID BATCHELOR: I had been playing house for a couple of years by this stage, and I was so frustrated at all these purist DJs playing Sixties and Seventies music that myself and Simon Gordon [who he started the night with] decided to start Hedonism almost as a stance against all that. I think Hedonism for me was the first time people saw the potential

87

of this music. All of the DJs were there, all of the Kiss FM DJs, all the promoters – it was full of London's, I suppose you'd call them, 'movers and shakers'. A lot of those people were still very much on the rare groove tip, they were still funky cats, and many of them became converts overnight. It was the changing of the guard. Hedonism was that key for me.

JAZZY M: I went to the first Hedonism, which was a hugely important night. I think it was the first proper acid house warehouse jam in London. I remember going in to see Johnny Walker in the offices at Polygram or Polydor and he showed me tickets for Hedonism, and I was like, "Wow, what the fuck is Hedonism?" and he said, "Do you want to go?" "*Fuck, yeah!*"

Justin Berkman and Kid Batchelor played, but the really important thing at Hedonism for me was the John Dean soundsystem, which was a very famous soundsystem. It was the first time I'd ever, *ever* heard acid house on a proper soundsystem and that in itself was mind-blowing. I still remember hearing 'Break For Love' in there and the way I heard that drum breakdown come out separately through this huge soundsystem was just mind-blowing. I almost started laughing to myself: "Ohhhhh, *I see*, ha ha, so *this* is how it's really meant to fucking sound! Ah, *now I really do get it*. So I was right in fucking loving it in the first place!" I just had this really warm feeling about myself, like, "Fuck me, Jazzy, this is great! This sounds unbelievable. It always sounded great, but now it sounds unbelievable!" Because it's club music, it's designed to be played in clubs on huge systems. You have to remember when it came to clubbing we were so far behind in the mid Eighties compared to America; most of the clubs in this country had shite soundsystems, so you couldn't ever hear anything properly.

MR. C: The Hedonism parties were great parties. They were the first warehouse parties that were purely house music all night long. You could also argue they were one of the first warehouse parties in which ecstasy was really prevalent, although the gay clubs had been on it since 1985. I MC'd at a few of the Hedonism parties and DJ'd at a few.

I know what Jazzy M means about that system, although to be fair I had also heard house on the Soul II Soul, Family Funktion and Shake'n'Fingerpop soundsystems, as all of those parties would feature a bit of house music. At the second Hedonism it was absolutely packed but the guys operating the John Dean soundsystem had to pack it up at 6a.m. in the morning because they had another booking, and as they were packing up at one end of the room the Soul II Soul boys were setting up their system at the other end of the room, so we could all carry on. There was a half-hour gap in between and the whole packed warehouse started clapping and bashing cans and chanting as one. It was absolutely mental.

TERRY FARLEY: The last Raid Club* was in Marble Arch at the start of 1988, and myself and Andrew Weatherall did the door. We were both wearing Duffer doughboy caps and I remember a group of lads turned up, all in bloody ponchos and dungarees, and I recognised one of the lads from football – he was a Millwall fan – so we were like, "Nah, nah, you're not coming in." A month later, Gary Haisman took me to Shoom and it blew my mind, and all those same lads were in there in their ponchos and dungarees and I thought, "Shit, I've misjudged this badly!"

Gary Haisman had been bullying me for ages to go to Shoom. I didn't want to go because it was in south London. You had the west London scene and everything was there. No one went to south London then, it was a wasteland; there's the Tate Modern and Borough Market now but there was absolutely nothing there then – that part of London was still Dickensian. But Haisman dragged me down there and within 20 seconds of walking in you were sold. I've always been impressed by fickle things such as fashion, music and dancing, and as soon as I walked into Shoom that whole package was there in front of you, and it all made sense. I couldn't believe it. Especially when you realised the 100 people in this room were the only ones in the country onto this. That's

---

* The Raid Club, started by Paul Dennis and Gary Haisman, was an influential club which just preceded the acid house explosion.

what made it feel really special, and you just thought, "Fuck 'em... fuck everything else!"

ANDREW WEATHERALL: Terry phoned me up and said something like, "You've got to come, it's amazing! There's loads of kids from football taking ecstasy and listening to that weird music you like!", which obviously sounds frightful so I said, "Nah, you're alright." I think it took him two or three weeks to finally persuade me, he kept going, "Look, you've got to come to this, you will love it." When I did go, I just couldn't believe it. I'm a confused punk soul boy, and to me it was the confused punk soul boy's dream come true. I just could not fucking believe the mix of music. I was standing on the dance floor listening to the music, thinking, "This is The Residents [the group and art collective]." I was a jaded clubber by the age of 24 or 25; before Shoom I thought my clubbing career was coming to an end. I was a little bit bored. It was getting a bit purist for my liking, the whole rare groove thing. Part of me hates purism and part of me admires it. I do envy purism in a way and I wish I could do it.

Everyone says when you go to back to your school you can't believe how small everything looks, and Shoom feels like that now, looking back — it really was small. It was about twice the size of your front room, and there was a smoke machine on constantly so you couldn't see anything. I remember being really out of it, in the smoke, and thinking I don't need to hug someone, I just need to touch someone to know there are other human beings still here and I'm not just dancing in smoke on my own. It was just a crazy mix of music, of proto-house and techno records and indie dance, for want of a better phrase. I didn't know at first they were all records they'd brought back from Ibiza. I didn't know the history of it or who these people were, I just knew I knew more about the records than probably Terry did because I had the indie side, which I think is why Terry invited me. I didn't know who Danny Rampling was. I didn't know why I was dancing to those records on that first night. I probably said to Terry, "Why are they playing these records?" and he'd explained the Amnesia story. It was predominantly kids from the Roundshaw estate [large housing estate in the London Borough of Sutton]. They were the faces of that scene. There was a smattering of London clubbing faces there quite quickly as well. I don't know if I saw Boy George on that first night but if not, it wasn't long before he tipped up. There were various other people whose names to this day I don't know, but you recognised them. It was 99 per cent kids, blaggers, chancers, football hooligans and girlfriends of hooligans, then a few faces.

CYMON ECKEL: Shoom had been going a few weeks by the time I went. Terry Farley had gone down the week before with Paul McKee, and I had them both on the phone first thing Monday morning for an hour and a half individually, raving about the night they'd had on the Saturday. In the end I felt like I'd been there before I'd even stepped in the place, if you know what I mean – you still get that fervour to this day from the people who went to Shoom. They'd talk about the pills, the smoke, the fact you couldn't see, 16-year-olds sitting in speakers with their feet hanging out of the bass bins, the array of records being played – because it wasn't just acid house, it was that Balearic mix. So I felt I'd already been there, but when I went down the next week it just blew my mind. People only did one pill; you only needed one because they were so strong. I hate it when people always say that, but it's true.

STEVEN HALL: When Danny started Shoom, Terry was the first to go. Terry always tells the story that the first week he went in his rare groove clothes and the next week he was there in dungarees, a pair of Converse and a baggy shirt. He went down there and just completely flipped; he said, "It's just not like anything I've ever seen, the range of music, the drug taking…" That was another eye-opener, the fact that in The Project and Shoom you could openly take drugs, unlike every other club you'd ever been to. I'd been clubbing since the late Seventies and I'd never seen that. Even the warehouse parties a year or two before, people were a bit cagey if they were doing drugs. I'd never seen anything like Shoom. I'd never seen completely open drug-taking.

I went down first with Andrew Weatherall and Cymon Eckel. I

only went because they twisted my arm. I was 26, working at British Airways, I'd just moved into a flat with my girlfriend and I can honestly say I thought my clubbing days were over. Back in those days you'd get to that age and think, "I've had enough now, I'm not interested." I hated rare groove and that scene because I don't like anything retro; I don't want to go out and listen to old records and wear old-fashioned clothes and pretend it's years ago. The younger kids were into electro, which I should have been into, but at 26 I felt too old for it because they were all teenagers. At that time people weren't still clubbing at 26, so if you went to a club you would stand out, you would look almost unsightly.

ARTHUR BAKER: Shoom was loud, man. It was crazy. I can picture now the basement and the smoke and steam pouring out of it. I went down with my friend Sophie Bramley who had this show on MTV called *Yo! MTV Raps*, and as we walked in and went down the stairs this heat just hit you. I wasn't doing drugs, but I thought I was when I walked in there. You couldn't see shit in there, man – the smoke was so thick and the strobes were on all the time. If there had ever been a fire there it could have been a fucking disaster. It was great.

TERRY FARLEY: I remember Robert Elms down at Shoom very early on with Graham Ball. I think Graham saw a chance and generally really got it and went on to promote Miami Is Your Friend at The Park, which was a really good club, and Choice, which was also great. When we did the Bognor *Boy's Own* weekenders later he also helped us out with the logistics on those.

I've heard Robert Elms on the radio saying he went down to Shoom but hated it and never went back again. I think he actually got the whole thing totally wrong and didn't like the fact that instead of being on the guest list he was now in the queue. I think he couldn't hack that. It was the absolute reverse for us. When acid house exploded we went from being the footsoldiers to, I wouldn't say generals, but at least Corporal Jones. But some of those other guys couldn't hack it. Boy George absolutely loved it and threw his heart and soul into it, God bless him. 'Generations Of Love' (released by Boy George in 1989) is still probably one of the best house records ever made by anyone in Britain and his voice was, and probably still is, really soulful. Paul Rutherford from Frankie Goes To Hollywood was there every week and he made a few amazing records as well. Michael Clark, the ballet dancer, was there every week. Dirtbox Phil was down there. Bananarama were down there early on, as was Martin Fry from ABC. Gary Crowley [broadcaster and DJ] was down there early on and I ended up holding his hand at the end of one night to Joyce Sims' 'Come Into My Life'.

MARK MOORE: People you didn't expect to see turned up to Shoom, not just Boy George and Paul Rutherford but Michael Clark, Patsy Kensit, Keith Allen. Some of the West End crowd poked their head in just to see what the hell was going on. Some of them stuck with it and some of them just thought, "This is not for me." Michael Clark later did a show at the Barbican or Sadler's Wells and incorporated a bit of acid house into the ballet, which was great.

If you asked me to pinpoint it, I'd put the explosion at March 1988 probably. That's when it really took off. Big time. As Sheryl Garrett said, once that happened, all the West End trendies who had been the 'in crowd' suddenly looked like dinosaurs.

ANDREW WEATHERALL: I think the first night I went to Shoom I went over and said to Danny, "Fucking hell mate," and said how great it was. Then shortly afterwards, I was playing a party just off Chapel Market in Islington. There was a guy called Skater Bobby, who was an actor and skater and was in *Starlight Express* – his mum had a caff on Chapel Market and he had a party above it on a Sunday night. I got the train in from Windsor with my Woolworths plastic record box and a plastic bag full of records. I think I played at about 4a.m. when there were lots of people just sat around spannered, and I played all sorts and then I put on 'October Love Song' by Chris & Cosey, which everyone really loved. It went down really well, but then again I slightly suspect everyone was so spannered I could have probably got away with playing anything. But I played Chris & Cosey and I played some dub and then when I finished Danny came over and said, "What was that record?" and I said, "Oh, it's Chris & Cosey," and we just got talking about music and he said, "Oh, you'll have to come and play at the Shoom," but I didn't really think anything of it – I thought it was just one of those 5a.m. conversations.

TERRY FARLEY: Shoom was definitely more spiritual than the other clubs that came along later. Danny was really into the spiritual side of things, he really believed in it. That came through in his music, and his ethos definitely spread through the club and through the people. I made friends with people at Shoom who I am still really good friends with 25 years later, and you definitely share a real deep connection with those people that you just don't really get with other clubs, so there was definitely something else going on there. Some of those early Shoomers were almost like disciples of Danny's; I remember one girl telling me she could see his aura while he was DJing, and do you know, to a certain extent maybe you could. He had great hair, he had a great dance, he wore brilliant clothes and Trash Can jeans with Jesus on, so that religious theme was really going through.

BOY GEORGE: That period, when it all started kicking off, was just a very exciting time for me. I'd stopped officially being a pop star, as I wasn't getting played on the radio and [Culture Club] had kind of fallen apart. I had a lot of time on my hands so I just started clubbing again. There was an unbelievably great vibe and I just fully embraced it. Although the first time I went to Shoom they wouldn't let me in because she said I would get beaten up – there were still quite a few, football hooligans in there who hadn't quite made the switch. Jenni was like, "They'll beat you up."

★

As the *Boy's Own* crowd – Terry Farley, Andrew Weatherall and Cymon Eckel – each had their own road to Damascus moment with acid house, the sea change was reflected in their magazine. Within the space of one issue it changed its direction.

TERRY FARLEY: There was a whole new language surrounding those early acid house days, which we adopted in the magazine: phrases like, "Get right on one matey!", which came from Chris Butler. I remember him shouting that in the club and then all these other people joined in: "Get right on one matey!" So we stuck it on the front cover of the next issue of *Boy's Own*. Then the following edition we apologised for it: "Sorry, we let ourselves down badly there." We started the backlash immediately. We were always very big on backlashes; we would start something and then start the backlash on it almost immediately, before everyone had a chance to jump on the bandwagon.

We had the first article about this new scene, which Paul Oakenfold wrote, although he said we couldn't put his name on it as he didn't want to get into trouble at work because of the drug connection. Paul's always been a bit cagey like that. We called it 'Bermondsey Goes Balearic' although we couldn't even spell Balearic so it actually said 'Bermondsey Goes Bala-eric'. We did it all cut-and-paste ourselves with Letraset, and my mum worked in an office so we'd take things in and get a girl to type it up in her lunchtime. We'd cut pictures out of magazines and take it down to the printers like that. We'd had a few editions before but after that we became, by default, the in-house fanzine for acid house.

ANDREW WEATHERALL: It affected us all. Although I was around for glam rock and punk rock, I was still quite young. I was 13 in 1976 so I was still laughed at a bit. I was like a mascot. Although I thought it was my thing, it really wasn't because of my age. When acid house came along we thought, "This is our thing," and we did get a bit overprotective about it, a bit wanky about it. Maybe I've got a bit more of a puritan streak in me than I like to admit. Even though I was a little late to it – I came in a few months after it kicked off – to us it was still 'our scene'. It's that classic thing we all do; anyone not into what *you're* into is a fucking idiot, but as soon as they say, "I get it, I'm into it now," you turn round and say, "Oh, I'm not into it anymore, I've moved on." So that's exactly what we were like, telling everybody, "Come on, you've got to get into this," and as soon as people got on board we were like, "Oh, fuck." It's classic human nature isn't it? You want everyone to be into what you're doing but as soon as they are it diminishes that special magic.

CYMON ECKEL: Shoom was the context. There is absolutely no doubt about it. Shoom, as in the make-up of its constituent parts, being the people, the music, Danny, the loudness of the soundsystem, the fact you couldn't move in there because it was so full of smoke, that you'd meet people in there you wouldn't normally meet. It only held about 150 people; it was just a gym with a soundsystem in and it was in SE1, which back then you normally wouldn't go anywhere near in your fucking life. SE1 was a desert; there was nothing there. But Shoom brought everything together.

I don't think ecstasy was the absolute be all and end all, because look at all the creativity that came out of it. But ecstasy was definitely the touchpaper for a generation. We all know you can't continue to party. Although there were a few wasted lives, there was also a huge amount of positivity that came out of ecstasy. It was a touchpaper, it wasn't the fuel. Shoom was the medium. We went for eight weeks, and in that eight-week period it went from obscurity to overground.

TERRY FARLEY: Shoom changed quite quickly. Initially, it was south London kids, Special Branch kids and lads from football. Then some of the old school of the West End came down, and then it went quite gay. The crowd at Shoom went through several changes like that, and when it moved to bigger premises it naturally became a bit more mainstream and you got the second generation of Shoom coming in.

The original south London kids, the Roundshaw Kids, were the absolute coolest, they were the absolute bollocks. They were the kids who had been first out to Ibiza; *i-D* magazine did a piece on them and called them 'the Amnesiacs'. They were all about 10 years younger than me. I had no idea where Roundshaw was at the time, in fact I didn't until quite recently. Funnily enough, about a year ago my car needed fixing and someone told me there was a guy in Carshalton who fixed Volkswagen Beetles, so I took it round to him and he said, "It's going to take me the rest of the day, can you come back at five? You can get a bus to Croydon from here if you like." I thought I've never been to Croydon, I'll check it out. I got on the bus and went and sat upstairs and then we came to this estate and there was a sign saying: 'Roundshaw'. I went, "Fucking hell, so *this* is Roundshaw Estate." It was a really fucking crappy 1960s council estate, exactly like the one where I spent my teenage years in Slough, and I thought, "Oh my god," and I could see exactly why all those kids fucked off to Ibiza to escape the drudgery of a place like this in the Eighties. It wasn't the poorest place, but there was absolutely nothing there.

The other part of the crowd was the younger, madder element of Special Branch. That was basically it. Because it was in Bermondsey it was a bit of a south London thing at first. Then very quickly the top end of the football lads started coming down. The top boys of Arsenal came down early on, although they caused a bit of trouble and were barred.

BOY GEORGE: A lot of those people in the early days had been football hooligans, and from what I gathered they were initially pretty much drug dealers – they weren't interested in getting loved up. But then they started taking ecstasy and were seduced by it, and everything changed for them.

The early MDMA was very different; it wasn't very toxic, it was much purer. It definitely had an effect on people, it changed people. It's funny, people don't seem to have a problem talking about people taking drugs in the Sixties, they seem to view that era more affectionately, but for some reason people are less ready to talk as affectionately about acid house as an era. Which for me is really odd because it's such a monumental thing.

MR. C: On the first Monday of February 1988, I started a new night called Fantasy in Camden. It was at the HQ in Camden Lock and I got my boys Colin Favour and Kid Batchelor to DJ with me. That was every fortnight and we did about eight parties there. One night a couple called Paul Stone and Lou came down looking for Kid, as they wanted him to DJ for them. Paul's a bit of a gentleman and didn't want to just poach him, so he approached me and said, "Look, I'd really like to book Kid Batchelor for an underground warehouse party." I said, "Well, why don't you just book all of us – Kid, me, Colin and Eddie." He didn't realise I was a DJ as well, he just thought I was a rapper, so I said, "Hang around for a bit, I'm playing after Eddie." So he did and I went on and smashed it, as usual, and Paul said, "OK, I'll take all four of you on." That's how RIP started in May 1988. We did a couple of small parties in Eversholt Street near Euston, and then Paul found Clink Street, a disused space that used to be an old prison. RIP stood for 'Revolution In Progress', and that for me is where acid house rave culture was born. Clink Street is when things started to change.

The first Saturday was half full, the second one was almost full and the third one was roadblock and it just got more mental from then on. By June, Paul and Lou started opening on Fridays as well. Fridays were called A Transmission and were supposed to be a bit more techno and acid, and Saturdays more house and garage, but it could go in any direction on both nights. Then by August we had to open on Sundays, too. We called that Zoo, because anyone who was still going by Sunday night was an animal.

Comparing Danny Rampling's Shoom and RIP is like comparing night and day. Or lunchtime BBC Radio 1 and Kiss. Shoom was great and they used to book Colin Faver once a month and I'd go down and MC with him and we'd smash the place to pieces. I loved Shoom and they did a lot of good work, but it was more of a Balearic vibe. They'd play acid house but they'd also play Sam Fox and stuff like that. Clink Street was altogether more serious. It was Chicago house, techno, New York garage and a bit of electro thrown in. Unapologetically underground. It was dark, raw and nasty. No fluff, no commercial stuff, it was in-your-face psychedelia and it was dark as shit. The crowd was mental. Everybody was out of their minds on LSD and MDMA and we had everyone from poor urban kids to rich bankers in there, every race, colour and creed you can imagine. Shoom had a much whiter crowd.

Those parties really did push it over into the mainstream. We had people like Tony Colston-Hayter come down, or Tony Cost-Inflator as we'd later call him after he copied the vibe, put these huge raves on and jacked up the price. A lot of people, like Anton Le Pirate and [DJ] Tintin who did the Energy Parties, used to come down to Clink Street and that's where they were all inspired to do their own parties. So you could say that Clink Street was the birthplace of rave culture, the first in the world.

EDDIE 'EVIL' RICHARDS: To be honest, I thought those guys that went to Ibiza jumped on the bandwagon. They came back with a new scene, but it was nothing like we had at Clink Street. They were just playing pop music; it was like a wedding reception. I did go down there and I really liked the atmosphere, but I just wasn't into the music they were playing. I was definitely into blacker, groovier music.

GREG WILSON: The romance of the Ibiza story is a bit of a red herring for me. Yes, Ibiza is very important because of the spirit and the Balearic aspect, but the music was already in place. The same with The Haçienda. A lot of people thought The Haçienda was the first dance club in Manchester, which is nonsense when we had Legends, The Playpen, Berlin, Gallery, Rafters… going right back to The Twisted Wheel. Acid house could only explode in Britain because of what had gone before. That's why it happened here. It was a fusion between what was happening in America and what had happened here. The Ibiza story muddied the water for me, but I can see why people wanted to believe this romantic story about these DJs going to this sun-drenched island, finding a taste of paradise and bringing it back home. But that doesn't say anything about the whole acid house experience in the North and the Midlands. I also think Trevor Fung is the most important figure of that crowd, and both him and Nicky Holloway go back to the jazz funk days. Paul Oakenfold also had a history with the music.

★

By the first few months of 1988, The Haçienda was a changed club, completely colonised by ecstasy and acid house. As ecstasy became the staple diet for punters, the main protagonists in the scene, like Eric Barker and other loose associates of Happy Mondays, began to put on smaller nights and after-parties, which were often by word of mouth.

DAVE HASLAM: It's quite endearing looking back at it now. No one knew how to dress. People were thinking, "Do we wear shoes or trainers with this music? Do we wear jeans? Do I wear a T-shirt?" In early 1988, there were still people coming into The Haçienda in suits with shoulder pads, men who'd bought their first Hugo Boss suit that they were really proud of. And then all of a sudden it all changed and people were wearing dungarees.

No one knew how to dance. No one had ever danced with their arms in the air before. We'd had northern soul, which had quite an exhibitionist streak to it, and people were used to dancing on their own. But what I had never seen before acid house was a dancefloor moving together as one. It was like a wave, which sounds unfeasible but that's what it was like – the dancefloor moving as one, like a wave. People were locking into one groove and sharing an experience, and that hadn't happened before.

ERIC BARKER: The Haçienda was closing at 2a.m. and there was nowhere for people to go after ecstasy had hit; everyone would be saying, "There's nowhere to go, we need somewhere to go..." so I said, "Fuck this, I'm going to sort something out," and I started putting on my own nights. The Haçienda was also shut on Sundays then, and people wanted to party every single night.

The first rave we put on was me, Andy [Barker], Darren [Partington] and a girl I was seeing at the time called Leah. We had been looking around town for a place to have a party and found this place, a small warehouse on Little Peter Street, just behind the City Road Inn, just across from The Haçienda, which was perfect. There were quite a lot of empty buildings and warehouses around Manchester back then because the regeneration of the city centre hadn't started yet – that was still a few years away. We didn't even have a name for the party, we just told everyone in The Haçienda and all you had to do was walk out of the club and across the road.

Darren and Andy and the Jam MCs DJ'ed. It wasn't a big do. I'd only bought 48 cans of Red Stripe to sell as we didn't know how busy it would get, but we ended up with over 100 people in there. We had a generator in one room and we had to cover it up with a mattress, so you couldn't hear it because otherwise it was louder than the music since we only had a small PA.

DARREN PARTINGTON: That was the first party we did, in an old double-glazing firm on Little Peter Street. The idea was simple – find an empty gaff somewhere, clear it out, stick a generator in there, lock it up again and wait for the Haç to finish, then get everyone down there. The Haç shut at 2a.m. but no one wanted to go home then because you were still off your fucking nut.

ANDREW BARKER: The only other option was to go home and watch *Hitman And Her* [*see* page 176] and no one wanted that. What you would do is sneak around town looking to find a warehouse with a 'To Let' sign on – or somewhere that was suitable – cut the locks off with bolt croppers and stick your own locks on. You'd leave it a couple of days before coming back and if your locks hadn't been tampered with, you knew you were on.

At that first one someone got knocked back on the door – don't know who it was but they decided to phone the police to say there was an illegal party going on. So the police turned up in their vans. Eric bounces out in his silk pyjamas, daft hat and moccasins and tells them it's a private do, some works do. There were some nice cars outside, which were nothing to do with our party, and Eric just went, "Look at the nice cars, there's no scallies in here; these are nice people, it's nothing to worry about."

DARREN PARTINGTON: Eric blagged the police it was Veronica's leaving do or something like that: "It's dear old Veronica's leaving do, she's been with us for 25 years…", and they just went, "Alright, just keep the noise down," and got off.

At that stage ecstasy was also helping our writing process, definitely. Without a shadow of a doubt. If you'd been out on Saturday and taken it, you'd still be in that frame of mind. If you were in a normal mindset, you probably wouldn't let one part [of the song] run for four minutes on its own when you were writing a tune, you would think, "Nah, that might get a bit boring," but if you were still in that E frame of mind then you would [let it run] because you could lock into it. The E would still be in your system because they were that strong, and you'd think, "Just leave that running in there for a few minutes." Some of our early songs were 15–20 minutes long but they weren't songs really, it was acid noodling. You'd be thinking, "Right, if I was in a corner of the club now, dancing, I'd want the tune to do *that* – how do I make it do *that*?" and you'd figure out a way to make it do that. So it definitely helped the writing process. We're not talking about, "She loves you yeah, yeah, yeah," or 12-bar blues here; I'm not sure ecstasy would have helped in that case but it definitely helped you write acid house tunes.

★

In March, Nicky Holloway held another of his one-off Special Branch parties at Rockley Sands in Poole, Dorset. For many who attended, this was one of the key events which revealed the split between the old school and those embracing acid house.

TERRY FARLEY: The Special Branch Rockley Sands was one of the first times it seemed to click. It was one of Nicky Holloway's events and he and a few others had obviously been to Ibiza at this stage, so there was a real split in the crowd. A lot of his Special Branch crowd were real modern soul heads, guys in blazers, caps and brogues, really serious dancers, and then there was this other bunch, the ones who'd been to Ibiza in tie-dye shirts and all that gear, doing this really strange dance. When Danny started playing, one guy called One-Eyed Dan even got up on stage and tried to attack him for playing acid house. I also remember when Danny was playing and Johnny Walker actually crawled into a speaker and sat there and we were like, "What is he doing?!" Then there were other people like Chris Butler rave dancing. There were probably 20–30 people out of a crowd of about 600 who got it. There was a huge reaction against it from some people but within six months, 95 per cent of those who had been against it were in shorts and dancing round gurning, with all of us laughing at them. The thing was, everyone had a different entry point over those six months or so. I wasn't there right at the beginning either, otherwise myself and Weatherall would never have turned those kids away from The Raid.

That weekend at Rockley Sands was the first time we all did a pill and it worked properly, and we all got it. We went back to Gary Crowley's afterwards and someone, I won't say who, did a second one. We'd never seen someone do two pills in one night and we couldn't believe it. We were all like, "How could you possibly do *two* pills in one night? *How* could you do it? How? I don't think *I'll* ever do two." When everyone got up the next day, around lunchtime, we started playing house music again and people started dancing and saying, "Oh, it's coming back again! Yeah, I can feel it coming on again!" We were all dancing round and I think we really convinced ourselves that we were coming up again!

ANDREW WEATHERALL: That weekend was a rare groove thing and there were guys in spats dancing in formation and we just turned up with foam hammers and in dungarees – there's a picture of me and Cymon with a Timmy Mallet foam hammer. When ecstasy first hit there seemed to be a lot of dressing up and toys. It was quite infantile; people in dungarees and stuff – everyone looked like a kids' TV presenter.

CYMON ECKEL: For at least a year, we'd heard about pills but they were called 'X' then. You'd be out and you'd see a little crew falling all over each other and someone would say, "Oh yeah, they're on X," while everyone else was on acid or speed. The first time we did it at Rockley Sands, everyone else I was with was off their nut but all I could feel was a burning sensation in my nose. What had happened is I'd swallowed it and it had somehow bounced off my neck and into my nose. I was on the floor going, "My nose is killing me!" then I blew my nose and this fucking pill dropped out.

That Rockley Sands weekend was quite infamous. There were a lot of people watching us, saying, "They're on ecstasy," because before acid house took off, ecstasy was considered by a lot of people to be quite a naughty Class A drug. It was almost as if you were taking heroin because no one understood it; and I don't mean they didn't understand it in a loved-up way, I mean they didn't understand it because there was no context for it. Ecstasy needed acid house to make sense to most people, which was really interesting. There were a few DJs at that particular Rockley Sands who were like, "I'm never going near it," who ended up making a good few quid out of acid house.

ANDREW WEATHERALL: The first time I did E and it worked was at Nicky Holloway's Soul Weekender at Rockley Sands. I remember thinking this is amazing and someone said, "Do you want another one?" and I thought, "Oh no, I can't do another one." They ended up holding me down on the dancefloor and literally forcing a second E down my throat. Fast forward two years and I was the one holding people down on the dancefloor, trying to get their ecstasy off them.

TERRY FARLEY: I think that's why acid house spread too quickly, because whenever it hit a new town, it didn't matter if that was Cambridge or Plymouth, the first people in that town felt like *they* had the best secret ever. But it was a very evangelical secret, so they had this desperate itch to tell everyone and spread the word. Add to that the chemical reaction and you can see why it spread like wildfire. That kid in Cambridge or Plymouth reacted exactly the same as I did in Shoom when it reached him nine months or a year later. Everyone had their own little revelatory moment.

★

Having run Future in the back room of Heaven, in early April, Paul Oakenfold opened a new night called Spectrum in the main room of what was one of the largest clubbing venues in central London at the time. Some viewed it as over-ambitious within a month it was sold out, the clearest demonstration of how quickly the acid house scene was exploding.

ANDREW WEATHERALL: It still hadn't exploded by that stage – I think that happened over probably eight months or so. There was a little gestation period. It's not as if the Shoom opened and then the front page of *The Sun* was 'acid house frenzy' the next day; it took a little while. Spectrum was on Monday nights at Heaven. I just remember at the first one there were only about 100 people, and then I went about three weeks later and there was a queue around the block, and I'm not sure what that was. It hadn't hit the papers, there was no shock horror yet; it was just word of mouth and the spread of ecstasy.

TERRY FARLEY: The very first night at Spectrum I think there were 120 people in there, and they gave everyone a free pill. I was playing reggae in the VIP room with Alex Paterson* and there were about five people in there and just over 100 people downstairs. The next week there was even less and the week after that even less. Paul Oakenfold and Ian St Paul had clocked up this ridiculous bill and it looked like they might have to close. But then, and I don't know what happened that triggered this, the next week there were 300 people there, and the following week there were 1,000 people and the week after that there were 2,000 people. I think it was purely word of mouth because unlike other clubs that had gone before, it didn't seem to matter that there were only 100 people in there; it just meant you felt like you were part of a magic circle of 100. Then when another 10 people joined they were part of a magic circle of 110 – it just grew and grew like that, and I'm sure that was replicated in other cities.

MARK MOORE: I remember one night Leigh Bowery turned up to Spectrum. I remember everyone off their faces just crowding round him because he was covered in mirrors, and they were just touching him and he was really freaked out by their reaction. He was used to walking into clubs and people going, "Oh it's *Leigh Bowery*! Leigh, you look *amazing*

---

* Alex Paterson went on to form The Orb, who spawned the 'ambient house' genre. They had several big hits in the Nineties, including 'Little Fluffy Clouds'.

darling!", not all these people off their heads crowded round, going, "Oh my god, what *is* this?"

WAYNE ANTHONY, PROMOTER OF GENESIS RAVES: I had taken ecstasy in Tenerife in the summer of 1987 but it hadn't really done anything for me. Then someone took me to Future one night after it opened. I didn't really have any idea of what to expect. I turned up in a £3,000 suit! Everyone else looked like they had just come back from Ibiza. But I had half an E and was totally euphoric. There was a huge positive energy being given out by everyone and I just knew it was something special. I knew it could change my life.

TERRY FARLEY: There was a class difference between Shoom and Spectrum for me. Shoom attracted quite a lot of people who had gone to university and people from the countryside, whereas Spectrum was generally more working-class kids from London, Kent and Essex.

I remember one night at Spectrum, Steve Mayes [of *Boy's Own*] was on the door and a load of ragga kids tried to get in and he wouldn't let them, so they threatened him, saying, "We're going to stab you," and all this. At the end of the night you could see about 15 of these kids at the top of the ramp outside, waiting for him. Without even trying, they managed to round up about 20 serious football lads who were in the club, including some from Millwall, ICF [West Ham hooligan firm] and Gooners [Arsenal fans]; they all came out together and charged up the ramp and the kids just scattered. It was really strange to see that but within a few months, whatever town you went to around the country, you saw the same thing. All these football boys had replaced one buzz with another buzz, one drug with another drug.

ANDREW WEATHERALL: I was doing three jobs at once around that time: I was building film sets, DJing and, to augment my income, I was also selling about 10 Es a week. I was getting them for £15 and selling them for £25, which was the going rate, so I made £100 quid a week, which was more than enough to live on back then. I started to get bookings as a DJ but I still loved the set building. I worked with Cymon building film sets and stuff for adverts and was offered my first job abroad, which was a Fairy Liquid advert with Nanette Newman (the one where she walks down a table of cricket players and says, "And Fairy Liquid does this much!"), but I got bumped because the art director's brother was on holiday from university so he brought him in instead. I thought, "Oh fuck, the DJ lark can't be any less secure than this – I'll give it a go."

I was only getting £50 a gig at that time but spending £100 on records, so I still had to augment my income with 'pharmaceutical distribution'. I got introduced to a leading Millwall football hooligan, whose name will most definitely go with me to my grave. I remember meeting him outside The Trip and I just had all these visions of what was going to happen, like he was going to give me a supply [of Es] and then they'd all bash me up and I'd have to be their slave forever because I owed them all this money. But it actually turned out all right, and I was only selling about 10 or 15 Es a week.

That was until an incident involving a friend of mine, who was going out with the daughter of the head of the Coldstream Guards or one of the other garrisons at Windsor Castle. Her father came round to their house one day and unfortunately found some ecstasy. I actually hadn't sold it to them – it was nothing to do with me – but my name was put in the frame and it was quite heavy because he was based at Windsor Castle, so it was quite high-level business. The landlord of my local pub then took me aside and said, "Look, I've had quite high-level police in here looking for you. I know what you get up to, I'm not stupid, but you wouldn't do it in here, would you?" and I said, "Nah, nah," which we didn't. So he said, "Don't worry, I told them you didn't, it was just a malicious rumour, but just so you know, you're on their radar." Shortly after that, Cymon and I decided to move out of Windsor to Battersea.

I'd been going to Manchester for years, way before acid house; I had friends up there in Moss Side. So because I knew a few people up there, I just thought, "I'll get 20 Es and take them up." When I walked into

The Haçienda, I saw this girl I knew and said, "Look, do you want to help me get rid of these?" We managed to get rid of them within minutes and I was a bit of a hero and taken to parties and all sorts, and I thought it was great.

So a couple of weeks later I decided to go back up to Manchester. By this time my name was in the frame with the police, and I remember being on the platform at Windsor train station and seeing these two or three guys who definitely looked like classic plainclothes policemen to me, so I thought, "Right, let's see what happens," and did that classic thing of getting on a train when it arrived then getting off again, two or three times, and they did exactly the same thing, so I thought, "Fuck, this is it." I somehow managed to lose them and get into London, then get the train up to Manchester, but when I walked into The Haçienda, to say I got a frosty reception was an understatement. I was trying to find this girl to help me sell the Es and I finally spotted her: this guy was holding her by the throat, up against the wall. It looked like a cartoon – her feet were off the floor, kicking in mid-air. He was giving her what for and then he pointed at me, and I thought, "Oh fuck," and I just legged it. In a matter of weeks I'd gone from hero to most definitely zero. So I did dabble in the criminal lifestyle when I was young but I definitely wasn't cut out for it. I haven't got the bottle, fortunately.

★

On 30 April, S'Express scored 1988's first acid house hit single, reaching number one with 'Theme From S'Express'.

MARK MOORE: 'Theme From S'Express' had been on white label for ages and when it finally came out it just went crazy. At the start I viewed S'Express almost as a performance art thing, where we all just played the part of pop stars. That's what I told myself: "It's just a performance thing and *maybe* one day we will have a hit…", but then the first record came out and was a hit, and I was like, "Oh, hang on a minute… maybe I am a pop star!" Someone wrote to the Musician's Union, saying, "I read Mark Moore in this magazine saying he was a *non-musician* – he shouldn't be allowed in the union because *he's not a musician*," which I had said because Brian Eno and *My Life In The Bush Of Ghosts* was a big influence on me and that's what I was saying: "I'm a non-musician." Rumour has it that it was [pop producers] Stock, Aitken and Waterman who sent the letter, which is hilarious. But there was a huge resistance to this new music and way of music making.

When 'Theme From S'Express' got in the charts, Derrick May [aka Rhythim Is Rhythim] was really impressed and happy. He said to me, "Mark, it's like you've arrived at the party, and you're just waiting for everyone else to join you!" He thought it was really important that in America we signed to Warner Bros. and then moved to Capitol Records. Derrick and his American peers thought it was incredible that a major label would be interested because it meant there was hope for them as artists. He said, "We're playing 'Lollipop' in the clubs in Detroit." I was like, "What – the B-side from 'Superfly Guy'?" [S'Express' follow-up hit, which charted at number five in the UK.]

By the time 'Theme' was a hit, some people were already trying to protect the scene and keep it special, and I was part of that to a certain degree. Because I was the first person from the scene to get into the public eye, I didn't want to be the one that said, "Oh, yeah, there's loads of drug taking going on." I did get asked about it, so I'd say, "No, I've never seen any drugs! I don't remember any drugs!" I just didn't want to be the one that blew the lid on it, I didn't want that on my shoulders – let someone else do that. I figured it was all happening organically and that was the best way – a friend would tell a friend would tell another friend, meaning we were all linked in some way, rather than a group of lads hearing about ecstasy in the papers or on *News At Ten* and thinking "I want a bit of this."

★

In May, both *i-D* and *The Face* decided to run features on the emerging acid house scene. At the same time these features were going to press, Nicky Holloway was planning his first house club. He'd been offered a short run of Saturday nights at The Astoria, which is where he decided to try his first house night, The Trip.

NICKY HOLLOWAY: I wasn't sure I could fill the Astoria at first. I'd filled it a couple of times for one-off Special Branch events, but I wasn't sure I could fill it for house music. On the first night I decided to put a false ceiling in [with drapes], so if it wasn't that busy it wouldn't look too bad. But by the time we came to open we had 600 people queueing.

I was just really lucky with timing. The only two magazines that were covering this sort of music were *The Face* and *i-D*. I wasn't cool according to them because I took the whole thing big, I made it mainstream. Even though I was there from the fucking start, according to some people I wasn't cool. What is cool? Look at the line-up for the opening night of The Trip – Paul Oakenfold DJing and Mike Pickering playing live, and then in the other bar was Andy Weatherall and Terry Farley from *Boy's Own*. That's not cool? But oh no, I'm the guy who made it all uncool and took it to The Astoria, it was all that sort of bollocks. After The Astoria was doing well I was like, "Fuck you – you might have the cred but I'm making the money." That was the ultimate payback for me.

ANDREW WEATHERALL: When Nicky Holloway started The Trip, Terry and I were asked to play upstairs. We only got the gig because the guy who was supposed to play upstairs got put inside for a couple of years, so we took over for a bit and made it ours. We used to play a very eclectic slot.

I still continued to do a little distribution in pharmaceuticals but in a safer manner. I used to do it from the DJ booth at The Trip, just to people I knew, until one night I was DJing and I looked up and there was this guy there and he said, "I hear you've got some E," and I said, "Where did you hear that?" I looked at him and he had a denim shirt on that was tucked in really neatly, and then I looked over his shoulder and there were my mates Rocky, Clive Henry, Terry and about three other people all waving their hands and mouthing, "*No! No! No!*" Then this guy in the denim shirt tried to get in the booth and they all kind of blocked his way, so I legged it out the club. I was running down the stairs when I met my girlfriend and she said, "What's the matter?!" and I said, "Get the car round the back!" and I legged it out the fire escape and into Falkenberg Court and she brought the car round and I jumped in and we cleared off. I think that was my last such occasion. I'm quite good like that – if I'm sent omens that tell me, "Look, you're not cut out for this," then I take notice.

CHAPTER 5

Enjoy This Trip, Enjoy This Trip

"I remember standing in the club at its peak and thinking, 'It is never going to get better than this,' and it never did really, not for me."

Nicky Holloway

PAUL OAKENFOLD: I always had a day job and never really saw DJing as a proper job when I first started out. I was an A&R man working for Champion. I signed Will Smith, I was working Salt'n'Pepa, and then I was at Profile and Def Jam. I always wanted to sign the next U2 – that was the challenge and my dream. But you have to have luck to find that band – just look at what happened with [Creation records boss] Alan McGee, when he stumbled across Oasis as a support band one night in Glasgow; it's just about being in the right place at the right time, or it was then. Now it's more about surfing the internet for days and weeks looking for the next big thing. But that was always my dream, to find *the* band. Fingers crossed it may happen tonight, or maybe it never will.

But then, true story this, one day after I'd started Spectrum I woke up and it suddenly occurred to me: "*Maybe* I was born to be a DJ." I really love playing and sharing music and moving a crowd. I just thought, "This is it, I've finally found my moment and I've finally found what I'm supposed to do. *This is it.*" That's when everything changed. That's when all of a sudden I had 3,000 people coming to a club on a Monday night. On a *Monday*. People had never seen anything like it.

ANTON LE PIRATE, CLUBBER/PROMOTER: The first night of Spectrum was the first time I really felt, "Holy fuck, what the fuck is this?" A girl I knew said, "There's this new club and it's on a *Monday*." We went to the first one and it was pretty empty – the club holds 1,500 people and there can't have been more than 100 people there. We didn't really know what to expect. I had ripped jeans, and I think I was actually wearing boots. I remember two moments vividly from that night. The first was when I was stood at the bar with my mate Pat and there were three people on the dance floor, literally. Then 'Theme From S'Express' came on and the light show started, and I just thought this is too good, I can't stand at the bar, and almost ran onto the dancefloor. There was this big, round, empty podium and I thought, "I'm having some of that," and jumped up and started dancing in the lasers playing across it and had a real extraordinary moment to myself. From S'Express onwards, I couldn't stop dancing on that podium. Then Paul Oakenfold came on and slowed the music down and turned down the lights, and I thought, "This better be good." Then he dropped his first song, the lasers came on and it was such an extraordinary moment, such an unbelievable moment of music, sound and movement. Incredible.

I think there were 500 people the next week, and then about 900 people, and the week after that it was full. It just went 'BOOM', because all of us went away and told someone else about it. You didn't tell everyone, you just told the few who you thought could handle it, and we still didn't quite know what it was – we were still like, "What is this? What is this new thing we've found?" But word got out via Chinese whispers.

Once Spectrum was established it was an experience unlike any other because of its size. It was the flagship of the scene, it really was. It was a life changer. If you went to one of the Sunday all-dayers, by the time you came out your life had changed. They would start at 3p.m. and go on 'til 3a.m. They were so epic, so amazing, such an incredible experience. Twelve hours of clubbing on a Sunday! It broke all the rules. We just felt such a sense of liberation, as if the rulebook had been thrown away. We were coming out of Eighties Thatcher's Britain where we'd had so many rules regarding how we were supposed to live. It felt like that was all being swept away.

DES PENNEY, SPECTRUM REGULAR/MANAGER OF THE BAND FLOWERED UP: I wasn't a football hooligan but I knew a lot of people and I knew a lot of football hooligans, and I got on with a lot of them. I remember being in Spectrum one night with my mate Mark Camera, who was an Arsenal boy. We were upstairs and we just looked around in amazement because you had five or six of London's firms in there, like the real proper boys, and they weren't only talking and having a laugh, they were fucking dancing with each other. We knew it was down to ecstasy and the euphoric buzz it had given them all, but because we knew how serious these characters were, you still couldn't fucking believe it. We were like, "Fucking hell, if this went the wrong way, if they all got on a slightly different buzz, there would be a fucking blood bath in here." But it never happened. Personally, I'm 99 per cent convinced ecstasy almost stopped football violence.

RUSS MORGAN, K-KLASS*: English [football] clubs had been banned from Europe at the time. So the FA created this domestic competition [called the Mercantile Credit Centenary Trophy, to celebrate 100 years of the Football League] at the start of the '88–'89 season, with the top eight sides from the previous season. [Manchester] United played Arsenal at Villa Park and I went to the game. Even though I'd started going to The Haçienda, I was surprised to see load of United lads turning up wearing bandanas and smiley T-shirts and Converse trainers and I remember thinking, "What the fuck is going on? Something's wrong here," because no one would have worn a bloody bandana to United before then, but obviously all these football lads had been turned on to acid house over the summer and they'd turned up dressed differently

---

* K-Klass were a house group from Wrexham/Chester who scored a big hit in 1991 with 'Rhythm Is A Mystery'.

for the new football season. That was the first moment when I thought, "There's something going on here."

PAUL ROBERTS, K-KLASS: It's funny, because the police had been trying to clamp down on football violence in the late Eighties by increasing intelligence and introducing more banning orders. Then when the violence did start to drop off they obviously took the credit for it, but it wasn't them that successfully curbed it at all; it was the arrival of acid house that stopped football violence. Not just the United lads either, but smaller firms from clubs like Chester who would go to The Haçienda.

Growing up in Chester, or going to a club in any small town, there was always trouble at the end of the night. It would *always* kick off. So we always used to leave 20 minutes before the end to avoid the fighting when the club kicked out. The first few times we went to The Haçienda we left 20 minutes before the end as usual, especially as we were very aware that, being from Chester, we might have sounded a bit like Scousers, which could get you battered in Manchester. But after a few weeks it was so good that we *had* to stay until the end, and then we realised there was absolutely no chance it was going to kick off. Nothing could be further from the truth. As you got outside everyone was hugging each other, hugging strangers even, and just planning where to go to next. That was the magic of The Haçienda. It was so new, and so different to anything you had experienced and it felt like a secret world. You wanted to tell a couple of close friends about it and let them into this secret world, but apart from that you wanted to keep it secret and special.

★

By early summer of '88 there was a nascent house scene in London, and it was possible to go out several times a week and hear house music. Although many of the new converts to the scene would frequent more than one club, many declared their allegiance to one or the other and rivalry did exist between the clubs, even if the people running them were friends.

STEVEN HALL: When The Trip opened, a bit of a circuit developed with Future, The Trip, The Shoom and a couple of other things, like Clink Street. At first they were all in it together – the separate clubs – then a bit of rivalry began to surface. I'm not sure if when the four of them went to Ibiza they were ever inseparable best mates, like they were the Four Musketeers or anything, but everyone was together at first. A lot of the soundtrack at all four nights was taken from Alfredo's sets at Amnesia the year before, so they were all similar. Even though there were only about 200–300 people into it at that stage, rivalry came into it quite quickly. I heard about an alleged row between Rampling and Oakenfold because people were not being allowed into Shoom if they'd been elsewhere. So I think the first split was the Shoom crowd was definitely a Shoom crowd and then when Clink Street started, they definitely had their own crowd; a bit rougher, a few more bad boys – there were no 'Josephines' going to Clink Street, unlike Shoom. It was a younger crowd which had come out of electro and hip hop. We used to go there sometimes after Shoom finished and they wouldn't play any fluffy Balearic pop; they would play the hardest end of whatever was around.

ANDREW WEATHERALL: Because people could now put 'Shoom' or 'The Trip' after my name on flyers, I started getting booked for main slots, rather than just back rooms, so I thought, "Right, OK, people are going to be expecting something mixed now, I'd better learn to mix." I didn't even have decks then. I didn't have decks until at least two or three years into 'my career', when I did some sleeve notes for some Italo compilation for some record company like BCM and I asked them to buy me a set of decks for my payment. That wasn't until about 1991. Prior to that I was just letting one record finish and the next one start, because what I was playing was so disparate. Those early house records are difficult to mix because they didn't have MIDI. So a lot of those records are not in perfect time, you could be a beat out here and there. Because it was very difficult to mix what I was playing, I didn't bother. I remember reading one DJ say, "Mix what you play, don't play what you mix," which I thought was sound advice.

116

It's very easy to mix. I can teach anyone to mix in 10 minutes, tops. It's a piece of piss when you're in your house, when the decks are working properly and you can hear everything perfectly. But go out to a club where the decks haven't been serviced for months, the monitor keeps blowing up, it's louder on the floor than it is in the booth, there's no bass so you have to mix on the offbeat, on the snare, because that's all you can hear: that's a different thing... that takes years to master.

But if you can hear properly, then as long as you know your four times table and you know when two things are in tune, then it's a piece of piss. Things are usually four-beat, eight-beat or 16-beat progressions, there's an upbeat and a downbeat, and then you just make sure there's no key clash when you're mixing – it's pretty basic. When I first mastered it I thought, "Brilliant, this is a piece of piss." Then next time I got to a club I suddenly thought, "Fuck! I can't hear the monitor!"

MIKE PICKERING: Nicky Holloway booked me to DJ and T-Coy to play at The Trip. Only six months earlier I had played at the same venue and was booed off for playing acid house. But this time the crowd were all in bandanas and smiley T-shirts, trance dancing. I actually probably played 70–80 per cent of the same records I'd played six months previously but instead of booing me off, they went mental, as if they had always loved this music. Bloody cockneys... always late to the party!

PAUL ROBERTS: I came across The Trip, and acid house itself really, completely by accident. I was an indie kid originally and I'd first heard acid house on John Peel. At the time I was a real indie kid and I was working as a roadie for a band from Bristol called The Flatmates, who were part of that C86 indie scene [named after a cassette given away on the front of the *NME* and defined by jangly guitars]. I was a huge New Order and Factory [Records] fan. I missed very few of their gigs between 1983 and 1988. I would hitch-hike and sleep in train stations, whatever I had to do to get to their gigs. If only I'd known then that through acid house I would go from being the sycophantic fan to having New Order on *Top Of The Pops* miming to a bassline I'd written for 'Ruined In A Day'.

117

The first acid house record I heard was Armando's 'Land Of Confusion' and it literally sounded like something from outer space. I was like, "Wow, what the fuck is *this*?" It sounded like nothing else, and I just wanted to hear more of this music. So the next Saturday, when I went into Manchester to go record shopping as usual, as well as going to Piccadilly Records to buy indie records I went to Spin Inn, which was the specialist dance music shop in Manchester, to see if they had more of this music. I then started to listen to *On The Wire* on Radio Lancashire, because the DJ Steve Barker used to play some house music on there.

I then stumbled upon the first night of The Trip, completely by chance. The Flatmates had a gig at The Astoria in June 1988 and the drummer from the band said to me, "There's a really interesting club night going on here after the gig," because they used to close the venue after the gig on a Saturday night and then re-open for The Trip. The drummer would do a bit of speed now and then, but I would never touch drugs at the time. I grew up on an estate called Blacon in Chester, which I think was the second biggest estate in Europe after Wythenshawe [in Manchester], and there was a horrendous heroin problem there in the Eighties. People I knew well had died of overdoses or totally lost it, so at the time I was just thought anyone who did drugs was a smackhead. That night in the Astoria I'd had quite a few beers and the drummer persuaded me to have half a pill, saying, "This is this new drug everyone's on." I didn't think it had had much effect on me but I do remember having an amazing night and everyone getting on well. I got talking to some random guy who said, "You do know all this and better is going on up north, at The Haçienda?" I had absolutely no idea, so the next Friday we had off work we went to Manchester to The Haçienda and it was going absolutely nuts. That was it for me. The music was right, it was so much better than The Trip. It was properly beat-mixed and the whole energy and vibe was so much better.

NICKY HOLLOWAY: By the second or third week it was rammed. The Trip only actually lasted 10 weeks but its legacy is bigger than that because for a lot of people it was their first experience of acid house, and everyone always remembers their first experience. The amount of emails, letters and Facebook messages I've had from people over the years saying, "I took my first E at The Trip"; "I met my wife at The Trip"; "It changed my life," and stuff like that. I've got videos of The Trip with people like Rocky and Diesel [future DJs and members of X-Press 2] all on podiums in bandanas, waving their arms about.

When the club shut, everybody used to just pour out into the road and be singing and dancing. We used to play [The Rolling Stones'] 'Sympathy For The Devil' as the last record, so people would be dancing in the fountains that used to be at the bottom of Centrepoint, going, "Woo-woo, woo-woo." The police would just be standing there confused and laughing; they didn't have a clue what was going on at first – they didn't know what ecstasy was at this point so they just couldn't understand. They just thought it was funny because they could see no one was hurting anyone else.

We filled in The Astoria's 10-week gap and then they had this play called *Black Heroes In The Music Business*, which was supposed to have quite a long run, but it was struggling to sell tickets so they asked me to come back and take over Saturday nights again.

FABIO, BBC RADIO 1 DJ: The Trip was mental. It wasn't just the drugs. I think the timing and the social aspect were just as important as the drugs. It's difficult to remember now just what Thatcher's Britain felt like: a lot of people were unemployed and bored and felt very distant from everything else going on in society. A lot of people were searching for something, for a way out. It's difficult to recall how drab things were then.

Even when [acid house] really began to take off in the summer, it still felt like there were only a few thousand people in on it. Most young people didn't have a clue. You would come out of all-night parties and bump into people in the petrol station on their way to work, and they would look at us like we were zombies!

NICKY HOLLOWAY: I remember standing in the club at its peak and thinking, "It is never going to get better than this," and it never did really, not for me. For the first time in my life I was not only DJing at the biggest and best gig – the best club night in the world at that time – I was running it and making the money out of it. We moved the decks out into the middle of the dancefloor after a few weeks, so the DJ was in the middle, and I could look around and see everyone going nuts: people on the balcony, Lynn Cosgrove (who is now Carl Cox's manager but was about 17 at the time) bouncing up and down on a trampoline on the stage. I had to pinch myself. It was just mad. I just looked round and thought, "It is never going to get better than this," and do you know what? It hasn't. So far. It's been good but it ain't been *that* good.

Ecstasy played a massive part in it, obviously. It would be nice to think it would have happened without ecstasy, but no way would it have taken off like it did. Anyone who says it would have taken off without E is talking out of their arse; ecstasy opened up the parts other drugs couldn't reach.

CYMON ECKEL: I was a carpenter and I cut my fingers off in an accident on 5 May, 1988, so I had to disappear off the scene. Four weeks later I came out of hospital and acid house was in the papers: it happened that quick. You're talking about a trajectory of about 12–16 weeks from being nothing, from being something only a handful of people knew about, to being on the front page of *The Sun*. Then it had gone overground and I think we felt the honeymoon period was over. We weren't trying to protect the emotion or the idea of acid house; we were just trying to protect the great parties for great people.

When you think about it, you talk about word of mouth and you look at books that try and take an analytical view like the American contemporary philosopher Malcolm Gladwell's *Tipping Point*. To go, in those short weeks, from an obscure club to a place where Boy George, Fat Tony, Patrick Cox, everyone who worked at Vivienne Westwood – everything and everyone we were genuinely against, well we were against Fat Tony and Boy George at the time – were all clamouring to get in. How the fuck did that happen? Even if you had all the money in the world, you couldn't build a brand to do that today.

BOY GEORGE: Although clubs like Spectrum and Shoom were mainly straight clubs, there were also gay versions of those clubs as well like The Fridge, Sacrosanct, White Trash – all sorts of things were going on. The queens definitely had their own version of it but I was much more involved in the straight scene at the start. I really embraced it all. I wasn't someone who stood by the sidelines, I definitely threw myself head first into the scene – I wasn't peripheral in any way. I remember [musician] Guru Josh saying, "What the fuck has Boy George got to do with house music?" and *Boy's Own* wrote a really nice article saying, "Actually, he's got a lot to do with it, fuck off." Guru Josh later came up to me in Heaven and apologised.

★

It was Andrew Weatherall, in his *Boy's Own* column as The Outsider, who had taken Guru Josh to task:

> OK, you pyjama clad git, let's deal with your 'arguments'. Basically, Guru, me old china, Boy George has got more to do with the real club scene than you ever will ever hope to have.

ANDREW WEATHERALL: Guru Josh?! You know what I mean? Boy George already knew more about the underground club scene in London than Guru Josh would ever know. We did take umbrage quite a lot in those days because it was *our* thing. But we were probably as contrary as everyone else. That's the same with any small club scene: people are quite protective of it.

★

On 13 July, The Haçienda launched a new Ibiza-themed night on Wednesdays called Hot. A swimming pool was installed on the dance floor and ice pops were given out for free. The resident DJs were Mike Pickering and Jon DaSilva.

PAUL CONS, HACIENDA PROMOTER: Tony Wilson used to pay me to go to New York for a month each year for 'research' purposes, and the previous year I'd basically spent it all in the Paradise Garage on ecstasy, so I knew what was coming. I had this idea to launch the new night with a summer beach party theme.

PAUL MASON, HAÇIENDA MANAGER: Myself and Fred, the maintenance manager, erected this huge pool and connected all the hosepipes we could find up to the sinks behind the bars, then went to the pub for a few pints of Stella. We came back three hours later and there was just this puddle in the bottom of the pool. We ended up having to get someone to connect us up to the main water supply. Of course, the morning after Hot we then had this swimming pool full of tonnes of water in the middle of the dancefloor and we had a bloody gig that night so had to empty it quickly somehow. Peter Hook [from New Order] turned up in the afternoon and said, "I know what to do; my kids have got a paddling pool which is the same design, just smaller. You just take one of the panels out – it's much quicker that way." But we lost control of it and tonnes of water burst out of the cargo doors of the club. This little old dear had the misfortune to be walking past the club just at that moment, pulling her shopping trolley, and it washed her about 300 yards down the road.

JON DASILVA: It was Paul Cons who gave me my break. He came down with Vidal Sassoon for a party at Stuffed Olives; there were loads of pretty girls dancing and the place just went off. I was supposed to just play for 20 minutes that night but Dominic and Madhatter were like, "No, no, you stay on." That must have been very early 1988. So after that Paul brought me in to the Haç to do Hot. The first couple of weeks of Hot were reasonably 'normal', but from the third week it was mayhem. It was almost scary. It was so intense.

I was concentrating so much on the DJing at first I didn't really go out of the DJ booth, because me and Mike were doing 20 minutes on, 20 minutes off, which is a bit of an unusual arrangement for DJs. It was back to back essentially, all night, and we used to work it at first so one would start the night, the other would finish it. Then Mike decided to pull rank and he would always finish the night. I think it was the third week I ventured out during the 10 minutes or so I had to spare in between playing, and the whole atmosphere had completely changed. I came out of the DJ booth and there was this guy with dreadlocks who was almost hysterical, crying and laughing at the same time, just blown away by the atmosphere. You almost felt like you were missing out by DJing at Hot: you just wanted to be on the floor.

Prior to Hot and acid house hitting The Haçienda, people would just dance to records they liked, which meant there would be the big movements on and off the dancefloor as records changed, but at Hot the punters would be queuing up early, come in at 9p.m. as soon as the doors opened, start dancing straight away and stay dancing all night. The sights you saw around the club were just... there was a lot of people taking ecstasy for the first time, so there were a lot of very emotional, very happy people, and it was very intense. As I wasn't doing ecstasy myself it was very strange for me. I didn't quite know what was going on.

★

When Hot launched, Tony Wilson had been over in New York for the New Music Seminar, where he had been addressing delegates on the subject of sex. Upon his return, a friend advised him he needed to get down to The Haçienda and check out what was happening at Hot. Wilson couldn't believe what he saw when he walked through the door at 10.30p.m. the following Wednesday: "I looked around in shock because people were doing this dancing and there's this look in their eyes." For Wilson, New Order manager Rob Gretton and the band themselves, The Sex Pistols and Buzzcocks gig at the Lesser Free Trade Hall in 1976 had been the pivotal moment in Manchester music, inspiring everything that followed. Factory even held a festival to mark the 10th anniversary of the gig in 1986, The Festival Of The Tenth Summer. But when Wilson walked into Hot for the first time he felt history repeating. "Within seconds, I was like, 'Oh my God, wow, it's happened again.' It was more than just ecstasy – it was something else."

SASHA: Me and my friend Piers moved to Disley, Cheshire, because he had a flat there. He got us jobs in a call centre; we were selling adverts on LED boards in post offices and I had absolutely no interest in it at all. Piers was actually quite good at it and did quite well. I then got offered a slot on WBLS pirate radio station, so I decided to jack in the call centre.

Piers thought I was mad to give it up and stay up all night DJing for no money. He couldn't see how anyone would ever make money DJing. But that was the beginning for me, really.

I was living in Piers' flat in Disley but it was an hour outside Manchester on the train, a real pain in the arse, so me and my girlfriend decided to move into Manchester and, completely fortuitously, we ended up in this block of flats called Rusholme Gardens, where Jon DaSilva also lived. He was always my favourite DJ at that time anyway, from when I started going to Hot on a Wednesday night: he was the first DJ I knew who would mix in key and use sound effects and *a cappella* and just stuff that no one else was doing. He also had a different sound to Mike Pickering and Graeme Park, whose sound was really big at that point, whereas Jon was more into the Italian labels. I also preferred Wednesday nights because the proper heads came out on a Wednesday.

Jon kind of took me under his wing and little by little he started throwing me some bones, like warming up for him at one gig or covering for him at another, and we became quite good friends.

I then started my first night at The PSV Club in Hulme – I used to DJ with Andy Madhatter; we had a DJ partnership going for a while. We got a decent little crowd there. It wasn't a legendary night or anything, but it was certainly the first chance I'd had to build a set through the night.

FIONA ALLEN, ACTRESS AND COMEDIENNE, *SMACK THE PONY*: I used to sneak into The Haçienda when I was too young, but I wasn't overly keen on it then as it was mainly lots of people in long, dark overcoats trying to look cool. It was a really different club and a lot of the time it was quite empty. They had some good bands playing but the acoustics were rubbish.

My sister was already working there and I got a job through her in the cloakroom. It was a brilliant place to work because I was just working with all my mates really; it was like having a night out but getting paid for it. We loved it. Then, by the time acid house started, I'd moved to work on reception. Within a few weeks it all changed and the Haç just became really vibrant, and that was basically because ecstasy arrived.

That's what made it. I know it's an old cliché, but it made white people want to dance. When you walked in you could just feel this energy, this *life*. People jumping on anything they could to dance: podiums, the stage, anything. Mike Pickering, Graeme Park and Jon DaSilva suddenly became stars. Before acid house, Nude was the only night that people were really dancing at in the Hacienda.

Within a short space of time, the queues became so big that people were queuing from an hour and a half before the clubs opened. People would do anything to get in, and coach-loads were coming from all over the country. Everybody would try and do anything to get in, because Manchester is just full of byaggers: "I'm on the guest list; so-and-so put us on the guest list." "No, you're not on the guest list." "I fucking am, because my brother knows so-and-so and he sorted it out for me." It was a nightmare, but my job was just to get people in as quickly as possible so they weren't queuing up outside in the cold and the rain. Wilson used to stand behind me sometimes, just watching all the byaggers and observing it all, which was quite funny, because there was a framed picture of him on the wall where you had to pay, so Wilson would be stood in front of a framed picture of himself, leaning in exactly the same manner. Typical Tony.

I just got to know everybody, although Manchester is not a big city anyway, but everyone wanted to come to The Haçienda, so it was like one big party all the time. I'd always go out after the club closed and end up at some place, The Kitchen or some house party until 6a.m. You could do that every night if you wanted.

JOHN MCCREADY, DJ/JOURNALIST, *THE FACE*: It wasn't like anything you'd ever experienced in a club before. The clubs we'd been to previously were full of apprentices in pressed white shirts on the pull. Girls were huddled in groups like disorientated wildebeest. At The Haçienda it was almost as if a generation breathed a sigh of relief, having been relieved of the pressure of the chase. The baggy clothes de-sexualised the whole environment. The rising heat from 2,000 people dancing, even at the bar, in the queue for the toilets, damped down everyone. We all looked crap. If you held onto the handrail on the balcony above the dance floor your palms would be dripping in accumulated human sweat. Many of the records talked about dancing as working, like 'Work It To The Bone', and suddenly the original intentions of the music started to make sense. You could feel the down when the music stopped. The room quickly went cold as all the exit doors were thrown open and we were herded out. Back to forbidding reality. Until the next week. The whole experience was always far more addictive than the drugs. You started wanting it all to go on forever.

BILLY CALDWELL, HAÇIENDA REGULAR: The first time I heard house music was around late '86 or early '87, but I didn't really get it at first because I was so entrenched in soul. A kid I grew up with called Jeff Lowe would lend me tapes with stuff like early Trax records and Phuture, mainly out of Chicago. It was so foreign sounding; I didn't really get it.

But then the first time I heard it in a club was at The Haçienda and I totally got it. It was a Friday night and I'd been out to The Gallery and I was dressed like a soul boy in a Van Gils blazer, tie, white shirt, Aquascutum pants – I'm surprised they let me in! I was walking home past The Haçienda and I was pretty drunk and I thought, "You know what, I'm going to stick my head in and see what's happening." I just wandered in and the strobe lights were going and the club was completely covered in smoke. They were playing acid house and I'd never heard it in a club before, all those acid squelches – which I later learned came from the 303 – sounded completely alien. The dancefloor was packed and there were girls up on podiums and everybody in the whole club – 1,500 people – was going for it. I went upstairs to the balcony to try and get a better look at what was going on. I remember gazing out across the club and just thinking, 'What the fuck is going on?' I had never seen anything like it, or heard anything like it, in my life. I couldn't get my head around it at all. I had absolutely no idea about ecstasy at that stage; I don't think I'd even heard of it. Then I ran into this Rasta kid I knew from Hulme called Gary and he said, "Billy, what are you doing here?" and gave me some of his spliff. I said, "Gary, what the *fuck* is going on in here?" and he just said, "It's acid house, this is what's happening here."

I spent the rest of the night just staring at the dancefloor. It was so alien. Nobody was trying to chat anyone up, everyone was just kind of dancing on their own, lost in their own world. I got myself a drink and the longer I stayed the more I started to appreciate the music. I walked home that night and I couldn't get to sleep, all I could think about was this music.

Next morning the first thing I did was go round to my friend Jeff's house – I knew he frequented The Haçienda – and I said, "You've got to give me some of this music," and he played me stuff like Phuture and Adonis, and that was it. I was *obsessed* with this music – and started collecting it. I remember waiting for Eastern Bloc to open on the Monday morning and just buying up every acid house record I could get my hands on.

That week was a life-changing moment for me, and you can trace my life since back to that week. I think it's very rare in someone's life that something comes along and absolutely just knocks you off your feet, you just know that it's absolutely brand new and there's never been anything like it before. From then on I was a regular at The Haçienda every single chance I could get – three, sometimes four times a week. Right up until the club closed.

KARL BROCKBANK, HAÇIENDA REGULAR: When you walked up to The Haç, you could hear and feel the old doors vibrating and actually *see* the steam coming out from under the door. You just couldn't wait to get in there. Then when you walked in, there were these big plastic curtains and as you walked through them it would absolutely smack you right between your eyes. It was just electric man, *electric*. Absolutely. Greatest place in the world ever. It really was.

At the end of every night everybody used to say, "Where we going? Where's the party?" I was followed home when I was in a taxi sometimes because people thought I was going to a rave, and I had to get out of the car and explain to people, "No, I'm going *home*, mate."

MIKE PICKERING: That whole period just felt so special because no one had a clue what we were doing. The authorities didn't have a clue.

We used to come out of The Haçienda when it finished and go back to The Kitchen in Hulme, which was just two old council flats knocked together. Funnily enough, I bumped into Noel Gallagher recently and we were reminiscing about The Kitchen and saying how hardly anyone mentions it.

★

The Kitchen was located in Hulme, just south of Manchester city centre, in high-rise flats with deck access known as The Crescents, so-called because they were based on Bath's Royal Crescent and 'curved' in the same way. Constructed after the slum clearance of the Sixties, The Crescents were troubled from the start and within a decade were declared unfit for purpose. By the late Eighties, the blocks were almost exclusively occupied by Bohemian squatters and Hulme became a magnet for anarchists, artists, musicians and anyone else who fancied opting out of society, or simply living rent-free. The Kitchen was originally one squatted flat but became a notorious after-party. It was a favoured post-Haçienda destination and many members of Manchester's music fraternity frequented it, including DJs and members of New Order, The Stone Roses and Happy Mondays. When The Kitchen needed to expand, the squatters simply knocked down the wall into the next flat.

SHAUN RYDER: Hulme was pretty wild back then. The Crescents had been this big experiment in social housing in the early Seventies, which was supposed to be a vision of the future or something – it was all concrete walkways and stairwells. But by the mid Eighties it had failed and had been taken over by squatters, scallies and drug dealers. No one paid any rent, people just broke into flats and stayed there. Charles Barry Crescent was just full of squatters.

A kid called Jamie had one flat and he had a bit of a recording studio and a soundsystem in there, so it became a bit of a party flat. The DJs would DJ in the actual kitchen and so it became known as The Kitchen. There was hardly any light in there – it was really dark because they'd taken all the lightbulbs out – but the music was good because Chris and Tomlin used to DJ there. They had to knock through to the flat next door because it became so popular. Basically, half the flats were boarded up so if the one next to you was boarded up, you would just knock through and give yourself a massive extension, double the size of your flat. The Kitchen was great. We used to get down there sharpish after The Haçienda shut to grab the tables and chairs upstairs.

I remember being in there one night with [New Order's] Barney and Hooky and a few other Manc musicians – I think Chris Goodwin, who was in the Roses early doors then in The High later on, was there as well. We were all E'd up and just got up and had an impromptu jamming session, whichever Manchester musician heads were in there that night.

CHRIS JAM, DJ: I moved up to Manchester from London in 1986. Acid house hadn't really hit London when I left. I was working at a place called Mendoza's in Brixton, which was a kind of shebeen, and Fabio and Grooverider were playing there. Then just before I came to Manchester I went to a huge Soul II Soul warehouse party somewhere near Islington, which just blew my mind; I'd never seen anything like it. But acid house still hadn't hit.

Not long after I moved to Manchester I met Tomlin and we realised we had similar music tastes, so we started hanging out and playing together. It was Tomlin that introduced me to The Kitchen in Hulme. It was all quite disorganised and just a few acid heads, but we could see the potential for it so we decided to get involved. Paul Pryce and Timothy Williams were also pretty instrumental in getting it going, but loads of people who came down helped out or contributed something. It was just the right time to start it because people were desperate for somewhere to go late on, after The Haçienda and the other clubs had shut. Within a couple of weeks, Shaun Ryder would be in the corner with his pals, Ian Brown might pop in one night, then Mike Pickering would come down after The Haçienda, dripping with sweat from playing there and Sasha and Justin Robertson and a lot of those emerging DJs used to come down as well.

I actually had an office job in Haslingden when I moved up here, but within six months some weeks I was out Tuesday, Wednesday, Thursday, Friday, Saturday night. I'd get in at 5 or 6a.m., have a quick kip if I was lucky and then get up and go to work.

DARREN GREENE, DJ: I was DJing at The Kitchen one night and I was playing house music when someone started tapping my shoulder in the middle of a mix. I said, "Wait a minute, mate," but whoever it was just kept tapping on my shoulder so I stopped mixing and turned round, and this guy pulled a big shiny thing from down his pants. I thought it was a knife so I went to grab it to stop him stabbing me in the stomach. I felt a round barrel and looked down to see a pretty big pistol staring up at me. I instinctively put my hands up in the air and the guy with the gun, who had a Scouse accent, told me to play some hip-hop and give him "maximum respect" next time I saw him. Ironically, the tune I was trying to mix in was 'Back By Dope Demand' by King Bee. I didn't play again that night.

ERIC BARKER: I was down The Kitchen all the time. Jamie was a nice kid; I always got on well with him. We didn't have any mither at first, but after it became popular the police started raiding it. At one stage it felt like they were raiding it every night, so I said to Jamie, "Right, I've had enough of this, the dibble are spoiling my night out." So a few of us went and took the steel door off one of the other flats that had been boarded up and fitted it on The Kitchen, so the police couldn't raid us as easily.

BILLY CALDWELL: My grandma lived on The Crescents when I was growing up, so I knew them well. All of us who went to The Haçienda then started going back to The Kitchen. I ended up going on Wednesday, Thursday, Friday and Saturday night. It's still the best after-party ever for me. It was like a *Who's Who* of Manchester's music scene. Tomlin and Chris Jam were playing all these great house records but they would throw all these curveballs in there like Roachford's 'Cuddly Toy' – that was a big Kitchen tune. Then you'd go upstairs where they'd knocked through a wall to create a studio and any night there could be Bernard Sumner, Peter Hook, Shaun Ryder, Chris Goodwin and any number of Manc musicians, and they'd all be picking up instruments and just jamming with each other. It was just an amazing creative place and it was so inspiring to be around that sort of energy.

CHRIS GOODWIN: I had been going to The Haçienda since it opened, on and off, before the summer of '88 changed the club beyond all recognition: the music, the clientele, the atmosphere. When people nowadays ask me what it was like, I find it almost impossible to describe. It was like a whole new way of clubbing was upon us and we were the guinea pigs in the experiment – an experiment that went fantastically right! It's now 2013 and we have 3D this and High Definition that, but back then we had the ultimate 3D sensory experience that to this day hasn't been topped and is still chased by many. We had been looking for the perfect beat and found it in one blissful church called The Haçienda. That's how it felt. Clubs started springing up every week and you could go out every night of the week and find somewhere that was 'on'. If there were no clubs there was always The Kitchen or some shebeen in Moss Side. You dared not miss a night, in case it was a big one. It could be a rainy Tuesday night in The Brickhouse and people would be in [Factory-owned and run] Dry Bar the next day saying it was a classic!

I lived in Hulme on Epping Walk for a while; it was a big party house with a group of lads going out every night. One night the lad who owned it, Simmo, said he was having a quiet night in. We all went out and as we all walked over the bridge, we could hear a distant thud and the strains of 'Voodoo Ray'* floating over the estate from behind us. We turned round and we could see Simmo dancing in his front room on his own, strobe light on, hands in the air. We turned to each other, laughing, and said, "A quiet night in, eh? Ha ha!"

---

* 'Voodoo Ray' by A Guy Called Gerald was a seminal acid house record, especially in Manchester and The Haçienda. It soundtracked the summer of 1988 and became one of the first Hacienda anthems. It eventually reached number 12 in the UK charts.

CHAPTER 6

The Summer Of Love

"Fuck the hippies – they had nothing on acid house."

Darren Partington, 808 State

GRAEME PARK: Early in the summer of 1988 I got a call from Mike Pickering. He was going on holiday for three weeks and wondered if I'd like to cover for him on the Friday [at The Haçienda] because the guy he was DJing with had left to go to America. I said I'd bloody love to do it and Mike said, "Do me a favour, can you come up the week before I go away?" I said, "I've been to The Haçienda before…" And he responded with, "Yes, but you've not to been to Nude on a Friday night before, and you need to be prepared, otherwise you'll turn up and think, 'What the fuck is going on?'" So I went up with my then wife the Friday before I was due to start, and as I walked in the door, I just couldn't believe what I saw: the noise, the heat and the crowd. Mike was playing the same stuff I was playing in Nottingham, but I was playing it to 500 people who liked a drink and were quite a dressy crowd. Here, Mike had 2,000 of the scruffiest people I'd ever seen in my life, with pony tails, in tie-dye, dungarees and Kickers, going crazy, and the atmosphere was absolutely electric. It only took me about 10 minutes to find out the reason for this. Ecstasy. Mike just laughed. "See, I told you you needed to come up and

132

see it for yourself. Right, you need to have one of these..." I said, "No, no, no... I don't do drugs." Because even though I had been playing house music in Nottingham for a while, ecstasy hadn't hit Nottingham yet. But my ex-wife went, "Ecstasy? Yeah, fuck it, I'll have one!" and necked it. So I just went, "Whoa, hang on a minute! Right, give me one of those..."

Half an hour later we're down on the dancefloor, and I can remember distinctly the tune that Mike was playing when I got my first E rush, which was 'The Party' by Kraze, and even now, 25 years later, when I just mention that record by name the hairs on my arm stand up; whenever I hear it, it just takes me straight back to that moment. It was just an incredible, life-changing night. After The Haçienda closed we ended up at The Kitchen. It was all so... surreal. That night in Manchester, I realised I'd lived quite a sheltered life up until then.

I came back up and did the three weeks on my own, and it was just incredible. I can remember it really clearly, even the crowd response to individual records. It was also the first time I'd been looked after properly as a DJ – I'd given up the day job in the record shop by this stage and was starting to get guest spots in London and around the country, but I wasn't looked after anywhere like I was looked after at The Haçienda. It helped that I knew Paul Mason from his time in Nottingham. But all the punters would look after you. I couldn't understand it at first – I was a bit shocked that the punters would come to the DJ booth and offer you drugs. But I soon realised it was simply because they wanted me to be on the same level, the same high as them.

When Mike came back he asked me how it had gone. I told him it was the best three weeks of my life. Then he said, "How would you like to do it every week with me?" I just went, *"What??"* I couldn't believe it. That's how I started at The Haçienda.

DAVE HASLAM: Ecstasy obviously played a huge part in it all. Ecstasy intensified the experience and also meant the crowd were pretty responsive to dancing to music they had not heard before, which was very liberating, although sometimes I think you could have played a recording of a Hoover and 2,000 people would have screamed with joy.

When you DJ you're mostly faced with a crowd waiting to be entertained and it's your challenge to whip them up into a frenzy. But that early acid house era was different; you were faced with 2,000 baying people on the verge of such euphoria their heads were almost exploding. You almost felt like you had to hold them back a bit, like someone trying to guide wild horses. I was DJing at the Haçienda one evening and a girl came into the DJ box, lay down and took all her clothes off. She was naked and started pulling at my trousers. I was wise enough to know it was E taking effect rather than anything to do with me, but it was just one of those things; there was a lot of craziness in the air.

We were disconnected from the rest of the world really, or I was. If you'd asked me to name some other DJs back then I would have said Mike Pickering, Jon DaSilva and Graeme Park. I didn't know who Paul Oakenfold was until Nathan McGough, Happy Mondays' manager, told me they'd asked him to remix their work. I had a vague idea that I wouldn't be able to get into The Wag Club and I used to read what Jay Strongman would recommend in *The Face*, but we were on our own island in Manchester really. There was still no mention of this music in the *NME*. I'd pretty much given up writing for the *NME* at that stage because there was all this other stuff going on, which was far more exciting.

What might surprise people is there was never any discussion about music policy at The Haçienda. I think I had one conversation with the manager, Paul Mason, in all the years I was playing there. I never talked to the other DJs about music – I didn't know what the others were playing, and I didn't know what was cool. That was actually an important part of what made it good. So I didn't even know what Mike was playing, let alone anyone in London.

FIONA ALLEN: It was funny how the DJs became gods to people so quickly. Literally, people started treating them like absolute gods for playing records. I suppose part of it was because there were only a few of them back then that were any good, and we had them at The Haçienda.

JON DASILVA: After a while, Mike Pickering didn't come in until midnight on a Wednesday. I was living in the same flats as Sasha, so I would give him a lift into town in my taxi on the way to work and drop him off at the PSV, where he used to play for £25 a night. I said to him, "Look, I can give you a warm-up slot at The Haçienda." I told Mike, "I've got this young guy who's really good so I'm going to put him on for a bit."

SASHA: When Jon phoned me up I just thought, "That's it, my time has come!" Jon let the fucking genie out of the bottle that night and when I look back he must have thought, "What the fuck have I done?" I must have played every single one of his anthems back to back, every single one of his big tunes he'd built up over the preceding months, and I was scratching all his *a capellas* over the top. It was hilarious. He must have thought, "You fucking *twat*," but it kind of put me on the map because the place went absolutely fucking bonkers. It was an amazing night. I actually met some people that very night who've become lifelong friends; one of my best friends, Sparrow, who is a legendary character – I first met him that night.

★

After the success of Hot at The Haçienda, Paul Cons and Tony Wilson came up with the idea of a one-off rave at Hathersage swimming baths in Manchester, which was to be filmed for Wilson's Granada TV show, *The Other Side Of Midnight*. Playing live were The Haçienda DJs and A Guy Called Gerald with Graham Massey.

GRAHAM MASSEY: They were filming in there quite early in the evening and we were playing at the side of the swimming pool. The thing was, Gerald didn't have any health and safety sense back then, and some of his machines didn't even have plugs on – he'd just put bare wires into plug sockets. But they had a bouncy inflatable in the pool, water sloshing everywhere, and obviously water and electricity don't mix. God knows where health and safety were that night.

A GUY CALLED GERALD (GERALD SIMPSON), DJ/ PRODUCER: Not having plugs meant they were universal and you could go to Europe or wherever without needing adaptors. I kind of got used to getting the odd jolt now and then, so I'd almost expect it. But I'd obviously never taken so many electronics into a swimming pool before so I didn't think about it before we got there on the night. It was Graham who made me put plugs on the equipment after that night!

★

One of the first big illegal raves in Manchester was put on behind Piccadilly Station by brothers Chris and Anthony Donnelly. Called Sweat It Out, it was located in a railway arch on the site of what would become, 20 years later, the Warehouse Project.

CHRIS DONNELLY: The venue was right by me dad's scrapyard. We found this warehouse but it was a bit too knackered. So then we found this railway arch that British Rail were doing up. We broke into the warehouse with me dad and built a stage out of scaffolding. We had Mike Pickering and Jon DaSilva from The Haçienda playing, and we put a massive smiley face up on the wall that said, "Wait here." We had 10 strobe lights, which we had on all night. Tony Wilson came down to check it out and he loved the fact we had even built a little VIP area. Tony just loved it because he loved anything anarchic. He'd known us for years as Tracey's little scally brothers [Tracey worked at Factory], so he loved the fact it was two scallies like us putting on the first big illegal rave in the city centre. I'm pretty sure Wilson had a video camera with him, although I've never seen any footage of the gig.

Anyone who was anyone turned up, including the Mondays and Mani from the Roses. We only charged £3 to get in and there were about 300 people there. If you were there, I can guarantee you that it's the best £3 you have ever spent in your life because it was a legendary party.

In the middle of the night we ran out of drinks at the bar, but I had a load more outside in my Fiat Uno. I couldn't be arsed carrying them in, so I just drove the Fiat Uno into the venue with the hazard lights on, slowly across the dance floor to the bar. People were all dancing round the car and pressing their face up to the window and almost praying

136

to this Fiat Uno. I just drove through, unloaded it, and then reversed slowly out again with everyone cheering and patting the car.

The coppers didn't turn up until about 9a.m. when we were sweeping up and it was just piles of water bottles. The police were like, "What's been going on here?" and we said, "We've just had a private party, officer, but as you can see there was no alcohol, and Tony Wilson from *Granada Reports* came down as well," and they were like, "OK, fine." They didn't have a clue.

ANTHONY DONNELLY: We just dived straight into the scene, head first. It took over everything. It changed everything. We were complete converts; we didn't drink booze for over a year, just completely switched off the drink. We were like the Moonies, completely gone. I remember telling me mam we were going to pollute a reservoir with ecstasy, and we were serious. We thought it could change the world and we really wanted it to.

CHRIS DONNELLY: I seriously thought it was going to change the world. I remember sitting down with our Tracey and her boyfriend and saying, "Listen, he's *got* to take an E," and she said, "Why?" and I said "Because this thing is going to change the world." I remember trying to explain to him that if all the politicians and people at war would just take this tablet, it would solve all the problems. We were that deluded. Just absolutely puddled on ecstasy.

FIONA ALLEN: That little honeymoon period felt like one big party. We'd have a Hacienda night in Paris, so we'd all go en masse – it was just one big party, full of interesting, vibrant, exciting, fabulous people, *all* championed by Wilson, who was right behind anybody who said they had an idea. He wasn't the best businessman in the world but he was a very, very clever man, and he would always listen to people. Factory and The Haçienda stood for something, and still do to a lot of people. It was so different to everything happening before, and so well executed.

JON DASILVA: Dean Johnson, who was the Saturday night resident at The Haçienda for a long time, a soul DJ and real character, started telling me about this guy called Gerald [A Guy Called Gerald] who was living in Moss Side, making this amazing, out there music. I would walk round, trying to listen for strains of music coming from open windows because it was still very much a minority music. It turned out Gerald wasn't living in Moss Side anyway, he was living in Hulme. I was almost on a mythical search for him for a little while. But in the end it was him that came to me. One day he walked into the club, on one of the first weeks of Hot, with the first copy of 'Voodoo Ray', and hands it to me, not to Mike, simply because I opened the door. I just remembered putting it on the decks and playing it. I think it was the first time ever I'd been given a record in a club – a year later I was being handed stuff all the time. So maybe that and the fact Gerald looked like he did gave it more credence and made me want to hear it straight away. So I literally put it on straight away, and he's walking down the stairs from the booth and he hears his record come on in The Haçienda for the first time. The whole Gerald thing is kind of strange. He was a massive part of that explosion in the summer of 1988.

★

As acid house exploded in the summer of 1988, commentators began to draw comparisons with what was happening in the UK during that year and the hippies' Summer Of Love in 1967, of which San Francisco and Haight Ashbury was the epicentre. The parallels between the two hedonistic youth movements – the psychedelic drugs, the euphoria and empathy, and the almost evangelical vision of the future – led many commentators to call the acid house movement the 'Second Summer Of Love'.

DARREN PARTINGTON: I didn't like it when it was badged the second Summer of Love, and associated with Woodstock and hippies and all that – I hated that. For me it had fuck all to do with hippies. Me, Andy and Eric spending Saturday afternoon sweeping out a fucking industrial warehouse in the city centre and then installing a generator so we can have a huge party and have it right off that night – what the fuck has that got to do with middle-class hippies? Fuck the hippies – they had nothing on acid house.

★

The traditional music press had been extremely slow to pick up on house music, not least because the editors who had grown up on rock culture couldn't get their heads around the fact the DJ was the centre of attention, the DJ was the star. But they then found something that made much more sense to them: The Stone Roses and Happy Mondays. Both bands soaked up the influence of acid house and for some became default figureheads for the acid house generation. The Stone Roses had even considered bringing in DJ Pierre, the Chicago producer behind 'Acid Trax', to produce their debut album, although they settled in the end on John Leckie who had cut his teeth at Abbey Road, where he'd worked with George Martin, The Beatles (separately), Phil Spector and Pink Floyd.

In the summer of 1988, Manchester felt like the centre of the world: there was a palpable sense of things building week by week at that point. "At the time it felt great. It all came together," Stone Roses guitarist John Squire later said, "the people I was hanging about with, the clothes we were wearing, the records we were buying, the drugs we were doing." When the Bailey Brothers, directors who had shot most of Happy Mondays' promo videos, coined the term 'Madchester' slightly later, Tony Wilson jumped on it and the Mondays, while not particularly enamoured with the phrase, could see the benefit and acquiesced to their next EP, released on Factory in November the following year, being called the *Madchester Rave On EP*. With remixes by Andrew Weatherall and Terry Farley, it would give them their first Top 20 hit.

SHAUN RYDER: It was the Bailey Brothers who came up with the term 'Madchester' as a bit of a joke, but we were like, "Great, yeah, go with it," because Manchester *was* at the time, it *was* fucking mad. No one actually used the term Madchester in Manchester, unless they were a prick or a student, but it quickly became adopted by the media, who lapped it up. The *NME* even did a Madchester issue with me and Tony [Wilson] on the cover in front of a Madchester poster outside the Factory offices.

SARAH CHAMPION, AUTHOR, *AND GOD CREATED MANCHESTER*: I think 'Madchester' was born the night The Stone

Roses played a benefit gig with James at International 2 in May 1988. Something was in the water that month. Acid house had hit The Haçienda and my drink was spiked with my first ecstasy. We all ended up back at [Stone Roses' bass player] Mani's flat until dawn.

I was *NME*'s youngest writer since Julie Burchill, at 16, and my commissioning editor James Brown wanted me to move to London but I stayed in Manchester for a while because it just felt like the place to be. I remember interviewing the Roses in November 1988 and they asked me to meet them at Southern Cemetery, made famous by The Smiths' song 'Cemetry Gates'. We did the interview sat on a park bench and they gave me an early tape of the album and wrote the titles on a paper bag. They were very cocksure in that typical Mancunian way – Ian Brown said to me, "I seriously think we're gonna be huge." When I got home I played the tape and was blown away by it.

Excitement in Manchester was building week by week. It's not just myth, somehow the drugs and music were combining and something *big* was happening. We really felt we were the centre of the universe. It all peaked with Spike Island [the Roses' outdoor gig in 1990, *see* page 219]. After that, the mood changed in Manchester. The Roses and Mondays became huge and left town. The criminal element realised there was money to be made and moved in.

LEO STANLEY, IDENTITY CLOTHING: I was running my clothes shop, Identity, and a lot of people who went to The Haçienda would come and shop there. I first met the Stone Roses in the mid Eighties when they came into my shop in Affleck's Palace. Two girls worked for me – Tina Street and Debbie Turner – and all the lads fancied them. In 1988, Ian Brown asked if we could get hold of any Wrangler flares as they were really hard to get hold of and I decided to produce our own. As soon as Ian walked on stage wearing those flares, everyone wanted them.

I went down to Hot one night with Tina, and it was an incredible night. We were on ecstasy, like everyone else, and as we came out at the end of the night we were talking about the Soul II Soul T-shirts we were selling and she said, "We need to get on a northern tip, instead of selling these London T-shirts!" Because I was still high when I got home, I couldn't sleep, so I picked up The Bible and read, 'On the sixth day, God created Man...' and I just wrote down in my Filofax: 'ON THE SIXTH DAY, GOD CREATED MANchester.' I turned it into a T-shirt and they went mental – I couldn't print them fast enough. Everyone wanted one. About six months later, someone sent me a photograph from a French fashion magazine of Jean Paul Gaultier and Madonna at some party, both wearing 'ON THE SIXTH DAY, GOD CREATED MANchester' t-shirts.

FIONA ALLEN: They used to have all this Factory and Haçienda stuff hanging around the office and people just used to nick it. There was one guy in particular who worked there who had quite a big heroin habit and he used to ciphon off loads. It used to piss me off, so in the end I said to Wilson, "Why don't we open a shop in Affleck's?" And he said, "Yeah, good idea." So we found this space in Affleck's at the end of a corridor and I said, "I need this much to start it, and he said, "OK, there you go." But we didn't really think it through, because a lot of the stuff we were selling was very limited edition, so once we had sold it there wasn't any more. We'd have obsessive Factory fans with Bernard Sumner haircuts coming over from Holland or somewhere saying, "I have to have that *Technique* model," and I'd be like, "Oh sorry, I sold the last one yesterday." I thought, "Why don't we make some more, we've got the mould." But some purist Factory fan complained to Wilson: "I can't believe she wants to make more – that's against everything Factory stands for." Then the shop closed and I went over to work in the new Factory offices, which were just amazing: stunning Japanese oak doors, even the boardroom table was amazing, and everything was so tasteful. It just sums Factory up really – I was looking after merchandise and there was this massive office next to the boardroom and they just said, "Oh, you can have that."

ANDREW WEATHERALL: So I'd first met Danny Rampling at that party in Chapel Market where he'd asked me to DJ for Shoom. But the first time I actually got to DJ for them wasn't at a club, it was at a party they did out in the country in a farm. I remember getting off the coach with my plastic Woolworths record box and it burst and all my records fell out. It was hardly a glamorous DJ entrance to the party – there were just loads of people laughing and pointing at me as my records spilled out all over the road. Then they tried to turn the party into a foam party at the end, but it was in a fucking milking shed. I think you can see what's coming. Obviously they had cleaned it out, but you can't totally clean a milking shed; it's never going to be a pristine nightclub in Ibiza. So when this foam was pumped in, it brought up the remnants of cow shit and it all turned to mush. But I quite like that; it's so English – we're going to try and do a foam party but you're basically going to end up waist deep in this sludge. Ha ha! It was beautiful all the same.

Paul Oakenfold did a similar thing when he first tried to recreate Ibiza in that horrible little club in Streatham, Ziggy's, when he had Nosher Powell on the door. If you don't know who Nosher Powell is, he's this brilliant, notorious boxer and bouncer who has also done some acting; he's the guy in *Eat The Rich** who grabs hold of Shane MacGowan and says, "You, give him his country back, you, stop fucking about!" I just love the fact that you try and recreate Ibiza on Streatham High Road on a wet British evening with Nosher Powell on the door; it's so beautifully English. What we do well in this country is take exotic things and do our own ramshackle approximation of it. That's what acid house was in this country originally: a ramshackle approximation of something exotic. Then we send that ramshackle approximation of ours back out into the world and it ends up taking over the world. It happened with blues and punk rock. We had The Rolling Stones, The Yardbirds and Led Zeppelin and whoever doing their ramshackle approximation of the blues and it becomes bigger than the original. Same thing with punk to a certain extent. Now it's happening with electronic dance music, or EDM as the Americans call it. We did our ramshackle version of something American and exotic and we sold it back to them.

★

---

* *Eat The Rich* is a 1987 black comedy, directed by Peter Richardson.

In August, Tony Colston-Hayter hosted one of the first big warehouse raves at Wembley Studios in London, under the name Apocalypse Now, and let *ITN News* film the event, the first time news cameras had been let into a rave. On 17 August, *The Sun* published a story about drug taking at Heaven, which was owned by Richard Branson, claiming, "junkies flaunt their craving by wearing T-shirts bearing messages like 'Can You Feel It?' and 'Drop Acid Not Bombs.'" Branson gave an interview to ITN denying any link between the music and drug taking, although he did refer to it as 'acid rock'.

CHARLIE COLSTON-HAYTER, BROTHER TO TONY: I'm from Milton Keynes and when my brother Tony and I first started going out locally it was all false tans and shoulder pads, a bit like *TOWIE* is now. My brother was quite successful and knew a lot of people. One night when we were out someone gave us a 10-gram wrap of pure MDMA powder and we had absolutely no idea what to do with it. We were at a cheesy club called The Point and we just put a spoonful of it in our champagne glasses and then spent the night catwalking round to Madonna. Someone we met said there was this club called Shoom down in London where people take E, but it's a completely different type of club. We decided to go down and check it out, and it was such an amazing vibe; it was so completely different to the whole yuppie scene and crappy Stock, Aitken and Waterman music we'd grown up with. It was just 150 people, all dancing, holding hands and skipping round and it was just amazing. We just wanted more and more of it. The problem was we couldn't always get in; we weren't wearing the tie-dye gear at that stage, we were still a bit Milton Keynes, a bit shoulder-paddery, so it was a bit of a gamble, which is no good if you've driven 60 miles to get there.

So we decided to do a little party ourselves at Le Beat Route on Greek Street, which was only meant to be a private thing for mates, but then their mates found out and then their mates, and it just escalated. After that Tony and I got introduced to a guy called Roger Goodman and we decided to put on a party at Wembley Film Studios, which was the first Apocalypse Now. That was amazing. We were just kids really, and from just wanting to put a party on it spiralled out of control. It was a film studio so it had white walls that slid into the floor and we had a smoke machine, so people couldn't really see and ended up walking into the walls.

MARK MOORE: That was when it exploded. They told everyone they'd invited film crews down and Jenni Rampling was saying, "Do not go, *do not be part of this*." But I went anyway. Then when the programme did go out, it wasn't showing what a wonderful scene it was, like the promoters promised; it was more shock-horror coverage like, "Your children are all on drugs!" That's when it changed and all the shock tabloid headlines came out. It was a wonderful, beautiful period before that happened, but it was inevitable: there was no way we going to be able to keep a lid on this thing.

PAUL OAKENFOLD: As usual, the tabloids blew everything up out of proportion and sensationalised it. They tried to use the drugs issue, which was sensationalised and highlighted to put pressure on Richard Branson to close down Spectrum, but to his credit he wasn't having any of it.

STEVEN HALL: Because Apocalypse Now let ITN in, it sounds fucking pathetic, but there was a Shoom boycott and none of us would speak to them. To be honest, who wants to be interviewed on drugs anyway, but you knew something was suspicious because you could see them filming people collapsed in corners. The Shoom black-out held firm and no one we knew was interviewed on that programme.

CARL COX: Because I was tied in with Paul Oakenfold's nights with my soundsystem, I was still primarily a warm-up DJ. But a DJ with my own soundsystem and music. So Tony Wilson (the DJ, not Factory director) used to get me to play all these warehouses parties in east London, which became something of a phenomenon. I was still living in Brighton then and I was the only person playing acid house music on the South Coast – every other DJ was playing funk, soul or hip-hop, end of story; there was nothing over 90 bpm. I'd come in and play house music and it freaked everybody out. I would find a warehouse or wine bar or even a pub where I could play, and it would be free entry. I was playing tracks like 'Washing Machine' by Mr Fingers or 'Voodoo Ray' by A Guy Called Gerald, real classic stuff, and people wanted to hear it – they'd never heard it anywhere else. So eventually I got a gig at The Zap Club in Brighton on a Thursday night, playing this music religiously. If Graeme Park had The Haçienda, then Carl Cox had The Zap Club in Brighton, and that's how it went.

★

While Cymon Eckel was recovering in hospital after his carpentry accident, he met someone who offered him a venue that was too good to turn down. It led to *Boy's Own* holding their own small-scale party.

CYMON ECKEL: I had my hand sewn in my groin because it needed to get the blood supply from another part of my body, so I was kept in for a few weeks. I met this guy who was a couple of beds down from me in the same ward. He was into his old school blues and rock'n'roll, and hospital's a great leveller; you suss out who's on your wavelength in there. So the two of us started talking and then we started saving up a few bits of our Valium or opium, or this red drink which was an opiated paracetamol. We'd save up some bits for a few days and then we'd stay up late out the back with a spliff, and the nurses would leave us to it.

I told him about acid house and the clubs I'd been to and he said, "Oh, a friend of mine's got a recording studio with a barn and he has little parties there. I'll ask him if you can do a party if you like?" So when we got out of hospital we went down to see this guy and his place and I thought, 'This is great, we've got to do this!' We decided to call it the Karma Collective, and it was the first kind of outdoor rave really, although it wasn't meant to be a rave as such – it was just meant to be for the *Boy's Own* crew and everyone we'd met through Shoom and on our travels. It was just meant to be a mad night, a great night. I remember thinking, 'How are we going to decorate it? What's cheap? Let's just get some hay bales and put them round in a circle.

What are we going to do with this big space over here? Let's just get a bouncy castle.'

We booked some coaches from London and Windsor and everyone converged; there was about 400 of us and it was just a wicked party. By then acid house was the new cool thing to do, so we had people like Phil Dirtbox, [singer-songwriter] Pete Wylie, DJ Fat Tony, Boy George – a lot of that London music fraternity and the people working at Vivienne Westwood. I remember at one stage Boy George, Phil Dirtbox, Fat Tony and all these really cool crew and us lot all just lolling around on this bouncy castle, which is a mad image. But no one cared, no one gave a monkey's. In the morning, as the sun came up, the guy who owned the house was playing the saxophone and Boy George ended up singing 'Karma Chameleon' *a cappella*, which was amazing.

TERRY FARLEY: Cymon found this property in Guildford and we hired three coaches – everyone had to go on the coach, no one was allowed to drive. The guy had a big garden and a barn at the end of the garden, so we hired a bouncy castle, which is a watershed moment in rave culture. Then in the morning the guy whose house it was, we'd given him a pill and he was a bit of a songwriter and he started playing his guitar and Boy George was singing with him. Then the police turned up about 11a.m. and they just said, "How long are you going to be here, lads?" and we said, "Er, another hour?" and they said, "OK, there's some cans in the driveway – can you make sure you pick them up?" We were all sitting round gurning our heads off and just went, "Yeah, all right." They had absolutely no idea what was going on because it hadn't happened anywhere else yet. If it was a few months later they would have waded in wielding batons.

STEVEN HALL: That *Boy's Own* party was the first proper outside rave. I'd say there was about 600 people there. I think the guy who owned it was a bit of a hippie dude and I think he let us do it for a bit of speed and some draw. There were a number of early celebrities on the scene coming to everything and really going for it. Boy George, Martin

Fry and ABC, Pete Wylie, Paul Rutherford. I think part of the reason they enjoyed all the early parties is because no one treated them like pop stars. So there was a sprinkling of glamourous people plus a load of football hooligans, all the guys that became Flowered Up – a real mixed bunch of people.

CYMON ECKEL: Personally, I found the promoters' commercialisation and capitalisation of acid house quite abhorrent. I wasn't even mad about The Trip, when it reached that stage, although I only went twice and I met some amazing friends there, which made it worth it to me. But Tintin and Anton Le Pirate: you'd be at a party and they would be making so much fuss, like, "Look at me!" all the time, and I'd be like, "Get a grip, pull yourself together, what's wrong with you boys?" But it was obvious from early on that some people saw this as a platform to be famous or make a career out of it, but we were never like that. Yes, we were doing the magazine and putting on a few parties, but *Boy's Own* was never conceived as a commercial enterprise. I think that's what has helped us stand the test of time. We can still sell out a party overnight now. OK, it might not be the youngest party, but everyone is still there for the music.

CHAPTER 7

Moral Panic

"Jenni even had to print an open letter to Shoom regulars asking them not to give up their jobs, because so many [of them] were, so they could embrace this new life."

Richard Norris

The early press reports of acid house in the summer of 1988 had been quite gentle. Many seasoned cultural chroniclers observing acid house from the outside looking in suggested there wasn't anything necessarily new about it; they saw it as just another subculture, the latest fad of youth. "If they had been born 10 years earlier they would have been punk rockers," suggested the *Sunday Times*, "20 years earlier they would have taken LSD and listened to Jim Morrison." Those observers or academics closer to the scene, however, knew acid house was much more than another passing fad.

STEVE REDHEAD, PROFESSOR OF LAW AND POPULAR CULTURE, MANCHESTER UNIVERSITY: Their tale was that acid house was nothing new; it was merely another link in the youth subcultural chain, replaying and reworking the 1960s or the 1970s. But acid house is *not* a new subculture in this sense, nor is it the long-desired 'new punk' of the late 1980s.*

★

But as the Summer of Love faded away into the autumn of 1988, things would take a tragic turn. On 28 October, Janet Mayes, a 21-year-old nanny, went to a party at the Jolly Boatman pub in Hampton Court, Surrey. She took two ecstasy pills that night, rather than the usual one. She collapsed and was dead by the time she arrived at hospital. The police had actually been waiting outside the party Mayes was attending, ready to raid it, although after news reached them someone had collapsed inside, only a handful of officers went in to investigate. Mayes was actually Britain's second ecstasy death; Ian Larcombe had suffered a fatal heart attack in June: he'd swallowed 18 pills in one go after being stopped by the police.

On bonfire night 1988, a week after her death, Mayes' parents symbolically burned their daughter's flares and smiley T-shirts, declaring them to be "evil". *The Sun* then launched a 'say no to drugs' campaign, adopting a frowning equivalent of the smiley face as its logo. The newspaper also ran a front-page story declaring, 'Shoot These Evil Acid Barons'.

To the authorities, the national media and the general public, acid house ravers were now a classic case of a 'deviant group'. Sixteen years previously, the sociologist Stanley Cohen's landmark study *Folk Devils and Moral Panics: The Creation Of The Mods And The Rockers* had explained how certain groups of people throughout history become the focus of widespread fear and suspicion, usually informed by rumour or ignorance, which is utterly out of proportion to any danger they might pose. A moral panic then ensues regarding the perceived 'folk devil'. Like the mods and rockers and punk rock before it, acid house was now transforming into a true folk devil. And as the authorities grew increasingly concerned, the police were pushed to act.

* Quoted in Steve Redhead, *Subculture To Clubcultures – An Introduction To Popular Cultural Studies (Blackwell*, 1997)

149

From mid-October to mid-November, the national mood regarding acid house irrevocably changed. Stories appearing in the national press that month included:

'Evil Of Ecstasy' (19 October, *The Sun*)
'Ban This Killer Music' (24 October, *The Post*)
'Acid House Horror' (25 October, *The Sun*)
'Drug Crazed Acid House Fans' (28 October, *The Sun*)
'Girl Drops Dead At Acid Disco (31 October, *The Sun*)
'56 People Held In Acid House Raids' (7 November, *The Times*)

RICHARD NORRIS: When acid house first started it was completely unthinkable it would appear on the front pages of the tabloids or on national TV news, because for a few months it was only about 200 people. But as it began to explode, it was inevitable. I thought the reaction from the tabloids was quite predictable really, particularly as I was interested in previous youth cultures and scenes and I had read Stanley Cohen's *Folk Devils And Moral Panics*. The media's reaction was almost textbook.

ANDREW WEATHERALL: I think most youth cults are like that though, a bit symbiotic and mutually parasitic, because the people involved in the youth cult earn kudos and money by doing something dangerous and attractive to teenagers, and on the other side, the MPs or the councillors gain political kudos by getting on their moral soapbox. They feed off each other, and that's been happening since the Teddy Boys in the Fifties, it happened with punk rock – any youth movement you come to mention. It becomes political by default, it becomes a self-fulfilling prophecy because both sides profit from it. Managers or promoters in punk rock or whatever whip up some moral frenzy and sell gig tickets and records while the people in Parliament take umbrage, which increases their political power.

I think the police would be quite happy if there was a warehouse party in London because they'd know such and such a villain would be in there, and if they needed to nick 'em they could. Otherwise, who wants to be busy on a Saturday night? All these hooligans and ne'er-do-wells are all in this warehouse – they're not going anywhere and when they do come out they can hardly stand or talk, so they're not going to be a problem, let's just leave them to it. It's mass social control in a way. It's only when the tabloids get hold of it and start ranting about how it's the end of civilisation, and then someone sadly dies from a drug overdose, that [the police] have to be seen to be doing something. Otherwise I'm sure they would rather be sat outside in a van having a doughnut and a cup of coffee, thinking, 'We can nick any of these idiots anytime we want,' rather than have to pile in mob-handed.

STEVE REDHEAD: A chorus of celebrities was called to comment on the state of the nation's youth. [DJ] Jonathan King preferred to "call it rubeesh". Peter Powell, the Radio 1 DJ, thought it "the closest thing to mass zombie-dom". Matt Goss from [pop group] Bros told of his mate who'd been to an acid house club where everybody was "out of their heads" and sensible [pop crooner] Rick Astley astutely noted, "They may as well call it heroin house."

★

As a moral panic began to grip parts of Middle England regarding the perceived folk devil of acid house, the press coverage (which in some of the tabloids was predictably exaggerated and sensationalist to say the least) both fuelled the fear and spread the word to teenagers across the land.

ANDREW WEATHERALL: There were quite a lot of coach trips around that time. One week Danny Rampling was playing The Haçienda and we took a coach up there with a load of Shoom regulars. On the way back we somehow ended up in North Wales and it was September, so magic mushroom season, so we thought, 'Let's all pick magic mushrooms,' and all piled off the coach. If I take ecstasy or acid I tend to get into a character for some reason, and I remember looking at this coach load of Shoom kids and I decided to be the bastard schoolteacher. So I started barking, orders at them all like, "Look at all you simpering nancy boys! Come on, this is a bloody field trip, I want mushrooms!" But there was this one kid, called Andy something, and he was taking me *really* seriously, going, "I'm sorry sir, sorry sir…" and I was proper berating him, going, "You've let *yourself* down, you've let *the school* down…" All the proper nasty teacher stuff was coming out and he's going, "I'm sorry sir, I'm sorry sir…" Many months later someone said to me, "You know you made him properly lose his mind?" I said, "What do you mean?" "Well, he went to a really strict public school and he was bullied by one of the teachers; you totally took him back there." He was later spotted taking all his clothes off and running down the Portobello Road, giving all his money away. The coach trip had apparently been the tipping point for him.

RICHARD NORRIS: There's a famous story of a friend of mine walking down Portobello Road naked, the morning after Shoom. He definitely liked being naked. So some people did lose it a bit but that wasn't wide-scale. It's a good job ecstasy wasn't a stronger drug because there was a period when people really indulged… it's a good job people weren't taking similarly huge amounts of acid. Despite the fact that the music was called 'acid' house, it was quite rare for people to take huge amounts of acid.

ANDREW WEATHERALL: There was this proper old-school hippie couple called Roger and Maggie who had an old hippie bus, which even had the smokestack coming out of the side and everything. We drove out to Silbury Hill* just after Cymon had his accident, so he wasn't around but his girlfriend at the time was. We all went out there to take acid and stuff.

Silbury Hill is a big old mound, very steep with a flat top and sheep grazing on the top. So we all climbed up to the top and we had a pirate's chest full of dressing-up clothes (there was a lot of dressing up at parties we went to around that time). There were about 15 of us, and we lugged the chest up there and it was about dusk, and the sheep

---

* Silbury Hill is a prehistoric artificial chalk mound near Avebury in Wiltshire. A UNESCO World Heritage site, it is the tallest of its kind in Europe and forms part of a complex of neolithic monuments in the area.

dispersed. Out of the dressing-up box I picked a monk's robe with a hood and a shepherd's crook. From Silbury Hill you can see right down the Thames Valley, pretty much, and there was a storm approaching and it really seemed to us that every time I held my crook up to the sky, there would be thunder or lightning in the valley down below. Seriously, we all thought I was controlling the storm. We're almost in Julian Cope* territory here; I'd like to ask him what his ultimate psychedelic experience was, but I'd imagine it's something pretty similar, involving acid, a shepherd's crook and some neolithic stones!

Then, as darkness started to descend we all lit candles, but they started to go out, and as the candles went out the sheep got a little braver and started encroaching and coming a little closer to us. We're all tripping off our boxes and literally as the last candle went out, someone shouted in the darkness, "The sheep are going to get us!", which caused mass panic and everyone started running down the hill. But, as I said, it's really steep, so it was like those clips you see of that cheese rolling competition where people start running and can't stop and end up somersaulting and cartwheeling down the hill. We all tumbled down to the bottom, where there's a ditch, then a path and then the A30 or whatever road it is. Me and two friends fell into the ditch and I got it into my head that over the top of this ditch, which was only about two or three feet deep, was the end of the world. So we were lying there and peeking over now and again and going, "No!" We had our backs to this ditch for hours just talking it over, and we thought we couldn't move.

As the sun came up, we could see two grown men in their underpants, face down, spread-eagled, with their hands touching, saying random words to each other like "bollard" and pissing themselves laughing. Then this panda police car pulled up and they looked at us as if to say, "Looks like the hippie season has started again," and then they just drove off! I think they were quite happy to let us get on with it as long as we cleaned up after ourselves. A few months down the line it

* Julian Cope is a musician who first made his name as lead singer of The Teardrop Explodes. He is also an author and an authority on neolithic culture.

would have been a bit different, as travellers and hippies were getting a reputation with the police and were beginning to be seen as the enemy, but at that time there was a slightly more *laissez-faire* attitude taken by Her Majesty's constabulary.

There were a lot of fragile minds back then, and a lot of people who shouldn't have been doing drugs like acid.

RICHARD NORRIS: By the end of autumn 1988, I had moved up to west London and was definitely going out six nights a week. I think Tuesday was the non-clubbing night, but you could even go out on Tuesdays if you wanted to. Fridays was Love at The Wag, Saturdays was Shoom, Solaris on Sundays and then later on The Queen's Club, Spectrum on Mondays, Loud Noise.

At around the same time, pretty much all of the Shoom regulars had either lost their [day] jobs or found a way to create a new job, like making T-shirts, so they could embrace their new life to the full. Jenni even had to print an open letter in the fanzine asking people not to give up their jobs because so many of them were doing it. Some of them also began to show signs of heavy E use.

★

Despite of, or perhaps because of, the tabloids' interest, acid house parties just got bigger and bigger.

After the bad publicity surrounding the last Apocalypse Now party, Tony Colston-Hayter decided to rename his organisation 'Sunrise'. The first Sunrise took place on 5 November in the derelict Beckton Gas Works near Greenwich, where several films had been shot including the opening scenes of 1981's *For Your Eyes Only*, the 12th film in the James Bond series. The dramatic post-industrial setting had also doubled as a dystopian London for the film adaptation of George Orwell's *1984* and the Vietnam city of Hue for Stanley Kubrick's 1987 war film *Full Metal Jacket*. Derek Jarman shot part of the video for The Smiths' 'The Queen Is Dead' single at the gasworks and Oasis would later shoot the video to 1997's 'D'You Know What I Mean?' there. The Millennium Dome, built to celebrate the third millennium and originally housing

154

the *Millennium Experience* exhibition, would also be built nearby several years later.

Steve Proctor, Eddie Richards, Terry Farley, Trevor Fung and Phil & Ben were all on the bill. Riot police raided the party, but by 5a.m. they were completely outnumbered as partygoers found their way in. The police force had to withdraw.

CHARLIE COLSTON-HAYTER: We made Sunrise a private party and all of our friends ticket agents. We had Brandon Block as a ticket agent, Alex P, our friend Simon in Wembley – I used to sell tickets from my flat in Camden. We had all these people selling tickets and we put on coaches.

We had a boxing ring in the middle that was part of the dancefloor. I think Steve Proctor, Phil & Ben and Eddie 'Evil' Richards [were DJing]. But the police raided it. They turned up and they just didn't really know what was going on. But Tony was brilliant, he always knew how to talk to people to get them to do what he wanted. The police were trying to stop people getting in but they were just running and climbing over walls and fences and in the end the police decided it was best to just let the party continue.

ANDREW WEATHERALL: Again this is all a bit sketchy, but we used to get away with murder because the bigger raves like Sunrise were starting to be on the radar. I remember the *Boys Own* party out near Brighton, on the farm on National Trust land down near Sussex somewhere. We'd got it from the National Trust but, unbeknown to us, while we were blagging it Sunrise were planning a huge rave about five miles down the road on the same night, so obviously all the police were there and we were left totally to our own devices. That's what used to happen. The only time we got caught out was when we did one on a farm and it turned out to be the Queen's property – the farmer was a tenant farmer. We had an office in Kensal Rise and I remember that Monday morning the phone kept ringing off the hook, and if you answered it, it would be: "Hello, this is *The Sun* newspaper…" We'd just say, "I don't know what you're talking about," and keep putting the phone down on them. The next day it was on the front page – 'Rave On Queen's Land' – but we weren't named.

We were beginning to be infiltrated. By this time there were certain people on the scene who we thought were all right but they were actually selling stories to the tabloids; there was one guy in particular, who I won't name. There were also people on holiday from university whose parents worked for *The Guardian* and *The Observer* and they came down and started writing about it. I think Jane Bussmann was one of those; she did an article naming some of my friends for bootlegging records and actually got them in a lot of shit, which they managed to get out of. She painted a picture of them driving around in Porsches and stuff and making shit loads of money, when in reality they had a battered old Ford Transit van.

I'm sure there was a file on us, I'm sure there was a file on everyone. But in a way we managed to escape a lot of attention because we were only mobilising 3, 4, 500 people at a time – we weren't mobilising tens of thousands like those big parties. What I later heard second hand from the actual guy who was the head of the club squad was [the police] were putting everyone – DJs and promoters – under surveillance, filming them. It was overseen by the Met I think, but it was nationwide. I was told that what confused them, what they couldn't get their heads around, was these people had the power to mobilise 20 or 30,000 young people and get them in a field at the weekend, so they thought there had to be more to it than taking drugs to listen and dance to music; they were convinced there was some political element to it. But by thinking that, and treating it like that, it became a self-fulfilling prophecy: they *made* it political. They did it by default because they were chasing their tails so much it made them mad. So after the Poll Tax Riots* you then

---

* The Poll Tax Riots were a series of protests against the Community Charge or Poll Tax introduced by Margaret Thatcher's Conservative government in 1990. Protests took place across the country but the largest was on Saturday March 31, 1990, when over 200,000 protestors turned out, and there were violent confrontations between them and the police.

get the 'repetitive beats legislation'*. That's what politicised something which wasn't really political in the beginning, their refusal to accept it *wasn't* political; in the end, they themselves set in motion a chain of events which ended up making it political.

★

Inspired by what he'd seen at Spectrum and The Trip and a few early small warehouse raves, on 10 November, promoter Wayne Anthony held the first Genesis warehouse party in Aldgate East, east London.

WAYNE ANTHONY, PROMOTER/RAVE ORGANISER: I had already worked in the music business with [British pop duo] Mel and Kim. Once I'd been to a few acid house parties and saw it was just a sound system and a few lights, I saw there was an opportunity for someone to do it properly. A lot of the parties were in derelict buildings and quite unsafe, so I thought there was a gap to do this a bit safer. The police didn't have a clue, so once you knew how to placate them it was quite easy. We would look for a warehouse that was up for let and in decent condition and then we would break in.

At first we kept costs to a minimum. Drinks were on a sale-or-return basis, flyers cost about £80, the doorman was my stepdad, the bar manager was his sister Nikki, the DJ Tony Wilson was paid £100, and my mate Andy and me were on the door, taking the money. I chose the title Genesis because I thought it was a beautiful word that summed up the zeitgeist: this was an era that was dramatically changing millions of lives, a time of evolution and revolution in the mass consciousness.

It was a 'private party' as far as the law was concerned, so we printed the flyers as invites, with the phrases "No invite, no entry" and "Over-18s only". The only other promoter who was trying to do it on the same scale as us was Tony Colston-Hayter and his Sunrise outfit. Our

---

* The Criminal Justice and Public Order Act was introduced in 1994 by John Major's Conservative government, and brought with it a number of changes in existing law which pretty clearly targeted acid house or free parties, as well as the travellers. It famously referred to music that was defined by "repetitive beats", i.e. house music, rather than military marching bands.

157

first party was a couple of hundred people and then the second, a couple of weeks later, was over a thousand people, and it was amazing.

★

As this second wave of promoters began hosting bigger and more ambitious raves, a division grew between them and the founders of the first wave of clubs. Many of the early evangelists felt the new kids on the block were diluting what had made the embryonic scene so special, with opportunism and the desire to make money their only driving force. On the flip side, some of the new arrivals to the party thought of the original faces as overly protective and elitist; to them the acid house scene was something to be shared, rather than kept secret among a select few. The press coverage and explosion of public interest only fuelled the fire, on both sides.

STEVEN HALL: When the tabloids got hold of acid house, at first they were quite nice about it and thought it was OK. Then they started to get nastier when there was a bit of moral panic, around the time of Sunrise. I went to Apocalypse Now and the first Sunrise. Terry Farley DJed at that first Sunrise – people say it was Fabio and Grooverider but it wasn't; it was Steve Proctor, Terry and the more Balearicy sort of people. That was when the atmosphere changed I think, because all of a sudden it was a few thousand people in a disused factory going mental on drugs.

After Sunrise, that's when the division started, which I think is still there today. All the Shoom, Future and Ibiza crowds didn't want to go to the raves because they were too big and the security was heavy, but the people newer to the scene were happy to go. The people who started all those raves, like Tony Colston-Hayter and Wayne Anthony, were all people who had been at Shoom, Spectrum or The Trip. They all came from those three clubs.

NICKY HOLLOWAY: The *Boy's Own* lot were always very snobby about those big raves. I remember trying to book Terry Farley and Andrew Weatherall for some party and they wouldn't play because I'd booked Fabio and Grooverider: "We're not playing if they're playing," just because they'd seen those DJs' names on flyers for some of the bigger raves they thought had nothing to do with them. It was just snobbery: "We don't want our names on the same flyer as them." I just said, "Well, you won't be on it then, because they're already booked." I think they both realised it was a silly thing to say.

ANDREW WEATHERALL: I didn't go to any of those big raves; they just didn't appeal to me, it all just seemed too commercial. When I see footage, sometimes I wish I hadn't been quite so purist because some of them look great. What really strikes me when you see films of those old raves is how multi-racial they were. Stunningly so. I was slack-jawed in amazement at how multi-racial some of those raves were. I think it was only later in the Nineties when drum'n'bass started that things divided a bit more along racial lines. But at the time it was stunningly multi-racial.

MARK MOORE: When the big raves started, the elite would be like, 'Oh my God, you didn't go there did you?' They really looked down on it; they thought they were just full of the hoi polloi. But if you look back at footage of those first raves, everyone is completely off their heads but looks so innocent and natural. It was beautiful and I thought, 'This is a great atmosphere, there's nothing wrong with this.'

MR. C: I wasn't against the bigger raves. I played at the first two Energy* parties; I was MC at the first Sunrise and DJed at the second. I played a Weekend World, Back To The Future, Rain Dance. I played at a lot of those parties but I only did one or two of each of them. After playing a couple of them I was like, you know what? This isn't really me.

By 1989 rave music was starting and it was brash and childish, and everything I was against. I just thought all the DJs were competing against each other to have the loudest and most brash sound. I think the record that really started rave for me was 'Cubik' by 808 State. It was

---

* Energy was launched by Quentin 'Tin Tin' Chambers, his school friend Jeremy Taylor and clubbing face Anton Le Pirate, who Chambers met through clubbing at Shoom and Spectrum.

an alright tune and I played it a bit, until everyone else started playing it and then I dropped it like a ton of bricks.

CARL COX: I used to shop at Jazzy M's shop in Croydon called Mi Price, and they wanted to open a franchise of their shop in Brighton, and me being who I am, it all fell in my lap. If any new records came in, I was the first to get them. For two years I did that, and it really bolstered my record collection.

At the same time, these big raves like Sunrise and Energy were starting and because I lived in Brighton, I became a ticket seller for the South Coast, for Brighton and places like Worthing, Littlehampton and Bognor Regis. Anyone wanting tickets from those areas would come through me; I had a number for them to ring and they'd come and pick up the tickets from my house in Brighton. I'd have 200 or 300 tickets, sell them all on the South Coast, and organise drivers or coaches to take them to those acid house parties. But for me, when I was acting as a ticket seller all I really wanted was to be able to play at the party. So the organisers of parties like Sunrise would be like, "OK, no problem, we can just stick you on early." Little did they know that as soon as I went on I would have my fanbase – the 200 or 300 people who'd come with me, who'd be dancing as soon as I started playing.

As I began to make a name for myself, eventually it got to the stage where I had to choose between being a DJ and my sound system, and as you can imagine, I chose to be a DJ.

★

Carl Cox wasn't the only one to make professional gains through his devotion to acid house. As the media continued to shine a spotlight on what they saw as the evils of the culture, so the A&R teams up and down the country saw an opportunity and began to hone in on the talent driving the scene.

Having been recording mainly hip hop music under the moniker Hit Squad Manchester, Graham Massey, Martin Price and Gerald Simpson (A Guy Called Gerald), along with DJs Darren Partington and Andrew Barker, had by now switched their sound to acid house and their name to 808 State, taken from the Roland TR-808 drum machine.

GRAHAM MASSEY: Because acid house was getting more attention, Martin Price managed to convince Nine Mile distribution we were the hottest acid house band in the UK. Which was probably true, because we were probably the *only* acid house band in the UK at that time. So they gave us about £500 to make an album, which became *Newbuild.** We didn't have a name or any songs but we just went into the studio and started jamming. We'd never been able to afford a sampler and all of a sudden we've got this new toy we can play with. A lot of those early 808 records were six or eight-hand records because we recorded them live, so it was six or eight hands on deck – everyone had a role and we'd be like, "Right, this is the take."

When *Newbuild* came out, our first priority was to take it to Stu Allan at Piccadilly Radio. It didn't really get much of a reaction outside of that, but John Peel played a track off it, which felt really important because that was going national.

DARREN PARTINGTON: At first we had these machines but because they were so limited, you'd get the best out of them and you'd all be competing against each other. We only had four machines and we were trying to outdo each other. Me and Andy would be like, "Leave the basslines and beats to us and then you can put your mad shit on it and get Graham to mix it." It had to be funky and it had to be cool, and it couldn't sound white. We were determined it wouldn't sound white or remotely indie – we'd be sat at the back in the studio, saying to each other, "It sounds too white." We'd get them to fuck about with it until it got our seal of approval. Sometimes we'd be sat there listening to

---

* 808 State's 1988 debut release, *Newbuild*, was named after a co-operative housing project in Bolton, which band member Martin Price was involved with. It was released on Creed Records and only on vinyl, making that pressing somewhat of a collector's item today.

beats going, "Shit… good… shit… good"; it had to have soul and sound electro and dark.

Manchester was very white. Eastern Bloc [record shop] used to make all its money out of indie kids then – it didn't make a bean out of dance music, it was dance music that brought it to its knees at first. But then it's what made it in the end.

★

Around the same time that the members of 808 State were discovering their musical kinship, several other individuals began making house music before founding their own group. Interstate, an acid house group from the English/Welsh border, were later to evolve into K-Klass, and would go on to have a number three hit with 'Rhythm Is A Mystery' and record several albums together.

PAUL ROBERTS: I got made redundant from British Telecom, partly because I'd lost interest and kept not making it in [to work] after being out at The Haçienda. They said, "We either move you to Telford or we're making you redundant." Moving to Telford is a death sentence for anyone, so I took redundancy and went out and bought a crap keyboard and a Roland 505 drum machine. Russ [Morgan] also had a little bit of equipment so we started trying to make our own music at home.

We also used to go to a club called The Blast in Chester, which was run by a guy called John Locke. He would have people like [DJ] Laurent Garnier playing with him, and a couple of house DJs from Wrexham, one called Gary Jones who went on to DJ at [Liverpool nightclub] Quadrant Park, and another guy called Matthew Roberts, who later did some co-production work with us and also recorded as King Unique and Bottom Dollar and had quite a successful career of his own.

One night we saw 808 State playing at The Blast, supported by a group called Interstate from Wrexham. There's always been a bitter rivalry between Chester and Wrexham, so the only contact we'd had with people from Wrexham previously was knocking lumps out of each other twice a year at the football. But like I say, by then everyone was pilled up and chilled out, and the football violence thing had fallen by the wayside a bit.

Interstate at that stage was Carl Thomas, Andrew Williams and a third guy called Deggsy. Even though they were daft buggers from Wrexham, we actually thought Interstate were better than 808 State that night. Interstate were closer to the sounds we were hearing from Chicago and Detroit, while 808 State had kind of put their own British stamp on it.

The following night we went to The Haçienda and we saw the Wrexham lads in there and went over and said hello and told them we thought they were great. They said, "Oh, we thought we were crap," and we were like, "No, honestly, we thought you were better." So we got chatting and when The Haçienda closed, we were all still bright-eyed and bushy-tailed, shall we say, so we went back to their studio in Wrexham. They had a 909 drum machine and we were like, "Wow, that's the sound… that's the sound on all those records." We just started writing music there and then, and made the bones of our first EP right then. We decided that very night we were going to work together; it's dawn, everyone's in the moment and in a bit of a state, so we all agreed. They would have probably said no normally!

★

The *Jack The Tab* album that Genesis P-Orridge, Richard Norris, Dave Ball and others had collaborated on took several months to come out. When it was finally released, the *NME* put Norris on its cover, perhaps swayed by the fact that most of the album's musicians came from more of an indie background, thus helping their readers to relate to this 'acid house' record.

RICHARD NORRIS: In between going in and making the album *Jack The Tab* (which took two days) and it coming out, we actually heard house music for the first time, so we then added a sample from Adonis. We were put on the front cover of the *NME*, which was pretty unheard of for an unsigned band. Then by October 1988, we'd won a record deal with Warner Bros. We were surprised because it wasn't something you'd expect Warner to be interested in – it was still quite an underground thing, and a very odd record. They were quite a straightforward record label and we were pretty much coming from an avant-garde tradition, and didn't really have a pop sensibility at all. But their A&R guy had worked at Bam Caruso and was from the same area as me. I hadn't really wanted to play him *Jack The Tab* because I didn't think he'd like it but he loved it, and he signed me and Genesis as The Grid.

Genesis was really strange in the meetings with them – I couldn't really work out what it was about and then he kind of backed out of the project and I thought, "Fuck, that's it, that's my chance of signing to a major label gone." But the label said, "That's fine, we'll just do it with you."

The original idea was I would work with lots of different producers and produce a New York house track, a UK house track, but then Mark Kamins* beat us to it with *United House Nations Project*, so I ended up working with Dave Ball from Soft Cell because we'd done ['Meet Every Situation Head On'] together on *Jack The Tab*. We hadn't got on well at first because despite being quite a garrulous young teenager, I was also – and still am – quite shy, so I was a little in awe of him: "Wow, it's the guy from Soft Cell." So we didn't really talk that much during *Jack The Tab* and then I didn't really want to bother him when I remixed it, but he was really offended by that.

★

Although a few house records had made an impression on the charts, and the tabloids had covered the embryonic rave culture, it still hadn't seeped out into smaller towns. Even for those who had heard the music and were quite clued up, it wasn't always easy to see how the different elements could provide a perfect storm, especially if you were unaware that one of those elements was ecstasy. Every initiation was slightly different, although most can pinpoint one moment when it all made sense.

---

* Mark Kamins was a hugely influential DJ and producer in New York City, who helped launch his then girlfriend Madonna's career. He died in 2013.

MOONBOOTS (RICHARD BITHELL), DJ: I heard 'Jack Your Body' and 'Love Can't Turn Around' when they first came out, but I never really realised they were part of a bigger thing. I was going out in Wigan where we had to dress in posh shirts and shoes to get into clubs. Then one day I remember reading in *The Face* about 'acid house' and I thought, "Eh? That was that record I had last year. We've done that, it's *old news*. Aren't we on to something new now?" I presumed it was a bit of a London thing, but then I went to The Haçienda for the first time one night and stood up on the balcony. They were playing acid house, and I remember looking at the dance floor and thinking, "This is rubbish, I really don't get this. We've done all this, why are we digging it up again?" But then you would notice more and more records appearing in the shops.

When I first started going to Hot on a Wednesday night at The Haçienda, Jon DaSilva played a lot of different records that no one else would, but I still didn't get the real acid part of the night. And to be honest, I didn't realise it was Jon playing them when I first went there. I didn't know who was DJing or if there was one DJ or three DJs. It took me about three weeks to come down from the balcony and have a bit of a jig about on the dance floor. I must have been quite naïve because even then I didn't realise that everyone was on E, I just thought everyone was really *friendly*. Then in the car going home to Wigan one night, my mate Baz said, "You know they're all on that weird drug ecstasy, don't you?" I didn't.

Then a couple of months later I was with my mate Chris and we bought a pill between us in The Haçienda. For £20. I remember waiting and waiting for something to happen. And then it did. And everything made crystal clear sense. It was a revelation. I can even tell you the record, it was 'The Dance' by Rhythm Is Rhythm. Within the four minutes of that song my life completely changed, from being a normal bloke to being someone completely different. It felt amazing, unbelievable.

The thing about The Haçienda is it was a huge cavernous club, with a huge dancefloor, so there was always this feeling of group unity, it always felt communal. It was a big club but everyone was loving it. It was amazing, absolutely amazing. That night I went home to my mum and dad's house in Wigan and I couldn't sleep. I just laid there on my bed just… happy.

It changed everything. I'd been quite an angry, aggressive young man up to that stage. I was a bit of a pisshead who would be up for a fight and it knocked all that out of me. I stopped drinking for a start. For two years. I even went on holiday with my mates to St Tropez once and even though I wasn't taking E when we were there, I only drank Ribena.

I got up the morning after that first night and went to college and felt incredible, no hangover, no nothing. It changed everything. I grew my hair, and it seemed to grow really quickly, it seemed to grow overnight. My clothes got baggier. I started buying more records and hanging out in Eastern Bloc loads.

It still felt like a secret. I used to go watching football, both Liverpool and Wigan Athletic. After I got into acid house, I stopped wearing all the old football clobber and I remember going to the match in Wigan in dungarees and pink Converse trainers and my new wavy hair. Absolutely ridiculous clothing. But because I was wearing that when I went out to The Haçienda and fitted in there, I thought I could get away with it, but I remember these young kids saying, to me, "What the *fuck* are you on?" Because acid house hadn't hit Wigan yet. They didn't have a clue. But within six months they were all at it, and even organising raves themselves.

It made me realise that Wigan was a really small, irrelevant place. Before that it had been the centre of the universe to me. But when you started going to The Haçienda and Dry Bar and Eastern Bloc, you met all these fascinating people and it made me want to leave Wigan and come to Manchester. I know that's only 15 miles, but it felt like a thousand miles away at that time. There were 1,200 people in The Haçienda. But that was it really. It wasn't like there were another 1,200 people at home who hadn't come that week, because *everyone* would go *every* week. That wasn't even 1,200 people from Manchester, there was also a bunch of people from Wigan, Stoke, wherever… so there were 1,200 people into it in the Northwest at that point.

★

On 12 November, *The Guardian* reported the following:

> The acid house record 'It's A Trip' has been banned from BBC
> Radio 1 after an MP's claim it encourages children to take drugs.
> The station is also reserving judgement on a new version of the
> record due to be released next week. "Its explicit message is to
> encourage children to take the hallucinatory drug ecstasy," Mr John
> Heddle, Conservative MP for mid-Staffordshire, said yesterday.
> A Home Office spokesman said the government had no power
> to stop the sale of the record and it was up to radio programme
> makers to decide if it was suitable for broadcasting.

Geoff Simpson, Radio 1's publicity officer, was quoted as saying: "It will not
be picking up any more airplay on Radio 1 because we don't feel it would
be appropriate in the context of the publicity acid house has received."

As word about the first acid house warehouse parties began to spread,
enterprising individuals around the country began launching their own
parties.

DAVID DORRELL: There was a huge excitement in the air and
warehouse parties were springing up everywhere. You would get a
phone call and you would be off, and you'd find yourself in a warehouse
party in a business park in east, *east* London. It was thrilling because you
didn't know where you were going to end up or who would be there.
Previously I'd been part of quite a tight-knit central London scene, but
now I'd left that safety zone and was going out into the great unknown
and it was thrilling. Suddenly the Summer Of Love vibe started to suck
in these tribes from all over, from south London and north London – the
previously soul crowds.

SUDDI RAVAL, TOGETHER*: I had a funny introduction to acid
house. I got into it quite young, when I was around 15, so because

---

* Together were formed by Haçienda regulars Suddi Raval, Jonathan Donaghy and
Rohan Heath. Their debut single 'Hardcore Uproar' reached number 12 in 1990.
Donaghy died in a road accident in Ibiza in 1991.

of my age my introduction was in my bedroom rather than clubs, listening to *The House Sound Of Chicago* compilations on FFRR Records and Stu Allan on Piccadilly Radio. I really don't think Stu Allan gets enough credit. If you speak to a lot of people in Manchester and the North, they originally got into acid house, and even electro before that, through listening to his shows. But he doesn't really ever get the dues.

When I got into music I had loads of ideas and I actually wrote to FFRR* as a teenager in 1986, with an idea on paper, which I now realise is the most pointless thing ever. The idea was to use Wally Jump Jr.'s 'Turn Me Loose'. If it did actually reach Pete Tong he probably picked it up and thought, "What the fuck is *this*?" As if a record company was going to sign a kid from an idea on a piece of paper! The funny thing was, I eventually did end up signing to FFRR four years later.

I became so obsessed with acid house so quickly that my family became a little bit concerned, as I changed the way I dressed and everything overnight – it was just so exciting. I was living in Ashton-under-Lyne, outside Manchester, and I would buy *The Face* and *i-D* magazine and read about the mystical clubs like Shoom and just think, "Wow, *there's* a place I'll never get to go to." Even The Haçienda, even though it was only just down the road, seemed this distant magical place, another world. A place where great people went and great things happened. It felt like an absolute other world.

In the end, the first rave I went to was one I actually organised myself with a couple of friends, at a club called The Riverside in Hyde, near Ashton-under-Lyne, on December 8, 1988. We didn't have a name for it, in fact I think we simply called it 'Rave'. We actually managed to book some pretty big names: Stakker, The Spinmasters, Darren and Andy from 808 State. We were only kids so I'm not sure how we managed to pull it off, particularly as we hadn't even been to a rave ourselves at that stage! I'd only been to cheesy nightclubs

* FFRR (Full Frequency Range Recordings) is a subsidiary of London Records that was founded by Pete Tong in 1986.

like Rainbows and Butterflies in Oldham. Butterflies was cheesy chart music upstairs and you had to wear a suit, shirt and tie, and shiny shoes to get in, but they did have a basement bar that played underground music.

We managed to get Stakker because my mate Jonathan was at Salford Uni doing a course in music production, and his tutor was called Brian Dougans, who bizarrely was Stakker. So we'd got to hear his tracks and demos, and obviously 'Humanoid' is an absolute classic, and to watch that go from being a demo on cassette to being released and then getting to number 20 in the charts was really inspiring. It made you think it was actually possible, we might be able to do that. I realise now it's not as simple as just releasing a tune and it getting into the charts, but when the first person you know to record a song gets a Top 20 hit, it so inspires you. Especially as I already had loads of ideas myself, I just thought, "This is something I've got to do." But that first rave, we did all the right things; we were just a little bit before our time.

★

In London, Tintin Chambers, a Shoom regular, had gone into business with his old school friend Jeremy Taylor and they held their first party at Brixton Academy. Taylor had previously organised Gatecrasher Balls (not to be confused with the Sheffield-based house club which started in the late Nineties) with his mate Eddie Davenport, which were parties specifically catering for wealthy teenagers; a kind of shamelessly gauche and libidinous unisex Bullingdon Club. The press reported the parties were full of 'unbridled lust among upper-class Lolitas and public school Lotharios' and that at one party at Davenport's house, 'the swimming pool was turned into a 'gigantic punchbowl' by filling it with 1,000 litres of cognac so his party-goers could row in it'.

JEREMY TAYLOR, PROMOTER/RAVE ORGANISER: The first events I put on a few years previously were the Gatecrasher Balls with Eddie Davenport, who is now residing in jail for fraud.

Having made a lot of money in various ways, they caught up with him eventually.*

I was on holiday with Tintin in August of 1988 and he was raving about going to Shoom and these parties. When we arrived back from holiday my business partner at the time had run off with all the money, so I said to Tintin, "Come on then, let's have a proper look at these raves and see if we can put one on." The first one we put on was at Brixton Academy in November that year, which was called Hypnosis and was a fully legal rave.

DAVID DORRELL: A friend of mine called Rod Marsh and I got talking and said, "We've got to do our own house night." So we talked to Chris Sullivan at The Wag and he gave us Friday nights, because they weren't really happening. We opened after Spectrum and called it Love At The Wag. We spent two days crafting the letters 'LOVE' out of giant polystyrene blocks, which we painted baby pink and hung over the door, and the opening night we had a line down to Leicester Square. It was mental from day one and immediately became the busiest night at The Wag, and we had guests like Steve Proctor and Paul 'Trouble' Anderson.

Ecstasy played a huge part in the explosion of acid house. What had happened on the dance floors at Shoom and Spectrum was replicated on the dance floor at LOVE. The smoke was super thick, the strobes were super fast, and the E were super strong and everyone had a big smiling face. The fabled story of the football hooligan who becomes a 'Smiley Ted' is absolutely true. I met plenty of people who previously looked forward to beating the shit out of someone on Saturday who now only wanted to hug people on a Saturday. I met people at LOVE who had just come out of prison that day and were desperate to sample this new thing.

★

---

* Eddie Davenport was convicted of tax offences in 1990 and spent two weeks in prison. After various other court cases in the ensuing years, he was jailed for eight years for a £4.5m international fraud scam in 2011.

Towards the end of 1988, Eric Barker, one of the first acid house evangelists in Manchester, teamed up with two other characters on the scene, Jimmy Muffin (Jimmy Sherlock) and John The Phone (John Kenyon), and decided to launch a club called The Thunderdome in Miles Platting, a down-at-heel area in the north of the city centre. Muffin and John The Phone, associates of Happy Mondays, were T-shirt bootleggers and among the first to see the potential of the exploding scene in Manchester. They would later promote the biggest Madchester gig, two nights of Happy Mondays supported by 808 State (*see* page 217) at the G-MEX (now known as the Manchester Central Convention Complex). The Thunderdome building had originally opened as The Royal Osborne Theatre in 1896, when *The Era* newspaper said, "It is situated in a district which, though densely populated, has hitherto been singularly destitute of public amusements." Little had changed in this respect in a century. The building had suffered various incarnations, including being used for wedding receptions, Irish dances and a roller disco, that is until Barker, Muffin and John The Phone got their hands on it. They installed Eric's younger brother Andrew and his DJ partner in The Spinmasters (and member of 808 State), Darren Partington, as the resident DJs alongside Steve Williams and Jay Weardon.

There was, and remains, a north/south divide in Manchester and although Thunderdome was less than a mile from Piccadilly Gardens, it was another world, particularly for students. Manchester has one of the biggest student populations in Europe, but most of the 60,000 students stick to the 'student corridor' of Wilmslow Road and the city centre. You can count on the fingers of one hand the number who venture to the north of the city. So The Thunderdome drew much of its clientele from the surrounding council estates and the music, like the regulars, had a harder edge than other clubs in Manchester.

DARREN PARTINGTON: We'd done all sorts of little parties around Manchester. We'd done a few illegal gaffs with Eric, and we used to do this little Sunday night party at a gaff called The Stables, which was a tiny place facing the Apollo, next to Kwik Save supermarket. It was hangin', that place; the only flat surface to set the deck up was on top of this freezer behind the bar, so every time the landlady had an order for a burger we had to lift the decks up so she could squeeze her hand into the freezer to get one. Then Eric got us a night at this gay gaff called The Mindshaft, this old gay club. In the other rooms on the same night was a bondage night and a leather night, and Eric said, "Nip next door and see if they've got a canister for the dry ice, Daz," and I've gone next door and there's all these guys in leather chaps with holes cut out. I'm only 17 and I'm thinking, "What am I doing here on a Monday night?"

So when we got to launch The Thunderdome, that was really important to us. The thing about The Thunderdome is it was *ours*, it was full of *our* people. A lot of those people might not have got into The Haçienda, but they were all welcome at The Thunderdome. It was full of all sorts of lunatics, hooligans and vagabonds, but that didn't matter because everybody had come to dance.

SHAUN RYDER: I did go to The Thunderdome, but I didn't really go there much. The Thunderdome was a really moody gaff, surrounded by a council estate, and there were some pretty naughty north Manchester lads in there. You wouldn't catch many fucking students up there, let's put it that way.

ANDY SPIRO, BUGGED OUT*: The Thunderdome was totally different. It was great but it wasn't for everyone. It was much more of a local crowd. I remember being in there one night and seeing three generations of one family going for it, all off their heads. The son must have been about 16, his dad was about 35 and *his* dad was about 50, and they were all raving together, sweating – I've never seen anything like it. It was like an acid house scene from *Shameless*.

SUDDI RAVAL: The Thunderdome was the scariest thing I'd ever seen in my life. It was in this really dodgy area, full of dodgy people;

---

* Bugged Out is one of the UK's longest running club nights. It was originally started by John Burgess and Paul Benney in 1994, and put on early Chemical Brothers and Daft Punk shows. Burgess and Benney also launched seminal dance music magazine *Jockey Slut* (see page 233).

I didn't know at the time what people were doing but people were doing smack and whatever... scary people in scary parts of town, but I still went. There was something about being young and very naïve and unaware of what dangers there might have been. I remember going to parties in some really dodgy places and I can't believe I used to go to some of those things. You have no fear when you're a kid, do you, and it was like I really had no fear.

★

Emboldened by the success of their first party, Wayne Anthony and his friends at Genesis planned for another one. The second Genesis took place in an empty warehouse near Clapton Pond, in north Hackney.

WAYNE ANTHONY: Within a matter of weeks we had become the biggest promoters. We found this amazing warehouse venue in Hackney, and on Christmas Eve we had nearly 1,000 people in there. I was up all night and went round to my mum's for Christmas dinner but didn't end up eating much. Then we had another one on Boxing Day and 2,000 people turned up. We had quite a few celebrities that night, including Matt Dillon, Milli Vanilli and Boy George. Some of the West End's biggest club owners came down to, in their own words, "see what all the fuss is about". They'd come to see where all their punters had disappeared to and were gutted to find they'd lost them to a party in a warehouse on a back street in east London.

★

In Manchester, the Donnellys were organising a second rave after the success of their first, Sweat It Out. If the early clubs like Shoom, Spectrum and The Trip defined the Summer Of Love, the summer of 1988, it was the large outdoor raves that came to define 1989. They polarised opinion among the early protagonists on the existing scene, and also became the focus for the authorities and police.

CHRIS DONNELLY: The second party we did was on New Year's Day and that was hard work, that. It didn't help that we'd been up all the night on New Year's Eve, the night before. I think we called it Sweat It

173

Out II, like *Rocky II*. That one was in Ardwick, just near The Apollo, and it got the police angry. It was in a warehouse on one of the upper levels and you had to access it through a service lift, so what we did is once we got people inside, we left the service lift at the top with the door open, which meant the police couldn't get up. The police were there all night, frustrated. Mike Pickering played again – Mike was always there at the early parties and usually played them. He was like the Che Guevara of acid house.

DAVID DORRELL: 1988 and 1989 were the best years. But by 1989, divisions had already sprung up and obviously the term 'Acid Teds' had been coined by some kids from Slough, Mr Terrence Farley and Mr Weatherall, among others. I've never been quite as judgmental as that; I try to take people as they come. But they obviously saw these people as an incursion on their territory and a watering down of whatever ideals they had about the music being played by them and Danny, etc. But once the box was open, everyone could play with what was inside.

JUDGE JULES: There was quite a lot of antagonism between *Boy's Own* and Shoom on one side and the bigger raves on the other, about what the raves stood for. I went down the rave path and was a bit slated by them for doing it. But in retrospect, going from playing in my bedroom to playing to 10,000 people in a couple of years makes me look like the sensible one. *Boy's Own* used to slate the Acid Teds who dressed in purple and wore Travel Fox trainers, which looking back was a weird look. It's a shame there's not more footage of those raves because there were some right sights, of people with sunken faces and pupils the size of goldfish bowls... it's probably best for them that there isn't.

CHAPTER 8

Rave On

"Oh, is this the way they say the future's meant to feel?/ Or just 20,000 people standing in a field./ And I don't quite understand just what this feeling is/ but that's OK 'cause we're all sorted out for E's and whizz."
'Sorted For E's & Whizz', Pulp, September 1995

MIKE PICKERING: By 1989, Manchester was crazy. I was living at Cromford Court [housing association flats] on top of the Arndale. I would get up on Saturday and still be buzzing and you'd walk round town and see other people looking and feeling the same. It was a bad idea if you went clothes shopping still buzzing though; I saw Steve Geese* recently and said to him, "Some of the clothes you used to sell me!" I remember Graeme Park staying with me and we went shopping the next day, still buzzing, and went into Geese and saw these tracksuit bottoms with big fuzzy felt stars all over them and we both bought a pair. Monday morning Graeme said to me, "Have you seen those pants we

---

* Geese was a hugely influential Manchester clothes shop, run by Steve Caton for two decades from the mid Eighties. Geese held fashion shows at The Haçienda and dressed many of their staff and clubbers.

bought on Saturday morning!??" and I went, "I know! There is no way I'm *ever* wearing those fucking things!"

★

On Wednesday, 18 January, 1989, *The Hit Man And Her* came to Hot at The Haçienda. Presented by Pete Waterman (The Hit Man) and Michaela Strachan (Her), the show, which ran from 1988 to 1992, was usually broadcast from cheesy discos in small towns and offered a taste of late-night clubbing, including crowds dancing, party games and the odd celebrity appearance. It had never broadcast from a club playing acid house, like The Haçienda, before. At the end of the night Strachan and Waterman were pictured sitting downstairs, a little shell-shocked.

JON DASILVA: Hot was only supposed to go on until August, but Paul Cons let it run until December because it was so successful, so it had lasted much longer then it was supposed to. Then me and Mike made a definite move away from what we perceived as the more fluffy, kiddie-like music because we were having a lot of problems with underage kids getting in, and the club was attracting stick. Paul Cons had nothing to add to the concept of the new night, which is why we decided to call it Void. Musically, however, I think myself and Mike were probably more in tune than ever.

★

On 27 January, 1989, Boy George was the 'castaway' on BBC Radio 4's *Desert Islands Discs*, presented by Sue Lawley. Though he discussed his life and music, there was no mention of acid house, and when asked by Lawley, "I believe you've been clean for three years?", George agreed.

BOY GEORGE: Well, I wasn't going to go on *Desert Island Discs*, which is quite a traditional show, and talk to Sue Lawley about ecstasy. Even by 1989, you didn't really talk to people who weren't really part of it about what was going on, it was a private thing. But the other thing is I don't think I viewed ecstasy as a drug at that point, I just saw it as a pill. In my little head it wasn't really a drug, it was a harmless little pill. I wasn't the only one thinking like that, a lot of people thought, "Well, it's not coke, it's not hard drugs." That's how we rationalised it to ourselves. So when I said that to Sue Lawley, I was probably really convinced it *was* the case. With hindsight, I'm not so convinced it was... now I'm in full recovery, I look back at that time as not being as clean a period.

★

As acid house continued to spread across the UK, new venues emerged and people increasingly travelled further afield. Across the Pennines from The Haçienda, The Warehouse was Leeds' foremost club in the mid to late Eighties, but as acid house took hold other venues emerged. The Twilight Zone had previously been a reggae-blues shebeen in Chapeltown but now began playing acid house. In November 1991, one of its regulars, Dave Beer, and his late friend Ali Cook, with Ralph Lawson as resident DJ*, started the night which would come to define Leeds clubbing in the Nineties: Back To Basics.

DREW HEMMENT, DJ/ACADEMIC: I was from the south but got out as soon as I could. I ended up in Leeds and was hanging out in record shops and started DJing at a hip hop night. Then I went record shopping in Manchester one day and met DJ Martin, who was the engineer on all the early LFO** stuff and a really established hip hop DJ. He was the coolest kid on the block. I started hanging out with him and he would play me tapes of early LFO stuff, which sounded amazing.

I'd already heard acid house at the Mutoid Waste parties and a few of the gay clubs in London. Then Martin was invited to DJ at this place in Leeds called The Twilight Zone. It was basically a shebeen in Chapeltown, which had originally been a reggae-blues party, but it was the first place to play house music in Leeds. Martin stuck with it for a couple of weeks but he didn't really like the dub scene part

---

* Ali Cook and Ralph Lawson's girlfriend, Jocelyn, were killed in a car accident in March 1993. Dave Beer was also injured but survived.
**LFO, an electro-dance group, were formed in Leeds by Mark Bell and Gez Varley in 1988. They took their name from the abbreviation for low-frequency oscillator, an electro synthesizer. Their self-titled seminal debut single went to number 12 in the UK charts. LFO is now Mark Bell's solo venture.

of it, so he said, "Right, it's yours, you can have it," and I became resident DJ there. I used to do eight hours on a Friday and eight hours on a Saturday. I suppose it was basically Leeds' equivalent of The Kitchen in Manchester. A lot of people from the Yorkshire side of the Pennines who went to The Haçienda would go back to The Twilight Zone after.

After a while I noticed some of the regulars weren't coming on a Saturday, so I asked them, "Where have you been guys, what's going on?" and they started telling me about these raves in Blackburn. At this stage it was very early on but it sounded really special, it sounded like something amazing was going on, so I decided to check it out one Saturday. Blackburn started in early 1989 and just got bigger as the year went on.

★

The Blackburn raves were started by a collective including Tony Creft and Tommy Smith in 1989. The first few were smaller events, for friends and friends of friends, but as their reputation grew they soon began to attract people from Manchester, Leeds, Liverpool, Blackpool and across the Northwest, and later even further afield. Cars of clubbers would descend on the Lancashire town from across the North.

SASHA: It was through Blackpool I got invited to play Blackburn, and I think I caught the last 10 or 12 parties in Blackburn, including the one that got raided at Nelson [near Burnley]. I'd gone as a punter a few times before I played there, and most of the fun of the night was the chase and the convoy getting there and trying to find the warehouse while evading the police. The dummy convoy would head off and hope to take the police with them, and the rest of the convoy would go in the opposite direction. There was just this great illegal party vibe to it, which is unlike anything else.

I was still very wet behind the ears then. Dave Beer [who founded Leeds club Back To Basics] says he's got a video he took of one of those Blackburn raves and I'm stood behind the DJ staring at him, with this longing look in my eyes. He didn't know me then, he was just filming

178

Acid house party at Slough Centre, 1989. CAMERA PRESS/GAVIN WATSON

Paul Oakenfold, Lisa Lashes, Ian St John and friends, at Shoom, 1988. DAVID SWINDELLS/PYMCA

Danny Rampling (white t-shirt) in the crowd on the dancefloor at Spectrum club night at Heaven, London, April 1988.
DAVID SWINDELLS/PYMCA

Original Shoom flyer.

The Trip. DAVID SWINDELLS/PYMCA

Boys Own. DAVID SWINDELLS/PYMCA

A Guy Called Gerald and Graham Massey from 808 State play live from Victoria Baths in Manchester during Tony Wilson's Other Side of Midnight show, Manchester, 1988. PETER J WALSH/PYMCA

DJ Trevor Fung playing at an early acid house warehouse party. CAMERA PRESS/GAVIN WATSON

Bez and Deborah Faulkner in the Hacienda, July 6, 1988. CAMERA PRESS/IAN TILTON

Dancers, including Bez, in one of the infamous alcoves at the Hacienda, Manchester, July 6, 1988. CAMERA PRESS/IAN TILTON

Early acid house flyers and *News Of The World's* story claiming Richard Branson's club Heaven was 'DRUGS HELL'

i-D magazine cover.

The DJs and crew behind Spice in Manchester, including Justin Robertson, Greg Fenton and Moonboots.

Ravers at The Hacienda, February 22, 1990.
CAMERA PRESS/IAN TILTON

The second summer of love – 'DROP ACID NOT BOMBS' . The term generally refers to the summers of both 1988 and 1989. Leaning against the wall are Lee Thompson (left) and Chris Foreman who'd left Madness to form Nutty Boys then Crunch.
CAMERA PRESS/GAVIN WATSON

the DJ, but he later realised it was me and I'm staring at the DJ with this look in my eyes that says, "I fucking want that job."

★

On 25 February, 1989, the first Biology, subtitled World In Action (and using a bastardised version of the current affairs programme logo on the flyer) took place at Linford Studios in Battersea. It was organised by Jarvis Sandy, a customer at Jazzy M's record shop in Croydon.

JAZZY M: Biology at Linford Studios was crazy. It was organised by Jarvis Sandy, who used to come into the shop and buy tunes. He was a larger than life character, a very colourful character, and he wanted to put a party on, so I ended up renting the back room of the shop to him, and he set up the party out of there. I was probably a bit more of a pushover back in those days because I was such a friendly soul that I never saw bad in anyone, but you couldn't help but be charmed by him.

Biology was the night of Bruno v Tyson*, which got a bit hairy. The fight was supposed to be shown in the main auditorium where we were playing, but the projector broke because it was too hot in there due to it being so overcrowded. It was so full I could literally have walked off the stage and just walked across people's heads and out of the door; that's how tightly packed it was. People were starting to get irate because the boxing wasn't coming on the screen and it was so packed. Then the worst thing was we heard cheers coming from the VIP room, because they still had the boxing on in there, which wasn't good. I thought, 'Oh fuck!' and my first thought was to stick Nitro Deluxe on, which I did and within the first 'bum bum de bum' of the b-line everyone had forgotten about the boxing and they just screamed and started going for it. Sticky situation avoided!

STEVE PROCTOR, DJ: Once Shoom moved to the YMCA, I was playing there regularly. But when I started getting more work outside

---

* In February 1989, Frank Bruno challenged Mike Tyson to the unified World Boxing Association, World Boxing Council and International Boxing Federation heavyweight titles. Tyson beat Bruno in five rounds.

Shoom than Danny [Rampling], and after saying they wanted me to be resident, one day Jenni came to me and said we want to change it and we want to go with Mark Moore. So Mark came in and I got pushed out. The fitness centre [Shoom's original home] was empty and the guy who ran it, Jim, would ring me and say do you want to take it on. But I didn't at first, out of respect for Danny. Then my wife said, "Look, you're not going to get any more work out of them because they're scared of you." So I started Promised Land at the fitness centre in 1989.

★

808 State's second release proper was the EP *Quadrastate*, which started life as a John Peel session that was never broadcast and was eventually released as an EP. One song from the EP, 'Pacific State', became a huge hit in Manchester, particularly at The Spinmasters residency at The Thunderdome where it was played at the end of the night. It was eventually released as a single in its own right in 1989, reaching number 10 in the UK charts.

DARREN PARTINGTON: I remember being really shocked one day when Graham pulled out a saxophone in the studio. I said, "What the fuck are you doing? You're going to put a *real instrument* on one of our tunes!? Put that sax away you dick! What do you think it is, a brass band, you knobhead?... Oi, tell him we're not a brass band!" But then I did get it, and realised OK, you can use real instruments on house tunes. At first we were anti-everything: "Put a *guitar* on there? Nah, guitars are for people who wear cowboy boots!"

ANDREW BARKER: 'Pacific' was big in Manchester and huge at The Thunderdome, but it really took off when Radio 1 DJ Gary Davies heard it in Ibiza and starting playing it on his show. I quit my job as a roofer, and suddenly we were on *Top Of The Pops*. It all happened really quickly and I remember my mam saying, "What are *you lot* doing on *Top Of The Pops!*?" There was an amazing creative energy in Manchester at the time; not just for musicians, but all sorts of people just decided what they wanted to do and felt empowered to go out and invent their own jobs – DJs, graphic designers, clothes labels. Everyone decided to have a go, and for once there was no one telling you that you couldn't – "I'm gonna open a car wash," "Nice one, go for it, mate."

★

Despite the efforts and protestations of *NME* journalists Helen Mead and Jack Barron, who were converts, the *NME* still weren't regularly covering the scene in any great depth. Then The Grid's Richard Norris managed to convince editor Alan Lewis to send him to Ibiza to cover the opening parties of the 1989 season.

RICHARD NORRIS: I went to Alan Lewis and said, "You've got to send me out to Ibiza to cover this new scene." I might as well have said you need to send me to Saturn to cover this massive new dance scene... or Portsmouth, or somewhere just as unlikely; they didn't have a clue what was going on. But he let me do it, and I went over there and did this big roundup of what was happening in the clubs for the opening parties of 1989.

I went to the opening night of Amnesia, which was amazing. There was quite a few Shoomers there so there was a weird mix of pockets of people from south London and Manchester and then these older, moneyed Eurotrash-type people who seemed really old, but were probably only about 30. I remember meeting someone in Shoom who was 30 once and we thought that was amazing because most of the people there were about 17.

ANDREW WEATHERALL: It was towards the end of that summer I made my first trip to Ibiza. I'd made no arrangements for accommodation or anything. It was myself and my girlfriend at the time, Nina Walsh, a very lovely woman. We had two suitcases and we went straight to [club] Space from the airport, checked the suitcases in the cloakroom and preceded to get properly at it. I remember the DJ playing 'How Soon Is Now?' and then he played something else and I was like, "*What the fuck is this?*" and I just climbed up this speaker stack to get to the DJ and ask him what the record was. In the film version of this story the speaker stack will probably be 25 foot high and in my mind it was 25 foot high but in reality it was probably about 10–15 foot. But I climbed up it and got to the DJ and asked him, probably in an annoying Englishman abroad point-and-talk-loudly-and-you-have-no-need-to-speak-a-foreign-language manner, despite me thinking I was a sophisticated clubber, "WHAT. IS. THIS. REC-ORD!!?" and in the end he showed it to me and I wrote it down and it was 'Los Niños Del Parque' by Liaisons Dangereuses, and I climbed back down again. We piled out of there with two suitcases and we got the bus into San Antonio town and found this horrible room there, but we just dumped the bags and went out and did some more acid.

I went to Amnesia for the first time on that trip, and I've got a couple of vivid memories of it. There was a foam party and I was wearing that famous Westwood–McLaren shirt with the image of two cowboys, with their hats pushed back and their knobs out which are almost touching, and it's got a quote from a Joe Orton book underneath. I was wearing that shirt, much to the delight of the Ibizan queens, and I just remember being chased through the foam by these screaming queens.

My other memory is of being with Kevin Sampson, the writer, and this was just after *A Short Film About Chilling** came out, where apparently I'm the voice of reason because I say, "Oh, it's just a Club 18-30 for people with Gaultier shirts," which was my slightly cynical viewpoint. Kevin and I got on well because we were both slightly, if not cynical, then the voice of reason. I remember being in Amnesia, this beautiful whitewashed club, and Kevin is going, "Oh, you're a bit more clued-up than me," meanwhile I'm drinking La Mumbas, which is a Spanish cocktail of brandy and chocolate milk, and as Kevin Simpson is telling me what a great clued-up guy I am, and how I'm not like all

---

* *A Short Film About Chilling* is a 1990 documentary film that focused on the blossoming club scene in Ibiza. Directed by Angus Cameron and commissioned by Channel 4, it followed the stories of several young British people heading out to Ibiza for the magic summer of 1990, before the masses descended and commercial mass clubbing as we know it today took hold. It also features performances and interviews with many of the scene's best-known faces, including A Guy Called Gerald, 808 State and *Boy's Own*.

the rest, I had to go, "Excuse me Kev," and leaned over his shoulder and threw up about three pints of chocolate brandy all over the newly whitewashed walls of Amnesia. Which I think may have changed his opinion of just how clued-up I was.

★

While the first people on the scene were finding new ways to publicise the movement, so too were other acts finding ways to pay homage to acid house. Boy George had been a regular on the scene since the early days and decided to make a slightly tongue-in-cheek record reflecting the movement with his old friend Jeremy Healy, MC Kinky and producer Simon Rogers, going under the name E-Zee Possee. George was credited as 'Angela Dust' on the record, which was released on his new label More Protein. 'Everything Starts With An E' first reached number 69 in the UK singles chart in the summer of 1989 but would go on to become an acid house anthem despite being banned, by the BBC. It was re-released in March 1990 and this time made it to number 15, staying there for eight weeks.

BOY GEORGE: I was friendly with Paul Oakenfold and all the other guys who ran Spectrum, and I just threw myself into house music because it was the most exciting thing happening at the time, and so much more exciting than being in the band. We then had the idea to do a record, which became 'Everything Starts With An E'. It was a weird set of circumstances that led to that record. Jeremy [Healy] was working with this guy who had this weird Ronald McDonald album on which he says, "Everything starts with an E," so we sampled that. I already knew Caron [Geary, aka MC Kinky] who had sang on my last solo album, and I just had this mad idea of sticking Caron on a house record. Jeremy came up with the name E-Zee Possee and the track was a bit tongue in cheek and just a kind of observational thesis on what was happening – everyone was necking ecstasy and gurning. I remember Fat Tony used to laugh and say, "Peace?!!... peace off!" There's a fantastic clip on YouTube I saw recently of a rave around that time and you're like, "Oh my god."

What was really funny was when I took the record to Virgin, they wanted to take Caron off it. That was their bit of good advice: "Just remove the rapper, keep everything else but remove the rapper." I was like, "*That's* the fucking record. You can't take her off, *that's* the record."

Nancy Noise was working in the dance department at Virgin and she was going out with Paul Oakenfold and I said to her, "Why haven't you given the record to Paul?" Then one night in Spectrum, Oakenfold came up to me and said, "What's this fucking tune, man? Graeme Park said he turned off all the music in The Haçienda at midnight and played this record called 'Everything Starts With An E' and the whole place went ballistic... *what is this tune?*" I said, "Your girlfriend is promoting it, why don't you ask her?" So it became an underground classic, and it was the success of that which prompted me to start More Protein records and Jesus Loves You [his post–Culture Club band].

★

Quentin Chambers, Jeremy Taylor and Anton Le Pirate had been looking for a venue for their first large-scale event, which they called Energy. They knew they wanted to up the production values and decided a film studio would be their best bet. They found what they were looking for at the Westway Film Studios in Shepherd's Bush, and booked the five-room venue for 27 May. All 5,000 tickets sold out and come the day, touts were selling them outside the event for £100, while ticketless punters, desperate to get in, were scaling the walls.

QUENTIN CHAMBERS, PROMOTER, ENERGY: I was totally immersed in the scene but I thought we could go one further in terms of production, in terms of the amount of people you could get into these events, and just make them grander, more of a spectacle, because up to that point most were quite seedy and dirty. I wanted to take it to a different level and give people a real visual and audio experience.

Podiums were big things back in '88 and '89, they seemed to be everywhere in clubs. The exhibitionists would be on the podium, and on the highest point of the podium possible. We wanted to build ourselves a big podium but we wanted to make it something a bit more special. So we built a 20-foot high temple made of Greek-style columns and built our podium around that, and we had the whole lighting rig with lasers inside the roof of the temple.

JEREMY TAYLOR: That was our first serious illegal one. That was the one where we had pyramids and Stonehenge and a scene from *Bladerunner*. People hadn't really seen the likes of that before, but that's what we wanted to do, rather than get everyone into some dusty old warehouse where you were lucky if you got a strobe light. We wanted to put on an amazing show. We wanted to have the best music, the best displays, the best lights and everything. We wanted to create a whole experience and we managed to do it with that first rave. It sold out pretty quickly, so come the night people were absolutely desperate to get in and were literally climbing the walls. We had to get security to hold them back, but it was great to have our first party be so popular.

JAZZY M: That first Energy party was great, but I remember it being very packed, probably over full. I was 20 foot up on scaffold, and I remember playing two copies of 'Strings Of Life'*. I was wearing my 'Jack Hat' – it was a Canadian Mountie's hat and I called it my Jack Hat. I have no idea why, it was just silly. I remember pulling the brim down and getting on the mic and saying, "Do you want it, do you want it?" and just holding the crowd back and teasing them and teasing them, before letting them have it. That was the peak of those raves.

JEREMY TAYLOR: The police were on our case after that because they could see we were quite a big player. We then did one at Heston [in Hounslow] which the police tried to stop, and then took the view that it was better to let it go ahead. I didn't get arrested for it but they turned up at my flat in Chelsea in an unmarked police car, which was a Citroen 2CV, which I thought was hilarious. They ended up

---

* 'Strings Of Life' is a seminal track by Rhythim Is Rhythim, aka Detroit musician and DJ Derrick May. Released in 1987, it was huge throughout 1988 and remains May's best-known track.

driving me to several police stations because they couldn't get the recording equipment to work. The two coppers that day were actually quite relaxed, and their attitude was more like, "Well, surely you can get a licence for it?" I used to bump into them at other raves after that and actually got on all right with them. They weren't trying to stop us, they'd just been sent to investigate it – they weren't really anti-raves at all.

Even later on down the line, I had quite a good relationship with Ken Tappenden [then Chief Superintendent of Kent Police], who I would speak to on the phone, trying to work out a way we could make these raves legal. The trouble is, he had everyone else who just wanted them stopped any way possible.

I think Ken could see the illegal raves were a bit of a time-bomb waiting to go off, and actually we tried very hard to make them as safe as possible. But when you've got the police running round trying to do everything they can to stop you, then obviously dealing with that takes up your time and makes it very hard to concentrate on all of the health and safety aspects as well. I think Ken saw us as quite reputable organisers, the problem was his brief was to try and stop them altogether. I think Ken would have liked to have been in a situation where he had certain people he knew he could work with. But every time you tried to get a licence you were thwarted by someone in the village, wherever the location was, who didn't want it on their doorstep, they just wanted it somewhere else. A lot of the MPs were also in favour of making some of the raves legal events, but the problem was you just couldn't get a licence due to the number of complaints, especially if you had ever held an illegal rave before, because they would use that against you. If you look at the way it's done nowadays for similar-sized *legal* events, the organisers get a licence, they pay the police to come along, and it works. They understand there's going to be an element of drug taking, and they understand they need to provide medical care to deal with that. They understand people may drink too much alcohol, and they need to have provisions for that as well. But above all, I think they realise that if you're going to stop something or outlaw it, it's only going to make it more attractive; tell the kids not to do something and they just want to do it even more. Nowadays there's a huge festival or outdoor concert of that size going on every weekend.

I got charged for conspiracy to cause a public nuisance on two occasions, for the Energy summer festival in August 1989 and then the Dance 89 festival about a month later, in September. I got done for both of those and they tried to give me a suspended jail sentence, but on appeal they then realised it was slightly over the top just for organising a party. I did 250 hours' community service in the end, which was about three times as much as anyone else I met who was doing community service, and *they* had all been done for nicking cars, welding two cars together, selling drugs, or all sorts of different things. But the authorities at that time viewed organising a party as far more dangerous than any of those things.

Community service was actually great fun. I had to do gardening on the canal around Portobello; there was a little park there and I had to do it every Wednesday, which was a lot of fun and I met quite a few characters. I used to invite all the others doing community service with me down to Fun City on a Friday night; they just had to come down and say, "I'm with the Gardening Club!"

★

On 24 June, 1989, Sunrise held their biggest event yet. Midsummer Night's Dream took place at the disused White Waltham Airfield, two miles south of Maidenhead. Taking over the huge Fairey Hangar, Midsummer Night's Dream attracted 11,000 ravers from all over the country, including a young Noel Gallagher. The thousands of cars caused a three-mile tailback. The next morning, *The Sun*, now vehemently opposed to acid house, dubbed the event 'Ecstasy Airport' and bizarrely wrote about "pilled-up partygoers ripping the heads off pigeons".

CHARLIE COLSTON-HAYTER: Midsummer Night's Dream was crazy. We had people trying to smash holes in the walls with mallets and all sorts to get into that party. This girl turned up in her pyjamas, wide-eyed. She only lived two miles away and she said, "My parents have banned me from going to these raves and said, 'You are *not* going out this weekend!' But I was in my bedroom and I could hear the music, so I just climbed out of the window and ran here!" I said, "Go on, you're in for free."

JUDGE JULES: Probably more than any of them, the Sunrise that was dubbed 'Ecstasy Airport' caused the stink. I think it was on the cover of *The Mail On Sunday* as we came out of the event the next day. The scale of it was incredible. E was obviously a big part of it, but not for me if you were the DJ. The funny thing was, as a DJ, you might be the straightest person in there.

PAUL RUTHERFORD, FRANKIE GOES TO HOLLYWOOD*: I went to a few of those early raves, and played at a few of them. But it just got a bit silly. You'd drive miles, chasing your tail to get to a field, only to find it had been cancelled and then you had to drive another 50 miles to another field, hoping that one hadn't been cancelled. It just got a bit ridiculous and in the end we were like, "Let's just go back to ours, get out of it and listen to music," which we did. I was living in a big warehouse space in Docklands and that quickly became a bit of a Saturday night destination for friends and close family. It became a regular spot, until it began to tire me out because when word got out, strangers used to start turning up: "I hear you've got a great night here?" "You're right, we have, but you're not invited." It got a bit out of hand in the end.

ANDREW WEATHERALL: To this day I'd rather DJ to 200 people. My favourite club is just a box with 200 to 500 people in it. Don't get me wrong; I love being part of something bigger than myself. As an experience, being part of a big crowd is great, but as a *spiritual* experience I don't enjoy it, I don't enjoy big gigs. Ask anyone: they'd rather see their favourite band in a small sweaty club with 200 people rather than the

---

* Former Frankie Goes To Hollywood backing vocalist and dancer Paul Rutherford later went solo, releasing an acid house album and several singles, including the 1988 acid house cult classic 'Get Real', which was produced by Martin Fry of ABC.

O$_2$ arena with 20,000 people. I want to see the whites of people's eyes... or the reds of people's eyes.

STEVEN HALL: I never thought about it from a political stance, although it did feel like 'Loadsamoney' characters were taking over. We weren't being purist for political or ideological reasons, we just wanted to keep it special for us. For selfish reasons, if you like. Because you didn't see it turning into the industry it has become, so if it was just going to be your social life, why not keep it the way you like it?

★

On 27 June, 1989, Mr John Wakeman, the Leader of the House, told the Commons that the Home Secretary Douglas Hurd "would consider the wider implications of acid house parties" after receiving a police report following the rave at White Waltham airfield, Berkshire. John Watts, MP for Central Slough, had asked the Leader of the House to discuss with the Home Secretary "the alarming reports of a major acid house party in Berkshire at the weekend, and whether adequate powers exist in current legislation to deal with this menace to society, or whether fresh legislation is required to protect young people from being ensnared in a vicious circle of drug abuse".

The party's organiser, Tony Colston-Hayter, emphasised to *The Guardian* that there were no arrests at the event: "The atmosphere was special: imagine, 8,000 people without a single fight." There were 10 security guards at the party, and nine people were thrown out for drugs offences. He also promised writs against tabloids who reported the event was "drenched in drugs".

On 4 July, *The Guardian* ran a leader which questioned the government and police stance on acid house parties, under the header 'A Touch Too Acid':

> Acid House parties, according to the tabloid trumpeters, are shocking 'monster rave-ups'. No wonder so many teenagers are ready to pay £15 for a ticket to events where they are only told the location by recorded telephone message at the last minute. The entrepreneurs have produced an attractive package for the

anti-authoritarian young: anarchic, mysterious and condemned by press, politicians and police. Yet the biggest danger, in fact, is that they will become a diversion from serious anti-drugs operations.

Last weekend most of the party-goers never got to the parties being organised in Wiltshire and Oxfordshire. The police closed exit roads off the M4 and set up road blocks on the rural roads leading to the sites. Between 1,000 and 3,000 harassed hedonists spent much of the night unsuccessfully trying to outwit the law. A less anarchic group might now be consulting civil rights lawyers. Although the High Court upheld road blocks during the 1984 miners' strike – on the Common Law grounds that there was an imminent danger of the pickets breaching the peace – the police could not point to similar affrays with Acid House parties. What has happened to the right to free association?

But it is not quite that simple. There are reports the landlord of the aircraft hangar in Wiltshire, who agreed to the party, had been misled about its purpose and had withdrawn consent. No licence for providing music and dancing had been applied for or granted. Local residents, who would have been subjected to loud music throughout the night, had not been consulted. In an era where Hillsborough has demonstrated the dangers of over-crowding and Bradford the risk of fire*, safety regulations for public gatherings no longer look bureaucratic. Over 8,000 people attended the Acid

---

* During the mid to late Eighties, football was marred with several tragic disasters. On 15 April, 1989, the FA Cup semi-final between Liverpool and Nottingham Forest was due to take place at the Hillsborough Stadium in Sheffield. The decision by Chief Superintendent Duckenfied to open an exit gate led to a crush in the Leppings Lane end, resulting in the deaths of 96 people and injuries to 766 others. In 2012, the Hillsborough Independent Panel concluded that the main cause of what was to become known as the Hillsborough Disaster was a 'lack of police control', while crowd safety was 'compromised at every level'. It is Britain's worst stadium-related disaster. Almost four years previously, on May 11, 1985, a fire at Bradford City's Valley Parade stadium during a League match killed 56 and injured at least 265. Both incidents led to an overhaul in stadium safety and crowd control in the UK, including the banning of wooden grandstands.

House party the previous weekend at White Waltham airfield in Berkshire. Such gatherings need strict rules about access routes for fire engines and exits for participants.

The biggest danger of the parties, however, is the hype about their drug-pushing purpose. *The Sun* described White Waltham as "a cynical attempt to trap teenagers into drug dependency under the guise of friendly pop music events". The idea that the big drug barons are behind such events is absurd. The insidious barons are far too discreet to get involved in such brash, risky effusions. Undoubtedly drugs are consumed at the parties, as they are at many events where the young congregate. But the pushers will be minnows. Entrepreneurs who can get 8,000 young people to pay £15 to turn up to listen to loud music in an aircraft hangar do not need the extra profit – and risks – that drugs might offer.

The parties provide the police with the tempting illusion of drug action. But Acid House parties should be recognised for what they are: a potential public nuisance if the noise is too raucous or the safety regulations are ignored. The parties are an irrelevance in terms of serious drug dealers, who want regular clients not kids who they are never going to see again. *The Sun* published an account of an Oxford ball at New College – "mayhem as drug and booze-crazed toffs traded punches" – on the same page as its Acid House account. No road blocks are expected in The High.

SHAUN RYDER: Just after Dry Bar opened, at the end of July 1989, we played at *The Other Side Of Midnight* end-of-series party at Granada. It was filmed in the afternoon and we played with Mike Pickering"s T-Coy and A Guy Called Gerald. They basically tried to recreate a rave in the afternoon in a TV studio. We did about four or five tracks including 'Wrote For Luck', which was the track that went out on the show. Fair play to Granada for trying to expose a mainstream audience to what was going on – Tony probably had a lot to do with setting that up, along with Nathan McGough, our manager. Granada were actually really good when it came to stuff like that, and always have been. It was them who filmed Bob Dylan when he first came over, and The Doors, and they even filmed a programme with Muddy Waters in Chorlton years ago. Someone at Granada always seemed to have their eye on what was happening with youth culture and popular culture, and they were pretty good at it. You wouldn't get anything like that from any of the other British TV companies.

I don't really remember the filming of that show, but that's because I was completely off my tits. Completely. I know Tony introduced us, and Bez wasn't there because he was stuck in Marseilles for some reason. I can't remember what happened to him that time but there were a few occasions when there were warrants out for his arrest for non-payment of fines or maybe missing a court appearance.

MIKE PICKERING: The funniest rave was when Chris and Anthony [Donnelly] were doing a party in Rochdale called Joy. They put my name on the flyer. When you came out of The Haç at the end of the night there'd be kids handing out flyers for raves, and I'd be handed five flyers for different raves and they all had my name on, and I'd be like, "I'm not playing any of them!"

So, it's Friday morning and I'm in bed in my flat above the Arndale [shopping centre]. Next thing, the fucking door gets kicked in and the police come steaming in. I'm like, "What the fucking hell is going on?" and trying to shove bits of dope into plant pots and stuff. They're like, "You've got to appear in court at 11a.m. this morning, Rochdale Council have got a restraining order on you." I said, "A) You've just kicked me fucking front door in, and B) What *are* you *talking* about?" They said, "You're part of this rave, this illegal one we're trying to stop." So I thought, 'Fuck, I better ring Tony.' So I rang Tony, and he just swung into action: "Great darling, don't worry…" He loved all that shit. So he got John Wilson, the Factory lawyer, on it.

So later that morning I'm in the bloody law courts on Spinningfield, just off Deansgate. Chris and Anthony are sat at the back of the court and Rochdale Council are there. The judge said my name was on the flyer so I must be involved. I replied, "Look, you come and stand outside The Haçienda or any other club on a Friday or Saturday night and you'll be handed several flyers with my name on, but that doesn't mean I'm playing them all." After a while the judge said something like, "Do you have to bring this case? It seems a bit odd." But anyway, I was handed a [24-hour] restraining order preventing me from going within a 20-mile radius of Rochdale, and I just thanked the judge: "Thanks very much mate, I've never wanted to go to Rochdale anyway." He was all right, the judge, and he replied, "I don't blame you."

So Tony did a piece on *Granada Reports* that night, with me in front of Manchester Town Hall with a copy of that day's *Manchester Evening News*, and then I had to get off and drive to Nottingham for the night. I couldn't even stay in my own flat because the centre of Manchester is within a 20-mile radius of Rochdale. So I just went down to Nottingham and played with Graeme that night at The Garage, then came home on Sunday afternoon. Hilarious.

DREW HEMMENT: The Blackburn raves just got bigger and bigger throughout 1989. After a while, whenever you got close to Blackburn on the night of a rave, traffic was converging from all over. Blackburn felt like an independent state. It was beyond the rule of law, beyond anything. I was quite critical of authority when I was younger and I met a lot of similar people there, and OK we might have been innocent idealists, but we really thought we were changing things and it mattered. It was a red torch of incredibleness.

I talked my way onto the decks at one of them by telling them I was a DJ and I ended up playing a few. The other thing about the Blackburn raves is they were quite tribal. The mates I used to go with were all Leeds United Service Crew [Leeds football hooligan firm], and the organisers would have known that. It only occurred to me recently that might have been why I got to play, because I turned up with a lot of football supporters. When I moved to Leeds a lot of the people who became my mates happened to be Service Crew, and those tribal dynamics were very evident in the room. I wasn't from a football world, but if you were there, those tribal dynamics would have been even more evident to you.

There were so many moments at Blackburn that were so humbling. Moments that, even now, if I talk about them my whole being just melts thinking about it. The music was a big part of it but a lot of it was just this amazing feeling that we had created this whole thing from nothing. Sometimes I used to turn up later, after I had DJed in Leeds, so the party would be in full fucking flow, and as you walked up to the warehouse the hairs on the back of your neck would stand up and you'd get this rush, even if you hadn't done any drugs.

SHAUN RYDER: Just after that, that young girl called Claire Leighton died in The Haçienda. By that time there were some pretty dodgy batches of E turning up. We always knew where ours were coming from, but you had no idea where all these other Es were coming from. I remember someone giving me a pill one afternoon and saying, "Try one of these." It was red, I think. I necked the fucker and an hour later I was walking down Oxford Road and I collapsed. I was on my own and I just blacked out. I don't know how long I was out for and I don't think anyone actually tried to help me. When I came round there were a couple of people stood just looking at me. I just got up and got myself together a bit and just got off. There were some pretty dodgy drugs going about at that time.

About the same time, I had another dodgy E experience when I was crashing on a pal of mine's sofa, Dave Reddie's, in Walkden, near Little Hulton. I woke up in the middle of the night because I was being dragged off the sofa and then round the living room by two big Alsatian dogs. They were dragging me round the room and ripping me apart, these two Alsatians. But while this was happening to me, and these dogs were dragging me around the room, I sort of got my head together a bit and said to myself, "Hang on a minute, I'm in Dave Reddie's flat, and I *know* he hasn't got his dogs anymore, he's got rid of 'em." Next thing, I find myself on the floor in the front room of his flat, having a fit, convulsing and frothing at the mouth. But before that moment of clarity, I absolutely thought I was being dragged round the room and ripped apart by these two Alsatians. He'd actually only just got rid of the dogs, so you could still smell them in the flat. I must have smelled them in my sleep, and that smell then triggered something in my brain, and the dodgy E had given me some sort of fit, and next thing I think I'm being dragged round the room... until I get my head together, the dogs disappear, and I'm left having a proper wobbler on the floor. There was definitely some pretty fucking dodgy E's going around at that stage.

★

In 1989, Jazzy M was handed a tape with one word – 'Chime' – written on it. It would become the first release from Paul and Phil Hartnoll, aka Orbital, who went on to be one of the most successful British dance music duos. They took their name from the M25, Greater London's Orbital motorway, which had become central to the raves and free parties around London and the Southeast.

JAZZY M: There was a young lad and I think he was called Jackmaster Jay, who was a crazy looking kid from Kent. He had masses of ginger hair and he used to bring me in tapes of music made by a friend of his and all they said on them was 'Paul from Kent'. No contact number, no nothing, just 'Paul from Kent'. There was all sorts of mad stuff on here. I thought, "Fucking hell, you're mixing up ska with electronic beats, throwing in bits of Clash, some of this and some of that?" It was fresh, he had some fucking mad ideas going on. Then all of a sudden, Jackmaster Jay brought this new tape in, and it just had 'Chime' written on it. I played it in the store and loads of people said, "I'll have a copy of that." I said, "You can't, it's only on cassette." We pressed up a few thousand copies of the cassette and then a bidding war started between Pete Tong and Johnny Walker.

I chose the name 'Orbital' because people were starting to talk about the Orbital raves around the London M25 Orbital motorway. It also fitted in with the idea of Oh Zone, which was the name of my record label: we are a cosmic label. It just worked; I just thought, 'Orbital is a fucking great name.' So I got an Orbital logo designed by a couple of lads who used to come in the shop and had a design company called Wandering Moonbeam. How could you not use two lads who called themselves Wandering Moonbeam? They were ya-ya Sloaney types, and when I asked them they were like, "Ya, ya, we'll knock that up for you, Jazz."

I knew 'Chime' was great. But I didn't think it was going to go to number 17 and they'd end up on *Top Of The Pops* wearing anti-Council

Tax T-shirts.* Paul was never of the norm, which is what attracted me to him in the first place. His zany and creative head was what attracted him to me. He deserves everything he has got. I had a really good relationship with Paul. I've still got the original contract [Orbital] signed with me.

Paul was very much pushed by his older brother Phil. I didn't know Phil existed until the record became big, then Phil came in and took over a bit, and took Paul away from me and got them managed by one of their mates. Which I found very sad, but it's typical of the music industry. I suppose Jazzy M and Ozone was a good starting point for them, and then they went on to something bigger.

BOY GEORGE: The bigger raves were great for a while but then they started to get nasty. I remember we were booked with MC Kinky to do 'Everything Starts With An E' at one big rave, and the promoter refused to pay us. There were about 10,000 people there but after we played they refused to pay out. It wasn't even much money, I think it was about a couple of hundred quid. It got really nasty and the guy running it threatened to kill me, but because I was on E I just laughed and was like, "You're not going to kill *me*? How are you going to kill *me*?" But in reality it was actually really nasty, and that for me was the beginning of the end. After that I realised it was just getting really ugly. There were bouncers offering you drugs, guard dogs, and it was just really awful. They ruined it. They killed it.

★

Meanwhile, the violence in Manchester was only escalating. The violence that was happening in Manchester exists in the nocturnal life of most major cities; the difference was that in Manchester it was bubbling much closer to the surface and happening on a much more regular basis.

MIKE PICKERING: If you think about Manchester geographically, the city centre was surrounded by gangs at that time. On one side you

---

* After the initial release on Oh Zone sold out, Pete Tong signed the record to FFRR. It was re-released a few months later, in 1990, reaching number 17 in the charts.

had Doddington and Gooch in Hulme, on another side you've got Cheetham Hill, on another side you've got Longsight, and on another side you've got Salford. The city centre was completely surrounded by different gangs and their patches. The police seemed to almost encourage it as far as I was concerned, as if the violence continued or escalated then they could just close everywhere down. They wanted it to get worse so they could close everywhere.

SASHA: The scene had turned nasty with the gangs moving in. In Manchester, you felt it wasn't just about the music anymore. That whole Summer Of Love feeling lasted maybe a couple of summers at a push – '88 and '89 – but by the time it came to 1990 the gangsters had realised how much money some people were making from what was being consumed.

DAVE HASLAM: It did start to spiral out of control. It's to do with the ecstasy experience. If you're dealing with a large crowd of people, many of whom are taking ecstasy, then there's going to be a wonderful intensity but there's also going to be an element of things spiralling out of control, either on an individual or a collective level. As a DJ you can ride that or try and channel it very positively, if you're lucky, if you're playing the right records and things fall right. But I also remember feeling there was something making me feel uneasy. I'm not talking about the arrival of gangsters on the scene, I'm talking about the collective intensity. I remember saying that to Tony one night – Wilson used to come down [to The Haçienda] occasionally and come in the DJ booth and say, "How are things? This is great. What are you playing?" or he might have some visiting dignitary, like [music entrepreneur and Vice President of Warner Bros.] Seymour Stein or someone in town.

Tony's ideal situation is when things are out of control. He loved the anarchy, that was the Malcolm McLaren in him. He came in when it was absolute chaos. The whole club was chaos, like a circus. I'll be the only DJ in this book who quotes T.S. Eliot, but there was a line by T.S. Eliot about being 'a still point in a turning world'. In The Haçienda at that point, you were 'a still point in a turning world', and all around you was bedlam, absolute bedlam and chaos. Everyone else is losing themselves, having the night of their lives, most of them are on drugs and there's so much sensory deprivation, from the smoke machines to the strobes, but you are the one who is putting on one record after another and making it all come together, this bedlam is in your hands. You did have to have the mentality to hold yourself and take a deep breath, and do what you needed to do to make the night work.

Anyway, Tony came down one night, and I said to him, "This could destroy itself," and he looked at me as if I'd broken the spell. He had walked in and the club was packed and he could feel the intensity of it, and he thought I was just putting a downer on it, which I suppose I was. I just needed to express to someone what I was feeling. I just simply said to him, "This could destroy itself…" and he looked at me and said, "You miserable bastard…" and walked out.

Then what happened was the fact there was an illegal drug being used by so many people in the club meant it didn't take long for other elements to realise how much money was being made in the club. So it started to attract those sorts of people, who weren't coming from where we were coming from. They didn't understand the idea of community; they didn't understand the idea of loving music, the idea that this was unique, the idea that this was an important project. So it did destroy itself.

FIONA ALLEN: Unfortunately, the mood in the club changed a lot quicker than most of the punters realised. Because I was working on the door, myself and the doorman got to know every little dodgy kid who was coming in there and what they were getting up to. Quite quickly the violence escalated, and almost every week I ended up driving someone down to casualty because the ambulances and the police, how can I say this, took their time turning up when we rang them. Either that or they just happened to be rushed off their feet every time.

One week I had to drive a doorman down to A&E, although that was because he had split the skin between his fingers punching someone, so I didn't feel that sorry for him. Another week I drove another doorman down to A&E and when we walked in there was a whole load of Moss Side gang members there who the doorman had just had a fight with.

It was just me, the doorman and about five of them, and the nurses and doctors ran behind a door and I just ended up shouting and screaming and managed to get a few of them to leave him by just saying it was between the two of them. It was just horrible.

I remember one kid, who was a lovely cheeky chappy, but like a lot of those kids he suddenly saw an opportunity to make some serious money for the first time dealing E, and it seemed like easy money. He had his own little patch in The Haçienda but, being a cheeky sort of lad, had ventured on to someone else's patch in the club and ended up getting stabbed in the leg, just missing a major artery. I was so used to it by that stage – I remember taking off my belt to try and make a tourniquet and as I was doing it I thought, "I only bought this belt today." That's how commonplace the violence had become, that you could have a thought like that while trying to stem the bleeding from a stab wound. The week before I had seen inside someone's skull after they'd been glassed in the club. Meanwhile, most people in the club are still having a euphoric, great time. The Haçienda was a wonderful club but it had already lost its charm for me by that stage.

Then the guns started arriving on the scene, and there was a murder.

One night there was a bang and I looked up and the doormen scattered and there was a guy walking across the road towards the club with a gun. The doormen have scattered and I'm on my own behind reception, so I desperately started pressing the button that closed the shutter over the main door and it was the slowest moment of my life as it came down. I was just pleading with the shutter to hurry up and close: 'Please, come on!' Then it did close and I remember thinking, 'I wonder if bullets can go through bricks?'

Another night a guy came in and I saw him threaten to kill a doorman and chase him, trying to get hold of him. That's the reality of what went on in that club, and they're only a few examples. People were either lucky enough not to see it, or they try and forget it, but I'm not forgetting it because it was horrible.

MIKE PICKERING: There were no police in The Haçienda and no help from them at all, until long after it started getting nasty. The first proper trouble I ever saw was at the end of a Wednesday night, and I was flying out to America on Thursday morning to join up with Paul Cons on the Haçienda tour, because we'd split it between Graeme and me. At the end of that night there was a real fucking ding-dong on the stairs behind the DJ booth. I'd never seen anything like it in The Haçienda. It was Cheetham Hill with the Haçienda security, and they'd battered one of them. I just came out of the DJ booth, saw what was going on and went, "*Whoa, whoa, whoa...*" and one of the gang turned round with one of those things that extend into a stick, and went, "Fuck you!" So I jumped straight back into the DJ booth.

Next day when I landed in Chicago, Paul Cons said, "How was last night?" and I said, "We've got a problem." He said, "What do you mean? You're just being paranoid." I said, "What I saw last night was not me being paranoid. What I saw last night is a fucking problem that is going to spread, a major problem." And I was right. It spread like cancer through the club.

It was all about money. It was all about drugs. Jeff Oakes was dealing in the club, so they got hold of his girlfriend, they held her in a pub somewhere to get the message across, and just said, "It's ours now... fuck off."

GREG WILSON: I moved to London when The Haçienda exploded, but I went there when I came back to Manchester and it was incredible. An amazing sight and an amazing time. I remember being in there with Kermit, and we were stood chatting in an alcove. As we were talking he put his hand in the air, saluting the start of a piano break, and all the people in the alcove did the same, and then I looked across the dancefloor and the whole club was doing the same thing. I'd seen a lot of things on dancefloors but I'd never seen total unity like that. It was like the whole club was saying together: "This is us... we are here now."

Not long after that, maybe six or nine months later, I was stood with Kermit in one of the alcoves again and I watched a guy pulling a girl across a table by her hair, really violently. Your natural instinct is to move towards that, but Kermit put his hand on his chest and stopped me and explained, "This alcove belongs to them," (it was either Moss

200

Side or Salford, I can't remember which gang it was), "and the reason we can stand here is they know who I am." The gangs owned all the alcoves and if you were naïve and just went and sat in there, you could be in trouble.

Ecstasy was a double-edged sword in Manchester and The Haçienda: the gangs quickly saw the money that could be made from it and moved in – £15 or £20 for an ecstasy pill was a lot of money. I also think to a small extent The Haçienda had courted those people. They liked having a rough element from Cheetham Hill or Salford in the club, as part of the mix of people, but it turned sour on them. That criminal element was in there, and when they saw an opportunity to make a killing from it they went for it.

The difference with Liverpool is the gangster element on the doors seemed more established there, but in Manchester it was more up for grabs. When I was first at Legends we used to take the Wigan door crew into Manchester. You would never have been able to do that in Liverpool, bring a door crew from outside. In Manchester the gangs were all of a sudden competing for control of the clubs, whereas in Liverpool it was more established who controlled what. Manchester just deteriorated really quickly and the wonderful vibe that had existed was killed. As soon as the police thought they had that first wave under control, there was an even more ruthless second wave.

CHAPTER 9

Loaded

"We didn't give a fuck what anyone thought, we were having too good a time."

Bobby Gillespie

Faced with increasing opposition from the Conservative government, and a Private Members Bill to clamp down on unlicensed parties, Colston-Hayter recruited an old friend of his, Paul Staines, to help with PR and fight the bill. The two created the 'Freedom To Party Campaign' and launched it at the Conservative Party Conference in October 1989. They organised two rallies in Trafalgar Square, the first of which attracted 4,000 and the second 10,000, although this was only a small percentage of those out dancing in the fields each weekend.

In January 1990, the group joined forces with Energy, Biology and other promoters to form the Association of Dance Party Promoters, in hope that a unified front would help them fight the authorities and the imminent changes to the law, in particular the Entertainments (Increased Penalties) Act that Graham Bright MP was pushing through. The government, and the supporting MPs, were open about the fact the Bill specifically targeted acid house parties; the official introduction described it as: 'An Act to increase the penalties for certain offences under enactments relating to the licensing of premises or places used for dancing, music or other entertainments of a like kind.'

Staines later wrote: 'The Association of Dance Party Promoters organised a "Freedom To Party" rally on January 27 in Trafalgar Square. But considering that between them the organisers could pull nearly 100,000 to their raves, the attendance of 8,000 people was a little disappointing. Amplified music was banned by the police so the main promoters gave speeches and there were *a capellas* from Debbie Malone singing "Rescue Me" and MC Chalky White, who was arrested as police brought the demo to a close.'

"I can't understand it," Colston-Hayter said afterwards. "We have a private party, 4,000 people come but it's all over the press and the police say there was 12,000. We have a public demo, 10,000 people come, there's no coverage at all, and the police say there was only a thousand."

JEREMY TAYLOR: The whole Freedom to Party movement was headed by Tony and Sunrise but was very much supported by Energy and Biology and other organisers. We felt we had to do something. It doesn't happen very often that a youth cult comes along and changes the law, does it? It does seem incredible really, looking back; I don't think there's been another time when it's happened that way.

★

Chris and Anthony Donnelly also organised a sister rally for Freedom to Party in the north, in Albert Square, Manchester. The Granada TV topical discussion show *Up Front*, hosted by Tony Wilson and Lucy Meacock, held a debate about rave culture with an audience of disgruntled Blackburn residents and ravers. When the question of drugs was raised, the Blackburn rave organiser Tommy Smith protested, "I don't need drugs, I'm high on hope." The phrase 'high on hope' entered many a clubber's lexicon and was widely used to market club nights.

CHRIS DONNELLY: It had gone to that next level because everybody had had enough and decided they wanted to take a stance. Colston-Hayter had been on Jonathan Ross' TV show and handcuffed himself to

Jonathan. Then Tommy Smith had been on TV having a heated debate. So when Colston-Hayter said they were having a Freedom To Party rally in Trafalgar Square, I said I would do one in Manchester and went to the Manchester Town Hall to book Albert Square for a demonstration, because it's your right, and they said, "What for?" and I told them it was for Freedom To Party.

We had a load of flyers printed and handed them out at clubs and put them on cars. We had a wagon booked with a PA. I went and picked Anthony up in this orange Beetle I'd just bought and I said to him, "What the fuck are we doing here? What if no one turns up?" Then we turned the corner to Albert Square and it was fucking rammed: people with placards, people dancing to ghetto blasters they had brought with them and stuff. As soon as we got out of the car, Granada TV were straight on to us, wanting to interview us. All I remember saying in the interview is, "All we want to do is dance… all we want to do is dance." Then we had to go on Piccadilly Radio and do an interview with them. As we were waiting to go on, The Charlatans were also there waiting to do their first radio interview. I was in the wagon later taking back a generator and I turned on the radio and the rally was all over the air, which was bizarre.

KEN TAPPENDEN, PAY PARTY UNIT: Maggie Thatcher's aides were ringing in to the Police Pay Party Unit* regularly because the Shires were getting upset. I say the Shires; call it Middle England if you like, the Tory voters. They were getting upset, well more than upset, they were beside themselves, and they were demanding action from the government.

It was raised in the House a number of times and the legislation was upped as far as taking possession of the party organiser's equipment, etc., but it all took time. We had to report back to government regularly: they wouldn't leave us alone. We were under scrutiny from quite a high level, because they wanted it stopped.

---

* The Pay Party Unit was set up by the police in response to the explosion in acid house parties throughout 1988, and increased pressure from the government to clamp down on the parties.

It was a moral panic. It was on the front page of *The Sun* and *Daily Mail*, and the press can flare anything up, and the government weren't going to have it. They weren't going to put up with this for people in the Shires. The life of Tory voters in Middle England was being disrupted, in a big way. Some of them got really out of hand. Suddenly residents had people shitting in their front gardens and all sorts.

★

On 3 February, *The Guardian* reported that the police feared an acid house boom in the spring:

> A confidential police report on acid house parties fears a rerun of last year's weekend police operations in the south-east unless action is taken before the spring. Far from suggesting that the parties were last year's passing fashion, the report, entitled The Way Forward, predicts a resumption of activity. It provides a battery of statistics to show that demand for the illegal events which attract thousands of young people at up to £25 a ticket has remained high throughout the winter months. The report, produced by the police acid house intelligence unit at Gravesend, Kent, and circulated to chief constables in at least 11 forces, details the pattern of parties over the past six months and suggests strategy for the future. It reveals that the phenomenon, which was largely confined to areas bordering London's M25 Orbital motorway, is spreading to the rest of the country. The report says senior officers must now either meet party organisers to negotiate acceptable safety standards, or 'target' them for prosecution. These range from "Stopped by police, punters dispersed, persons arrested" to "A party took place. No police action, all quiet."

The report also revealed that the unit had indeed compiled a vast database on the organisers and promoters of rave parties, just as many of the scene regulars had suspected.

> The other board lists individual party promoters by name, with similar boxes for comments. One reads: "imprisoned for three years." The unit has borrowed space on the Holmes computer

(Home Office Large Major Enquiry System), introduced after the Yorkshire Ripper inquiry. It holds more than 15,000 intelligence factors relating to the parties. In a corner of the room, a sophisticated radio scanner searches the pirate radio waves of South and East London for details of imminent parties. The unit also draws on the fanzines and underground magazines which popularise the warehouse scene.

KEN TAPPENDEN: One of the things organisers would do is pay the farmer who owned the land £2,000 in his back pocket to go to France for the weekend, so that I couldn't serve an injunction. I had judges and magistrates standing by every weekend for nearly two and a half years to give me warrants, but I was thwarted by the organisers if they took out the person I needed to serve the warrant on, which was quite a clever move. And if you're making £10,000, £15,000 or £20,000 a night, then to slip a farmer a few grand is nothing.

★

On 24 February, the end of Tommy Smith and Tony Creft's run of Blackburn raves was signalled at a party in a warehouse at Nelson, near Burnley. Two hundred riot police raided the party, which had over 10,000 people inside.

DREW HEMMENT: At the start of 1990, it started to get heavy. There was one rave that I wasn't at when a police car was first turned over, and I think another one might have been torched, I can't remember. Then Nelson was about three or four weeks later. I remember that very clearly. I didn't know at the time, but I heard later the police used these things called 'thunderclaps' [stun guns]. It was 7a.m. before they made a move, so a lot of people had already gone. As the door went up, they threw the thunderclaps in to cause confusion and then a line of police with shields linked, marched forward, banging their shields as they walked. People started to panic and in the middle of the crowd there was this tall Rasta guy who was shouting, "Calm down! Calm down!" They managed to get the back door open and people started pouring out, and the police were out the back taking swipes at them as they tried to get out. All of a sudden it was just very dark. The DJ was thrown off the top with his record decks. Overnight it went from the police never stopping it to a complete cat and mouse chase every weekend.

★

While the fight to keep acid parties alive was intensifying and getting more high-profile by the day (or night), more of the DJs and musicians were beginning to have success with their own musical releases. One record inspired by the Blackburn raves ended up reaching number 12 in the charts.

SUDDI RAVAL: When I formed Together with Jon [Donaghy, another Haçienda regular], it was him that had the musical equipment, access to recording studios and all the contacts. He knew Jon DaSilva and Mike Pickering. I met him in Blackburn when we were raving and I just spilled out all my ideas to him. He wanted to manage me at first but then we ended up forming Together. He was basically a sort of shortcut for me into the music industry – there's no way I could have done it without him.

We started writing the track that would become 'Hardcore Uproar'. Me and Jon were the only sort of permanent members of the band, but Mark Hall was also really important – he's the one that did the piano solo – and Stuart Q also never gets the credit. When we first wrote the tune we decided it needed the sound of a rave crowd at the start. The actual idea came from 'Don't Miss The Party Line', an old rave tune by Biz Nizz, and he said "That's brilliant, but instead of using an old football crowd, let's record a real rave... I'll ask the guys who run the Blackburn raves." As I said, Jon knew everyone. Because one of the names they used for the raves was Hardcore Uproar, they said we could [record the crowd] as long as we named the track after that night. I remember being really unhappy about that because the original title was 'Can You Feel The Beat?', which I thought was really cool. But we agreed anyway. So we went up there one night and we set up all the equipment to record and we asked the crowd to be quiet for a second, which is why it starts off quiet, and then all the shouts and air horns come in.

Obviously we didn't know this was going to happen that night, but after we recorded it we started to pack all the equipment away and literally 10 minutes later the police raided the party and started beating people. It was a good job we had just packed all our equipment away or we could have been arrested by the police as one of the organisers.

We recorded the rest of the tune that week in Spirit Studios in Manchester for £125, that's what the session cost, and then we paid for some white labels. But what happened was the pressing plants were getting quite wise to the fact that some kids were increasingly asking for white labels with no intention of ever getting the records pressed and it was costing them money. So we paid for 25 and we made a list of the 25 people we wanted to get it to. Looking at it now it has everyone from Jon DaSilva to Graeme Park to Andrew Weatherall to Paul Oakenfold, and we managed to get them to most of them, sometimes by just going down to their clubs and handing it to them and saying, "Here's a record we've made, will you please have a listen?" Jon DaSilva was the first person to tell us he thought it could be a hit, because he heard it on cassette before hardly anyone. He said, "You've got a hit on your hands here." Then when we gave out the white labels, I think Sasha was the first person to play it out – I remember seeing him playing it in Leeds.

Some other mad little things happened out of that. We gave it to Paul Oakenfold when he was playing in Manchester, and the next weekend was Stone Roses at Spike Island [see page 219]. Jon and I were in, let's say, a very happy mood that day anyway, but then Oakenfold played our tune, and it was the first time we'd heard it played, obviously, to so many people. I remember hearing people around us saying, "Oh, they're playing Star Wars..." But we knew it was the start of our record, and we were literally doing fucking cartwheels. We were dancing around like nutters and just couldn't believe it.

By the time we got the first pressings back there was a huge demand because those 25 people we'd given it to were hammering it, and they were playing quite large venues. We ended up selling some of the vinyl copies for up to £10 a time, which back then was a lot of money. But we were advised to then hold back and let demand build before we signed a proper deal, which nearly backfired because a few people did cover versions of it, including Pete Waterman and [Dutch record producer] Frank De Wulf.

★

Andrew Weatherall had been introduced to Scottish indie rockers Primal Scream by their press agent, founder of Heavenly Records and acid house evangelist Jeff Barrett, who envisaged the two working together. Primal Scream were late converts to the acid house scene but were now fully sold. Creation Records boss Alan McGee had given Primal Scream frontman Bobby Gillespie his first ecstasy pill in April 1989. "By about June, [he thought] he'd invented acid house!" McGee later said of Gillespie.

Weatherall's remix of the band's ballad 'I'm Losing More Than I'll Ever Have', from their poorly reviewed second album, 1989's *Primal Scream*, was to prove a hit. 'Loaded', as the remix was called, went on to provide the blueprint for the band's next album, 1991's Mercury-prize winning *Screamadelica*. The track sampled Peter Fonda's B-movie *Wild Angels*, summing up the stand-off between authorities and acid party-goers: "Just what is it that you want to do? /... We're gonna have a good time. We're gonna have a party."

ANDREW WEATHERALL: I used to go to The Future on the Thursday night, and Bobby and Innes from Primal Scream were both there, as was Jeff Barrett. I just used to think Jeff was a member of Primal Scream because he had a stripy shirt and long hair and a leather jacket, and then I started seeing him about. Jeff was Primal Scream's press officer, and I was the only man in the world who liked their album. I think that planted the idea of me maybe working with the band, but then Jeff and [*NME* journalist] Helen Mead came up with the idea of me reviewing a live gig for them for *NME*. I ended up going to review them at Exeter University, under the pseudonym Audrey Witherspoon, and I think the headline was 'Sex, Lies And Gaffer Tape'. I've not read the review since and I'm not sure I want to. I think people thought I was writing ironically in the style of a local newspaper review, they thought I was being arch in describing the journey to the gig and the psychedelic anorak [*NME* writer] Jack Barron was wearing that night, but I wasn't – I wasn't a good enough writer to be that arch and ironic at the time, although hopefully it still had some naïve charm.

Anyway, I went to the gig and they were still in rock'n'roll mode, but they were really living it; it was a wet Wednesday in Exeter but they could have been in Detroit in 1969, that's the feeling they gave off. That was the whole crux of the piece, that Primal Scream were doing this not because they wanted to but because they *had* to. I had long curly hair back then, and after the gig, Bobby Gillespie came in the dressing room and looked me up and down and said, "Cool hair, man... you look like Mark Bolan, is it a perm?" I was like, "Thanks, no, it's natural." I think I might have been wearing leather pants that evening as well, so I had all the right rock and roll accoutrements as far as they were concerned.

The next conversation I had with one of them was upstairs at Spectrum with Robert Innes, and he said, "We've got an engineer and the parts, just go in and do something." I'd done a previous remix for the West India Company, which was one half of [English synth pop band] Blancmange. I think it was Alex Patterson who organised that, because he lived in the same set of flats as me, with Youth.*

The first remix I did was quite respectful. I think all I did was keep the arrangement and put a whacking great kick drum underneath it. Just gave it a beat and kept it pretty much the same. When I played it to them you could sense they were a bit disappointed, and Innes just said, "Aw no, man, just fucking *destroy it*, man." It was Innes who said, "I've got this great sample you can use," which was the Peter Fonda sample from *Wild Angels*. I'd love to claim that was my idea but it wasn't, it was Innes. I played it at a Primal Scream gig at Subterranea, under the Westway, and the whole place went mental, all singing the "woo woos", that 'Sympathy For The Devil' thing, over the top. I think Bobby was double pleased because all the Shoom and Spectrum

---

* Youth (real name Martin Glover) was a founding member of the band Killing Joke. He went on to become an acclaimed producer and is a member of The Fireman alongside Paul McCartney.

kids there loved it, and all the fey indie kids were trying to get into the dressing room to ask, "Bob, what's the fucking disco shit?" So Bob was doubly pleased because in one sweep it had managed to please the cool kids and ditch all these fey indie kids.

What did surprise me was it was quite a slow record – it's about 95 bpm, so to get a reaction like that at peak time really surprised me. The tempo in London was maybe slower than elsewhere, but it wasn't *that* slow.

Even when it went down that well, I still thought it was a cool crowd, so I didn't necessarily think it would translate outside of it. I actually went to a job interview with a test pressing of 'Loaded' under my arm; I had no idea it was going to be successful and I'd had to sign off the dole by that point as I started getting letters saying, "Dear Mr Weatherall, we think that with your qualifications you really should be able to find employment," because I got an A at A-Level in Art History and Fine Art. I think I sent one smart-arsed reply back saying, "With my qualifications, would you really want to work behind the bar at so and so?" That probably didn't help – they probably thought we'll have you, you arrogant twat. I was probably then placed in the file marked 'Arrogant twats, to be followed up shortly.' As soon as I put the letter in the postbox I realised what I had done.

As I said, 'Loaded' was quite a slow record for the time, and I remember a review that one certain northern DJ gave it when it came out. I can't remember who it was but it was someone who worked at The Thunderdome or one of those proper full-on clubs, you know what I mean. He sent back his reaction sheet* and it just said, "Soft, southern, shandy-drinking shite."

BOBBY GILLESPIE, PRIMAL SCREAM: Punk's what made us want to be in a band. But when things started to happen for us with 'Loaded', it was like, "This is our time now." Everything we'd learned we were going to put to use. That's my band playing that song, just with a

---

* At the time, it was common practice for DJs to be sent a reaction sheet with promo copies of records, so they could fax back their reaction to the record.

breakbeat and Weatherall's visionary arrangement. But we didn't give a fuck what people thought – we were having too good a time.

★

'Loaded' was just one example of DJs from the acid house scene now making a name for themselves as producers. According to John Leckie, who produced the Stone Roses' debut album: "The technology has given us a new way of creating music. The great thing about acid house music is it doesn't try to be anything else, other than machines all ticking away, ridiculously loud hi-hats or bass drum patterns that no human being could play. It is a revolution, because it's so easy to compile a great-sounding track from programming or sampling."

Paul Oakenfold was another of the original house DJs who was now in demand. "The DJ has always been the man in the front line," Oakenfold explained. "He knows what the people dance to, the best parts of records. So when I was given the opportunity to go in the studio, I would say to Steve [Osbourne, his producing partner], 'I like this, don't like that, take all that off and replace it with this, this and this.' So we'd basically make the record work on the dance floor."

Suddenly, everybody wanted dance beats on their tracks. One joke had it that within months, every band would claim there was a dance element to their music.

At the same time, there was a slight splinter in the scene. Those DJs with more of a Balearic sound separated themselves from what they saw as the 'Acid Ted' mainstream house sound.

GREG FENTON, DJ: My musical background is quite varied and I don't like hearing one tempo all night. Me and Justin Robertson started talking about doing a night together, and the first Spice was at the end of January 1990 in a place called The Cavern on Piccadilly Gardens in Manchester, next to where the Wetherspoons is now. It was myself and Justin and a friend of Justin's from London called Carl Simmonds, and The Stone Roses and people came down. We wanted to do a more Balearic reaction to the mainstream house sounds being played at The Haçienda. We had a lot of negative reaction from people at The Haçienda

212

and there was a piece in [fanzine] *Freaky Dancing** that took the piss out of us. We did take our cue from *Boy's Own* somewhat. I remember Terry Farley writing to us, I've still got the letter somewhere, saying he had heard of us, and he wanted to take a picture of us for a new series on club gangs they were doing in the magazine. So Peter Walsh did a picture out of the back of Dry Bar.

We only did a few nights there and we then moved to a club on Deansgate, which later became Richfields. We then started to bring up people like Andrew Weatherall, Steve Proctor, Diesel. Steve Proctor was a very important DJ, as I'm sure he'll tell you himself, but he was, and very enthusiastic. This was the start of what people began to call the Balearic network. We brought them up because they had a similar sensibility to us. Danny Rampling had played The Haçienda for the first time towards the end of 1988 at Hot. I think Richard Bithell [aka Moonboots] was dancing along to Barry White's 'Ecstasy' in a poncho that night.

Konspiracy had just opened at this time, which was a wonderful club. I went down on the opening night. The Jam MCs were amazing DJs, kind of Balearic but not Balearic. It didn't feel threatening to me really. I remember seeing one of the doormen, who I got on quite well with, pull out a gun and tap on the manager's door when he went in to see him. He did it quite casually and I don't think he was even threatening him. It didn't surprise me too much, but if one of them was carrying a gun then probably all of them were, but I don't know. It does sound weird to say it was a wonderful club on the one hand, and then say there were people carrying guns on the other, but that's what it was like. I honestly didn't feel that threatened, no one ever threatened me personally in there. Upstairs Nick Grayson would be playing stuff like 'Acid Rock', downstairs The Jam MCs were playing, and then you'd

---

* *Freaky Dancing*, an irreverent fanzine started by Haçienda regulars, was aimed at people queuing to get into the club, the queue being so long now that clubbers had time to read a fanzine. A typical issue mocked up a cartoon of Happy Mondays' Bez on the TV quiz show *Blockbusters*, asking host Bob Holness, "Can I have an 'E', please Bob?"

go through to 'the caves'. We did get quite Balearic in there, which is probably why our room wasn't as packed as the others. Our crowd were slightly more dressy, with white jeans and long hair, which was another reason why some people probably didn't like us.

JUSTIN ROBERTSON: Konspiracy was great. I know a lot of people found it intimidating but I really enjoyed it. I was quite fearless when I was younger, I'm not sure I would enjoy that atmosphere quite so much now. The sound was harder there; if we played something too Balearic or fluffy they would throw cans at you. There was a cage around the decks so you didn't actually get hit. I remember saying to Greg Fenton one night, "Watch this," and I put on 'The Whole Of The Moon' by The Waterboys and then ducked, and sure enough several cans came whistling through the air.

★

After the success of 'Pacific State', 808 State signed a record deal with Paul Morley and Trevor Horn at ZTT Records. They went on to release four albums on ZTT, *Ninety*, *ex:el*, *Gorgeous* and *Don Solaris*, the first two of which went gold.

DARREN PARTINGTON: When we signed to ZTT they were telling us how they wanted to turn Derrick May [aka Rhythim Is Rhythim] and Marshall Jefferson [Chicago and deep house musician] into the black Pet Shop Boys. When we first played 'Cubik' to Trevor Horn, the look on his face was surreal. He'd just come off a boat with Rod Stewart, and he's now in a little studio with us four, and we played him 'Cubik' and he was like, "What the fucking hell?.... *how?!*"

ANDREW BARKER: ZTT went through Warners, so we used to go to Warners now and again to do press days. We went in to see Rob Dickens, the head, and he was sat there in his office, with his bike in the corner, and said to us, "I can't believe we've got a hit with a tuned fart." That was what 'Cubik' sounded like to him, a tuned fart.

DARREN PARTINGTON: What was great about that time was we got to meet loads of people we admired and respected, like Frankie Bones in New York or Derrick May, and it was mutual. They would tell us they admired us. When we signed to Warners in America, through Tommy Boy, they said, "Right dickheads, we want you to turn this acid house into John, Paul, George and Ringo and put a show on." They wanted to package us up and bring us on tour to the States. We didn't want to be The Beatles, we wanted to look like Earth, Wind & Fire, with loads of banks of keyboards and mad lasers. We wanted to be Manchester's Earth, Wind & Fire.

So we had to go over and do this coast to coast tour, and by the time we came back we were a proper band. But we were an acid house band. We had a computer on stage, with a fucking mouse and everything, and we were proud of that, we were proud that we went out live as a band, but we were an electronic acid house band and didn't pretend to be something we weren't.

Everywhere we went – Chicago, San Francisco – they put mad, elaborate parties on for us. We were like, "How the fuck do you know about us?" But in a way they weren't welcoming us, they were welcoming British acid house to America – we just happened to be the first people off the plane.

BILL BREWSTER: The first time I properly got acid house was at Troll, which is a club no-one really talks about. I went to Troll every week and the whole of our lives revolved around the club until it closed in August or September 1992. Troll was amazing, it was fucking incredible. The DJs were Daz Saund, an Asian kid from Leicester who became quite a well-known techno DJ later on, and Marc Andrews. But we weren't too bothered who the DJs were at that stage. I didn't know any gay DJs then, but subsequently I've met and interviewed quite a few and loads of them have told me that Troll was their temple. When I interviewed Klaus Stockhausen, one of the guys who was instrumental in introducing acid house to Germany, he told me, "Whenever I came to London, I always went to Troll." I'm sure Shoom was just as amazing, but I didn't go to Shoom, I went to Troll. Troll was my baptism. I also went to another gay club called Attitude, which was in Shepherd's Bush. A guy called George Mitchell who was in The Sharp Boys DJed there.

★

In London, Laurence Malice and Tim Stabler founded new gay club Trade – an offshoot of Troll – in 1990. Trade was pioneering because it opened its doors at 4a.m. on Sunday morning and stayed open until 1p.m. on Sunday afternoon.

BILL BREWSTER: Trade was opened off the back of Troll, and when Trade opened we used to go straight [there] when Troll finished at 3a.m. and stay until Christ knows what time, and then go back to someone's house and stay up all night. Trade wasn't as hard as people think. I went to the first night and the warm-up DJ was Smokin Jo and for the first few hours she was playing emotive New York garage. It was only later in the night that it got harder.

Acid house wouldn't have happened the way it did without ecstasy, definitely not. A lot of great music movements have a drug associated with them. Northern soul had speed, reggae had weed, acid house had ecstasy. Once you took ecstasy you wanted to dance to house music all night. I don't know fucking why. I can't explain it scientifically, and you can't really explain it to anyone who hasn't taken it. That first night I took it, I was completely blown away and became an evangelist. I would go round telling all my friends who hadn't had an epiphany yet: "You have *got* to come with me. You have *got* to come to Troll and you've *got* to do an E." I took one of my best mates from Hull down to Troll and gave him an E. He was sat down and we were like, "Do you think it's all right? Shall we check on him?" and I went over and said, "Are you OK?" It was the first E he'd ever done and he was really rushing, and looked like he wasn't enjoying it, but he just looked up and said, "It's not going to stop anytime soon is it?"

After that we were mad for it. Some aspects of it frightened me a little bit. One of my mates became a drug dealer for about a year, and some of my mates would go round to someone's house after the club on a Saturday and would still be up doing drugs on Monday morning, when they should have been going to work. That frightened me a bit. All of those people who really went for it burned themselves out quite quickly, and within a few years had given everything up.

I withdrew slightly and I always managed to go home at some point on Sunday, and go home and become 'normal' again. Then the whole rigmarole would begin again on Thursday.

★

In March, Happy Mondays, the first guitar band to fully embrace acid house, played their biggest gig to date.

SHAUN RYDER: G-MEX was the biggest venue in Manchester at the time, and when someone first suggested we should play there, [concert promoter] Simon Moran wasn't convinced we could sell it out. That's why we ended up doing it in-house and putting it on ourselves. Two pals of ours – Jimmy Sherlock, who everyone knows as Jimmy Muffin, and John Kenyon, who everyone called John The Phone – promoted it. They had a company called Nighttime Promotions, and they used to do all our merchandise as well, because we used to do all our own merch.

It did seem a little bit scary doing the G-MEX because it was a big jump up from the Free Trade Hall, which was the biggest venue in Manchester we'd done up to then. That's how quickly things had exploded for us. At the end of 1989 we did the Free Trade Hall, which was 2,000, and then at the start of 1990 we're doing the G-MEX, which was 10,000. We missed out doing those middle-sized venues like The Apollo. Outside Manchester, it was an even bigger jump – we'd gone from doing 500-capacity venues to arenas. We missed out your Apollos and stuff that's about 3–4,000 capacity, so it was quite a jump. The Manchester Arena wasn't built then, but now we've played that – if I go back to the G-MEX it looks small because the arena is twice the size. But at the time, playing G-MEX was a massive thing. It was the biggest venue in Manchester and bands like us just didn't play there.

Although it was a bit of a step up, we were well up for doing it, even though Moran thought we wouldn't sell it. Jimmy Muffin and John

The Phone got on the case with putting it on sale and promoting it, and next thing they turned round to us and said, "Look, we've done this, it's happening. Sold out. We're going to put a second night on sale." Which must have made Moran sit up and take notice, because [Muffin and Phone] weren't even promoters, really – they were ticket touts and merch sellers, and Muffin had promoted at The Thunderdome. But they knew what would sell at street level because they were tuned in to the vibe on the street and were confident it would sell out, and they were right.

As usual, we made a little bit of extra dough on top as well, especially after it sold out. I don't remember this, but Andy Spinoza said in *City Life* magazine that he stopped me on Deansgate the afternoon of the gig and tried to grab a quick interview with me, but I told him I didn't have time because I still had some tickets to get rid of for that night's gig. We were still definitely touting our own gigs at that stage, although I would have thought we would have had someone else, a grafter like John The Duck, who used to do merchandise and stuff for us, out on the street doing it.

We stayed at the Midland Hotel the weekend of the gigs, which is just across the road from the G-MEX. We knew there was potential for trouble if a lot of our fans managed to book rooms in there, or just even get in the doors. We knew there would be trouble, and the hotel would get robbed or whatever. We really tried to warn the hotel but they didn't take any notice. We said to them, "You want to watch who you let rooms to, and who you let in the door," because we didn't want it all to come back on our toes if it had nothing to do with us, because we'd been blamed before for the behaviour of our fans. By this time, we'd had police coming to see us about some of our fans and we were like, "What can we do? We don't know anything about it." I'm sure when Elvis played Vegas, if something got robbed the cops didn't drag bloody Elvis in and question him about the behaviour of his fans, or ask him about this firm or that firm, y'know what I mean?

So we'd been down to the Midland beforehand and actually had a meeting with them and stressed, "Watch who you sell rooms to, and watch who comes through the door, and we want you to know these people have got nothing to do with us." But they didn't listen. They just said, "Oh, it'll be fine, we've had The Who and Frank Zappa here and that was no problem." We tried to tell them that The Who is nothing compared to our lot, but they just didn't listen.

There wasn't an official after-show at the hotel or anything, but inevitably everyone piled back there. Bez probably invited hundreds of people back. The bar got rinsed and someone, I think it might have been Bobby Gillette, threw a champagne bottle or something, which smashed a mirror. The place got trashed. There were glass cases in the lobby with watches and jewellery in, and they all got robbed. Someone just opened them up, and took everything.

After the gigs, of course, someone from the Midland rang up complaining to us and we just said, "It's nothing to do with us, check with your Area Manager or whoever because we fucking warned you this could happen."

It's all a bit of a blur to me, though everyone says they were top gigs. I remember Eric Barker came on at the end of 'Wrote For Luck', whistling into the mic, and then Fonzo Buller* was giving it, "Manchester vibes in the area," although I think he said, "Happy Mondays in the area" that time. You couldn't stop Fonzo getting up on stage.

★

After Happy Mondays' huge gig/rave at G-MEX, The Stone Roses went one bigger by organising a huge outdoor gig at reclaimed toxic waste site Spike Island, in Widnes, Cheshire, on 27 May, 1990. Instead of booking support bands they booked DJs, as they wanted it to feel like a rave. The event was attended by 27,000 people and at the time was deemed somewhat of a failure due to sound issues. Since then, however, it has taken on a legendary status.

---

* Alfonso 'Fonzo' Buller was part of MVITA, a collective/group that took its name from Fonzo's catchphrase, "Manchester Vibes In The Area!", which was a call to arms heard regularly in The Haçienda and at other Manchester events during this period. It would also be used at parties or gigs in other cities or countries where a large Manchester contingent was present ("in the area").

DAVE HASLAM: The Stone Roses captured the wistfulness of Sixties bands like The Byrds, but in their music and at their gigs they also wanted that surging euphoric club buzz. So they decided that instead of support bands for Spike Island they would get a couple of their favourite DJs to play. They asked me because they used to come and hear me play at my regular night at The Haçienda, and they also asked Dave Booth, who had a psychedelic night at a Manchester club called The Playpen, which had previously been George Best's club Slack Alice and is today called 42nd Street.

When we got to Spike Island, the DJ set-up was 80 yards from the stage on a rickety tower, which was also home to the mixing desk and lighting desk. From the tower I could see the queues and what looked like acres of baggy jeans and T-shirts. Spike Island attracted a young crowd. People had travelled from all over, like pilgrims. Lives were being shaped.

To this day I'm convinced the Roses had asked Gareth to book Frankie Knuckles, but we got Frankie Bones. I can imagine his logic: he's American, he's called Frankie, and he's cheaper than the Knuckles bloke. Mr Bones got on the microphone, drawling that he was honoured to be in Wigan (Wigan? Someone had misplaced his atlas!) and giving shout-outs to 'Noo Yawk City'. The crowd were unimpressed, but slowly, collectively, us DJs began raising the atmosphere, with The Jam MCs working their magic and Fonzo ('MVITA') Buller rasping out his war cry, "Manchester Vibes In The Area". I remember by the time I played 'Cubik' by 808 State, the crowd were kicking up dust, dancing, a sea of [Roses' drummer] Reni hats and floppy-haired happiness.

★

That June, the FIFA World Cup took place in Italy. Salford's very own New Order were chosen to write England's official World Cup song and somehow managed to get away with an acid house-infused track that had the chorus, "We're singing for England" (or for those who got the reference, "sing 'E' for England"). 'World In Motion', which featured the 1990 England football squad and a rap from attacking midfielder John Barnes, was a massive hit, becoming New Order's only number one single.

Guardian journalist and football fan Ed Vulliamy noticed the mood had changed from the European Championships, just two years earlier:

> Unlike Germany in '88, the fans were bringing their lives with them this time: their daft T-shirts, their daft haircuts, their cassette tapes, their silly dancing. A few even brought girls along too. Acid House was a new ingredient: smiley banners draped the stadium railings. In the absence of lager, marijuana became a common match-day refreshment in the campsites and on the terraces.

At that year's Glastonbury music festival, at the end of the same month, sound systems like DIY and Tonka (DJ Harvey's sound system) made their first appearance, bringing house music to Glastonbury for the first time.

SHAUN RYDER: I'd been to other festivals before, but I'd never been to Glastonbury. I wasn't interested in the whole mystical side of it, and the ley lines and all that bollocks. To be honest, it wasn't a completely jolly experience for me. It rained, so it was muddy, but that didn't bother me much, apart from I didn't want to get my trainers muddy.

I spent almost the whole time on the tour bus. I didn't even go to the dressing room. Glastonbury in 1990 was still quite basic, it was closer to what it must have been like in the Seventies than to what it's like now. When I went back recently to headline with Gorillaz [in 2010] it was a completely different experience.

Back in 1990 we had a sleeper bus, but I also booked into a hotel so I could get off site for a bit. When I was on site I spent most of my time underneath our bus, in the luggage hold. You know when you have a panel on the side of the coach that lifts up and there's a big hold underneath for everyone's bags and stuff? I spent most of Glastonbury in there with about 20 other smackheads. We seemed to spend most of the weekend under the bus, in the hold, just smoking gear. Stick a gram on a piece of tin foil, smoke that; stick another gram on a piece of tin foil, smoke that. Just smoking constantly. It was a mad scene. We ended up with more and more of us under there because someone would have to go and get some more gear and they would come back with a few more hangers on.

My mam's got this great photograph on the wall of her kitchen which is taken from the back of the stage at Glastonbury while we're playing. You can see the back of me, and my Armani jeans, and then the whole of the audience and the tents behind them, a great crowd shot. I can't really remember much of the actual performance though, because I was so numb from the heroin. I think the most exciting part of the weekend for me was taking the bird back to the hotel for a bit.

Some of our lot were selling backstage passes as well, which we just turned a blind eye to. They were making copies from our backstage passes and banging them out. We also had people selling snide merchandise as well as the official stalls. Basically, you couldn't stop people selling snide merchandise, so you might as well sell it yourself. We wanted both ends of the market. So we had a few lads out there working, and what they would do is when they had made a certain amount of dough, they would go and bury it or stash it somewhere. One of our lot, John The Phone, was kidnapped. This biker crew – I don't know if they were actual Hells Angels but they were a heavy biker crew – kidnapped John and took him to this disused farmhouse nearby. They tied him up and had him in there for nearly two days, slapping him and torturing him, but you've got to give it to the little fucker, he told them nothing. So eventually they just let him go. He had a fair few cuts and bruises and I think they'd shaved a bit of his hair off, but he just brushed it off, went to the place where he'd stashed the last of his money, got it and brought it back to the bus.

We got asked to leave [Glastonbury] in the end because our lot had brought it a bit on top. They realised how many backstage passes we'd knocked out and in the end security surrounded our bus and made us leave the site.

★

In July, Graham Bright MP's Increased Penalties Bill was passed. The penalty for organising an illegal event was raised to a £20,000 fine and six months in prison.

On 21 July, 836 ravers were arrested and detained at the Love Decade party held at Gildersome in Yorkshire. It still remains one of the biggest mass arrests ever in British history. Only eight people were actually charged in the end.

DREW HEMMENT: Everyone was looking for the party, every week – is it on, is it not? And there wasn't a party for a few weeks. The first one after that was Gildersome, one that I [organised]. I found the venue in a horse gymkhana in a little valley just north of Leeds and I knew Tommy Smith, so took the venue to them. It took several weeks to plan.

We ended up taking decoy convoys over there on the night. When we eventually arrived, the police had beat us to it, so a line of us [party-goers] charged them. I knew a back way into the venue, so I led hundreds of people round the back way, and when we got in there the police were already taking down the decks and taking the PA apart. Someone just shouted, "Charge!" and we just charged these police and they got out of there. So we were left with half a PA and no decks, so I got a lift back to Leeds to get my spare set of decks, brought them back and got them wired off, and the event actually went off in the end.

But I lost my faith a little that night. I was young and idealistic and I lost a bit of my faith in some of the other people in the scene after that, because it became clear to me there was a core of people organising the parties who were really into the money. I had put my own money into making it happen, and people were getting charged on the door and there were bin liners full of cash that went somewhere, but I never saw any of it. After that it all got a bit dark. Up until Nelson [*see* pages 206–7], there was a regular income for everyone who was involved in putting on the parties, and that's fine, because they did take a lot of work, but after that it seemed like people were just in it for the money. I had organised collection boxes for a hospice for Leeds, and they also went missing on the night.

★

Greater Manchester Police had attempted to shut down The Haçienda after the previous summer's tragic death. The Haçienda employed George Carman GQ to fight its case.

MIKE PICKERING: Even now I don't think Factory could have done much more to stop it. They couldn't do anything. They were getting no help from the police, and you just can't deal with all those gang problems on your own. You couldn't really bring in a firm from outside to run the door at that stage. I remember The Thunderdome trying to bring in an outside firm to run the door, they brought in a firm of Scousers, and they just did a drive by and shot them. I think three of them got hit.

★

While the mood on the dance floor was growing ever gloomy, the law was closing in. On 12 August, the amendment to the 1988 Criminal Justice Act came into force. If convicted, organisers of illegal parties already faced six months in jail and a £20,000 fine. Now that penalty was increased to seizure of their profits (provided they exceed £10,000), if they were convicted of breaching licensing laws.

At the end of September, the Home Secretary, David Waddington, attended and addressed the Police Superintendents' Association conference, where there were calls for increased powers to deal with acid house parties. On 7 October, 1990, a police officer whose beat included the village of the Home Secretary collapsed and died on a canal bank beside a disused mill at Barnoldswick, Lancashire, during a police operation to stop a party. Five people were arrested for public order offences after organising the illegal party at Barnoldswick and another at a disused building in Accrington. In response, missiles were thrown at the police station in Barnoldswick.

The same night, at another acid house party in Liverpool, 13 men were arrested after clashes with 70 police in riot gear who had surrounded a derelict block of flats in Huyton, barricaded by 200 party-goers, some of whom threw missiles. *The Guardian* reported: "Police said men were preventing women inside a flat from leaving. The siege ended after two hours when the men let the women go."

SASHA: There was a certain period around the winter of 1989/1990 when I went a good few months without any gigs and I was definitely on the verge of having to sell my decks and get a real job. And then

The Haçienda shut down around the same time and I think a lot of us thought, "Fucking hell, that's it. It's gone, it's finished. Oh well, we've had a good two years, suppose it's time to get a proper job."

Then there was a big turning point for me, during the explosion of raves towards the end of 1990. As Blackburn was getting shut down, the rest of the country started doing a lot of big illegal events, and I remember one in particular, which was probably the one that put me on the map. Both myself and Jon DaSilva were booked to play this festival called Lifestyle 2000, on Christmas Eve 1990. By that time I'd taken a rap over the knuckles from Jon for playing all his big records before he went on, and we were doing a few gigs together and I'd learned how to do a warm-up set and got used to doing that. But Jon couldn't make this gig for some reason, so I went on my own and I got to play all the monster tunes. The people in the Midlands hadn't really heard all that music, all those massive Haçienda anthems, so I got to take all the glory and it absolutely put me on the map. After that I think I pretty much got booked every weekend to play in the Midlands, and things like Eclipse and Shelley's Laserdome in Stoke all came off the back of that, and by 1991 it had all started to take off.

When I started at Shelley's, The Haçienda was closed so everyone was absolutely gagging for it. I'd made a name for myself in Blackpool and Birmingham, so Stoke was kind of a perfect place for me since it was smack bang in the middle of the two, so right from the off we had a thousand or a couple of thousand of people outside trying to get in, and it just got bigger and bigger and crazier and crazier.

★

In October, the free party sound system Spiral Tribe held their first squat party, Detention, at an abandoned school house in London. They would go on to become one of the most influential soundsystems of the Nineties. On 24 November, 284 people were arrested as the police raided the Mad Hatters' Tea Party in Burnley, Lancashire.

KEN TAPPENDEN: In the rural areas in particular, we didn't know what had hit us. But I was determined it wasn't going to carry on. On a

Monday morning after a party on Saturday night, we could find people comatose in hedges, in ditches, in people's gardens. Their parents would ring up the police looking for them and we would try and protect the kids sometimes, we wouldn't tell their parents it was drugs, we would tell them they were exhausted through dancing. But I went to these parties and there is no way you can dance for 12 or 16 hours continuously, surrounded by fairgrounds and coloured lights, without getting out of your pram in some way.

In the end, we have 30 people working in the unit. Then Raindance rang me and told me they were bonking one of my secretaries and getting information from her. They were laughing, saying, "We're fucking one of your secretaries, Ken. You've got nothing secret there, she's told us everything..." She was pretty, to be fair.

I don't think a lot of the organisers, people like Raindance or whoever, realised quite how professional they were at organising their events. Hardly anyone had mobile phones, so it was all organised via public call boxes at the side of the road, and yet they could mobilise 10,000 to 15,000 people. Not only that, but they could do that and evade the police a lot of the time. We had radios, which we could talk to each other on, although they were intermittent and not as good as the ones the police have today. But we did have radio contacts, and yet [the party organisers] could outwit us. They could outwit the police, the fire service and all the local authorities responsible.

CHAPTER 10

Coming Down

"Pretending not to see his gun, I said, 'Let's go out and have some fun.'"
'The Perfect Kiss', New Order

On 3 January, 1991, The Haçienda won a licence reprieve for a further six months. As Wilson wrote in his 2002 book, *24 Hour Party People: What The Sleevenotes Never Tell You*:

> The real problem with The Haçienda was it was still not making money, even before they tightened the door. There were huge crowds and a great atmosphere, but it was all fuelled by ecstasy, not alcohol. We were spending money on the staff, the building, the DJs and the sound system, but most of the money spent by the revellers went to the drug dealers. And guess what? They didn't pass the money on to Wilson and Gretton.

Even the DJs, with their pulling power, weren't making any money. "We were still on about £40 a night," says Haslam. "The only people making money were the drug dealers."

On 26 January, The Haçienda's new head of security was threatened by a gunman with an automatic gun. "Someone who was turned away by a bouncer went back and got a machine gun," recounts New Order's

Bernard Sumner. "He chased the bouncer through the club, cornered him by one of the fire escapes and pulled the trigger, but the gun jammed. That cost us a lot.

"The head doorman was chased out of the club by an Asian kid holding an Uzi. The doorman ran out of the back door, jumped into his car, sped home to London and never came back. Poor bastard. That ended everything. The other doorman packed up and left too. Now we had no bouncers. Clearly we were fucked."

At an emergency meeting the next day, the decision was taken to close The Haçienda voluntarily, temporarily. Not everyone agreed. Factory director Rob Gretton was against the idea. The leader of Manchester City Council, Graham Stringer, and the Greater Manchester Police were also against the idea.

On Wednesday, 30 January, Wilson called a press conference on the Haçienda dancefloor to announce the club's decision:

> The Haçienda is closing its doors as of today. It is with the greatest reluctance that for the moment we are turning the lights out on what is, for us, a most important place. We are forced into taking this drastic action in order to protect our employees, our members and our clients. We are quite simply sick and tired of dealing with instances of personal violence… When we opened The Haçienda, we never thought we'd have to deal with the sort of people we've had to. We hope, we must believe, we can re-open The Haçienda in a better climate. But until we are able to run the club in a safe manner, and in a way the owners believe will guarantee the role of The Haçienda at the heart of the city's community, it is with great sadness that we will shut our club.

MIKE PICKERING: I'd had enough by then because I'd been threatened personally when I was playing. My guest list got smaller and smaller, because I used to have my sisters and friends on there, but I stopped them from coming. It got to the stage where people were getting mugged at knifepoint in the toilets, and I'm not having my sisters and my brother-in-law coming in the club when that's going on. I said, "Just don't come anymore." It had got lawless. Pete Hadfield and

Keith Blackburn, my management from Deconstruction, came down to the club for a night out and ended up banging on the door of the DJ booth, saying, "Fucking hell, let us in here, we're not staying out there, it's horrible." It was terrible. Such a shame.

JEREMY TAYLOR: Fun City, the club, always used to work quite well – that was quite good at making money. But all the problems with gangsters and police got too much with the parties. You were trying to run a business but you had so much to work with. It wasn't just whether you could put on a good event, it was all these other factors, and that's the bit which got to us in the end. We would make a lot of money on one event and then the next event would be stopped by the police or we would have problems with gangsters trying to steal the money. Then one of our security guards was shot dead and I thought, 'Do you know what? I don't actually need all this.' What happened was he stopped someone selling tickets at an event which they'd stolen from a record shop in north London. They'd had a bit of a fight outside the event. Then a couple of months later, after I'd stopped working with the guy, there was a sort of revenge attack, where these guys turned up at whatever nightclub he was working at, walked in with guns, and they just shot at him in front of everyone. He was trying to escape and fell off a balcony on to some railings below, so it was a pretty nasty end.

I did it from 1988 and then stopped in 1992, and there were a lot of gangsters and drug dealers around towards the end. All I wanted to do was put an event on, and make it fantastic fun, and have the best music and the best lights and all of that. I didn't want to get involved with any of the other stuff but it always ended up getting in the way.

RICHARD NORRIS: I think the halcyon period had finished by the end of 1990, when it became a bit darker. I think with all dance music scenes you get a few great records and a few great clubs, and then countless copies of those records and clubs, and then it should mutate into something else. Which it did, with the advent of clubs like Rage at Heaven, as harder versions of garage evolved into drum'n'bass and two-step and onwards. So I would say probably by 1990 it had started to change. I'm sure some purists would say by April 1988, but I think by 1990.

MEKON (JOHN GOSLING), DJ: I used to DJ at Biology and I went to a few of the other larger raves. A lot of people loved all that and everything that came with it, driving round the M25, chasing the party and dancing in fields, and it was really interesting, but I always prefer a club. Give me a dark, smelly basement over a field any day. I just prefer music in that smaller environment; I don't like festivals or big gigs either.

The honeymoon period of acid house finished quite soon for me. I'm always keen to move on to the next thing anyway, but I didn't like it when it became too big – I never like any scene when it becomes too big; I prefer to just keep moving forwards on to the next thing. If you want to go and dance in a field, fine, go and have a mental time, but I got bored of it after a couple of years. It became too commercialised. I can only do the same thing for so long before it becomes boring.

If you look at what it's become now, what they call EDM [electronic dance music], surely the [original acid house] DJs who are still playing and have started playing to those crowds are bored stupid. But maybe they're getting paid so much money that it dulls the pain. If you're being offered £50,000 or £100,000 a gig then it must be very hard to turn down, but I can't see any merit in it creatively.

LUKE HOWARD, DJ: I loved the initial explosion of acid house, and I grew a ponytail and became a raver, but that didn't last very long for me. Once it became huge and the big warehouse raves started it lost its appeal for me. Not because it had become popular or anything, it was more that I didn't want to take drugs anymore, so I was less interested in spending all night chasing the party around. I had the ecstasy experience for a while, and then I didn't really feel I needed to keep having it because I was so into the music and dancing anyway.

The music had also got harder and a bit brasher, I didn't like the way it had gone. We used to really take the piss out of it, you know that 'We Call It Acieed'; we thought it was a bit of a joke.

So I started to seek out different types of nights, like High On Hope, and I was much more into that mix of house music and disco music which was all about dancing and sweating and getting a release, but not in that very formulaic way that the raves were. When you watch some of those videos of those big fairground raves they look ridiculous.

What acid house did was get rid of a lot of the pretentiousness of nightclubbing. You could wear what you wanted all of a sudden, although there was a kid of acid house uniform that developed.

KEN TAPPENDEN: I really made an art of studying the social interactions side of it, and trying to control it that way, as opposed to using police power, because police power was ineffective. [That tactic] was years ahead of its time, and it got a lot of response from the organisers. I even held a few lunches for all the organisers of the parties at Gravesend police station.

I got to know the party organisers, although they weren't friends of mine. I know this sounds awful, but when I invited them to a lunch, there was always one or two I wanted to nick, so they would all come to the lunch but two of them might not go home afterwards! I would invite them to lunch and say, "I want you to run lawful pay parties. You're going to have electricity, you're going to have toilets, you're going to have health and safety, you're going to be in control of your event and you're going to look after young people... and if you can't do that then you're not having a party." A lot of them started to come on board because they could see it was the only way forward. So much so that when I retired from the police in 1992, Raindance even offered me a job as an adviser, to help them run legal parties.

By then we had driven it underground, and the worst thing we ever did was drive it underground because then the real violence came in. There were incidents of knee capping, smashing up of premises... A lot of the villains were using guns and took money off some of the young organisers. If you speak to people like Wayne Anthony, they were shit scared, and some of them are still scared now.

★

231

By 1991, Paul Staines, who Tony Colston-Hayter had presumably enlisted to help with his PR and lead the Freedom To Party campaign, was UK Secretary-General of the International Society For Human Rights and the editor of the *Human Rights Defenders Briefing Papers*, a series of six papers. He wrote a paper for the Libertarian Alliance entitled 'Acid House Parties Against The Lifestyle Police And Safety Nazis':

> Imagine a regime so totalitarian that it will not allow its young citizens to dance when they want. Imagine that this regime introduced a law which banned dance parties unless they were authorised by the state, and even then the parties would only be allowed of limited duration and on state-licensed premises. Naturally this regime would, in line with its ideology, only apply these laws to parties held for profit.
>
> The populist pro-government newspapers would of course launch a propaganda campaign against what it would call 'evil dance party organisers'. The pro-government press would conduct a hysterical smear campaign, describing the party organisers as 'criminals'.
>
> In order to combat the 'subversive profiteering free-market dance party entrepreneurs' the state would from Lifestyle Police. Using undercover agents, they would infiltrate the parties, discover where they were to take place and then, using helicopters and roadblocks, they would try to prevent the parties going ahead, by turning away thousands of dissident party-goers and arresting the organisers.
>
> This is truly a regime of which Stalin or Hitler himself would be proud, implementing socialist policies to protect the citizens from their own 'moral weaknesses'.
>
> Sadly, the above is not a fantasy, it is based on reality. In Britain in 1990 all this happened, not under a communist regime, but under an increasingly authoritarian Conservative government. What the tabloid press called the 'acid house party' generated a momentum for yet more restrictions on our civil liberties.

After including examples of who he deemed to be 'lifestyle police', including the National Viewers' and Listeners' Association and Mary

Whitehouse, 'the Lifestyle Policewoman par excellence', his slightly confused paper concluded:

> Uptight Conservatives are probably the people who would benefit most from taking drugs, particularly Thatcherites, with their machine-like obsession with efficiency and abstract attachment to the freedom to make money. I'm as much a believer in Capitalism as the most earnest of Young Conservatives, but couldn't we put acid in the punch at the YC ball and then really have a party?

PAUL ROBERTS: The Haçienda lost something from 1990 onwards for me. The gangs had started to creep in and the special atmosphere had gone. [K-Klass] were on the road a lot by that time, and I'd moved to Liverpool because my girlfriend at the time was at John Moores University so I thought I'd have a crack at living with her, rather than living at home with my mum and dad. So I started hanging out there more, and going to Quadrant Park, which was taking off and was a bit of a lunatic asylum. The energy levels in that place were fucking ridiculous. The DJs were John Kelly, Andy Carroll, Mike Knowler and James Barton, who was a young up-and-coming DJ. James had already ran his own nights at The Underground, and then became part-owner of it, at the age of 19. James was basically a very industrious young man who was always destined to do what he went on to do, which was build his own company, Cream, and sell it for millions of pounds.*

Our very first manager was a guy called Steve Williams, who never really gets mentioned. He was a really big part of the early Manchester scene. It was Steve who taught Sasha to mix. He really believed in the early scene but got very quickly disillusioned when it went commercial,

---

* Cream was launched at The Nation in Liverpool in October 1992 by James Barton, Darren Hughes and Andy Carroll. Paul Bleasdale was the main resident DJ. It became one of the biggest superclub brands in the world, not just another night out but a lifestyle that attracted thousands of dance music devotees and the best DJs from across the globe.

and basically sold his records to Sasha and stopped DJing. When that happened, Eric Barker took over as our manager.

At the end of 1990, we played Quadrant Park in Liverpool and James Barton really liked what we did. James was quite blunt and said, "Listen, Eric's great at what he does but he's taken you as far as he's going to take you." Then there was an incident in Brighton where we had hired a van from Salford Van Hire and he parked it outside the club on double yellow lines and I said, "Eric, you can't leave the van there." He said, "Yes I can, it's got 'Salford' on the side, no fucker will touch it." Lo and behold, we walked out of the venue later and saw it disappearing down the road on the back of a flat-bedded truck.

RUSS MORGAN: There was a similar incident when we were playing a gig in London around the same time, although I think it was a van from Manchester Van Hire that time. We were stuck in horrendous traffic somewhere near Marble Arch and Eric just lost it and went, "Fuck this!" and just pulled out into oncoming traffic and started driving up the middle of the road. People were beeping and shouting, and Eric just leaned out of the window and shouted, "Fuck off, can't you see what's written on the side here? We're from fucking Manchester!"

PAUL ROBERTS: Eric was brilliant, he took us from being a bunch of clueless idiots to being semi-organised. But James and a guy called Andy Carroll got interested, and at that stage we had the first version of 'Rhythm Is A Mystery', which really got them onside and really interested in us. 'Rhythm' was quite an underground sounding Detroit techno thing at first, much more minimal. We released that on Creed, through Eastern Bloc, and sold a ridiculous amount of records and weren't far off the Top 40. I think it sold about 30,000 or even 40,000. So anyway, James and Andy heard 'Rhythm Is A Mystery' and said we want to take you to another level.

John Berry had already suggested we go back in and make a more commercial version of it because he thought it really had legs. Mike Pickering had just started playing all the big Italian house records, so we were influenced by that. None of us had written lyrics before so we went out and bought *The Guardian* and read the arts section, looking for arty-farty words to use.

RUSS MORGAN: All we'd ever wanted was to hear our record in The Haçienda, and we heard a rumour they were playing it. We were stood up on the balcony and you heard the first tom roll come in and the whole place went up, then arpeggio synth and the place went up again, then the strings came in and the place went up again.

PAUL ROBERTS: The crowd noise was unbelievable. The response to our record was like someone scoring a goal at Wembley. We shit ourselves. We just couldn't believe it. We later heard it was Mike Pickering who had broke it in The Haçienda.

It took ages to organise the release on Deconstruction and then we heard a rumour that one of London's best-known bootleggers was going to put it out himself. So James Barton got on the phone to him and basically explained that we wouldn't be very happy, to say the least, if he put out the bootleg, and let's say James suggested this bootlegger might want to reconsider. Suffice to say the bootleg didn't come out. Rumour is the bloke had even pressed them up already but ditched them after he got that phone call from James.

When it eventually came out, we were hoping it would make the Top 40 because our previous two releases had just missed out, but then we thought, "Nah, it's us, something will go wrong, it always does." Then on the week it came out, Deconstruction rang me up and asked me to give them a seven-inch instrumental mix of the song, and I should have twigged then it was for *Top Of The Pops*. I was in a studio in Liverpool mixing it when I got the call from Deconstruction saying, "We've got your midweek, you've gone in at number 36," and I went, "Fucking great!" They said, "Nah sorry, I'm joking, it's actually number 20." I said, "Fucking hell! You're joking? That's amazing!" Then he said, "Yes, I am joking, you're actually at number six." "WHAT???!!"

I legged it round to the office and James phoned Russ, who had just got in from his post round, and told him, and Russ went, "That's all right, innit?"

James said, "Fucking hell, the postman says being at number six in the charts is 'all right'!"

Then a couple of days later, we were on *Top Of The Pops*, which was just surreal. We were on with Belinda Carlisle, Crowded House and KLF. Everyone else stayed behind for an after-party but we had to get back up north because Russ had his post round to do the next day.

Then we went in to record our debut album, and we'd read about the Mondays' escapades making their albums and we thought, "Well, that's obviously the way to do it," so we recorded it in Manchester and stayed in hotels and just got trashed every night. The recording was just a mess, a total cat's arse. We were up here for months and I don't think we kept one track.

I remember lying around in flowerbeds in Piccadilly Gardens at 5a.m. one morning, pilled up, and deciding to get our own back on John at Eastern Bloc, because we weren't convinced we'd been paid in full for the records we'd sold and we wandered down to the shop, got the number and name of the burglar alarm company from the box outside the shop then rang him up and pretended to be them, saying Eastern Bloc had been broken into. We then hid at the end of Oldham Street, sniggering as we saw him turn up half an hour later, having got up at 5a.m. and driven in from Bolton. I don't think he ever knew it was us... but he does now.

Then we went into the studio later that day and the engineer was reading the *Mirror* or *The Sun* and went, "What??!!" and they'd done a story on us, saying we'd been caught on *Top Of The Pops* doing drugs: "Cheshire rave act K-Klass are in disgrace today after being caught taking drugs on *Top Of The Pops*. A BBC spokesperson said curb your wild antics or you'll never appear on *Top Of The Pops* again."

We thought it was hilarious until the phone calls started, from my mum and my girlfriend's mum. James Barton went mad at me, saying, "This is your fucking fault, you've got a big mouth." Then he rang up the journalist who'd written the piece, Rick Sky, and had a right go at him, telling him it was slanderous and blah blah blah, and asked him where he got his info from, and Rick said, "It was you, James," and it turns out James had smoked a spliff during an interview with him, and told him we'd had a smoke at *Top Of The Pops* and stuff, so it was James' fault.

What 'Rhythm Is A Mystery' did is just take it up to the next level. We started playing huge raves, like Perception in King's Lynn, to 15,000 people. Scotland was always the best though… Ayr Pavilion, Kilmarnock Hippodrome, Metro Salcoats, Colours in Glasgow – all those places were crazy. We've got some video footage of us playing Kilmarnock Hippodrome and it looks like a punk video. There's a kind of mosh pit at the front – at a rave! – with all these kids surging forward. It must have been the biggest health and safety risk ever.

JOHNNO (BUGGED OUT/JOCKEY SLUT)*: The Haçienda's problems led to it closing down for several months in 1990. But it reopened in 1991 with a night called The Healing, and then that summer for me was a really good summer and they had that night called Shine. And 'Rhythm Is A Mystery' by K-Klass came out. It almost felt as good as 1989 for a short period, that was a real joyous period, before it all soured again at The Haçienda, and having not really indulged before, that's when I really started to get involved in the drugs.

MIKE PICKERING: Nowadays clubbing culture is completely different, it's all about guest DJs. So when people go to somewhere like The Warehouse Project, they go to see the guest DJs, they don't go to see the residents. When I was resident DJ, if I heard a great record my first thought would be, "I can't wait to play this at The Haçienda. You put your taste on the line, but the crowd trusted you, they knew what they were going to get. I would break a record by just playing it at peak time. People would come banging on the door asking what it was, and I used to have pieces of paper and a pen and I just used to write the name of the record down, and I knew when they were going

---

* *Jockey Slut* was an acclaimed specialist dance music magazine, launched by John Burgess and Paul Benney in Manchester in 1993. It was sold to Swinstead Publishing in 1999 and closed in 2004. Burgess and Benney were also founders of the club night Bugged Out!

to come banging and asking. I'd see Kenny at Spin Inn on a Monday and he'd say, "Fucking hell, you played that so-and-so track on Saturday, didn't you?" because he'd had a load of orders for it. I knew which new records were going to work most of the time. Almost all of the time. Because I knew the crowd's tastes and they knew mine. We got to know each other.

★

Just six weeks after The Haçienda had reopened, on Saturday, 22 June, a gang was refused entry on the door. They returned later that night and attacked the doorman with knives. Six doormen were stabbed. Two hundred Tactical Aid Group officers, armed with riot shields and CS gas, sealed off the exits to the club, while a helicopter circled ahead. The music was turned off and the crowd was eventually led out one by one through a gauntlet of police and riot shields, every face captured by the Greater Manchester Police video unit. Ten men were arrested in the crowd's controlled exit and four, from Salford, were charged with affray and assault.

Two months later, a doorman told Andy Spinoza of *The Face* that one of his colleagues was still off work. "He's had enough. He was stabbed five times and his lung is still leaking. That's enough for anybody, isn't it?"

MIKE PICKERING: The police all piled in the club and one copper came in the DJ booth and took the needle off my record and I went fucking ballistic, shouting, "Don't you ever touch my record!" He just said "Have you got a mic?" I said, "What do you think it is? 1985?" But they went and found a mic from somewhere and made an announcement to the club. Then we had to walk out of the club through this line of police and they were all banging their truncheons on their riot shields, and there was a helicopter overhead with its searchlight on. I remember turning and looking back at this line of police with their riot shields and the helicopter circling, and it looked like that Alan Bleasdale play about the police state [*GBH*], and I just thought this is over... this is definitely over.

BILL BREWSTER: That first period, the kind of halcyon days, ends in September 1991 for me. The reason is that prior to that, everyone was playing similar kinds of records. DJs had their own sound and their own signature records, but they were all drawing from roughly the same pool. After September 1991, it started splitting up and you got hardcore, the beginnings of drum'n'bass, techno got harder. The mood had changed as well. I didn't feel much peace and love when I went to the hardcore clubs like Roast and Rage on Thursday nights in Heaven. They were pretty scruffy and hard clubs. It also felt like there was more of a nihilistic edge to the drug taking, which reminded me of the way people were drinking in Grimsby, where I come from. I don't want to slate people in Grimsby, because I'm sure it's not just Grimsby, but there was a side to the drinking I saw there which was really destructive, and I started to see a similar nihilistic edge in some of the clubs in London. It didn't feel like anybody was celebrating on the dance floor in those places. Some of them looked like they were in a gym doing something they thought would make them stronger and better, which they didn't particularly enjoy.

Part of the problem was possibly that the drugs weren't as good. When I first started going out, you had one E and it lasted you the whole fucking night, and most of the rest of the next day sometimes. By 1992, people were doing several a night and would be like, "Shall we do another one?" and it started to get a bit like taking drugs for drugs' sake. I don't want to make out like I wasn't really doing drugs, because, I was, I just wasn't doing quite as many as some of my friends.

Then cocaine started to creep in. I had never seen cocaine in my life until 1991. When I worked as a chef in the mid Eighties, I worked for a musician in quite a famous live band and he was the first person I knew who was doing cocaine, but I didn't see any until 1991 because it was so far out of the reach of normal people like me. It was a mythical drug that you knew people did, but you'd never seen it. Then all of a sudden in 1991 it came into your orbit and people around you were increasingly doing it, which definitely had an effect on the mood in the clubs. It didn't feel like there was as much celebration going on.

FRED (PSEUDONYM): I got nicked in November 1991 and I got put away in July 1992 and came out in September 1993, so I did 14 months. I got caught with 100 ecstasy pills on me, and then they found another 30 pills in my flat, and I had about half a kilo of puff as well. I got 15 months for 10 ounces, three and a half years for the 100 Es and another three and a half years for the 30 Es, but all sentences were to run concurrent. I didn't know what concurrent meant, so I thought I was going down for eight years – I nearly fucking fainted when the judge read it out.

One of the well-known DJs on the scene knew one of the screws in Wandsworth, so they got me downgraded from a B-cat to a D-cat open nick after a few months, which was amazing. I was in Brixton at first, and then I got sent to Wandsworth, which was a fucking hellhole. It's a massive prison and a really violent place. One Saturday afternoon I was sitting in my cell when the cell door opened and two wing screws came in, and one of them said, "Do you know [name of well known DJ]?" And I said, "Yeah, I do." Then he said, "Well I went to school with him and I can get you out of here. Where do you want to go?" So I got moved to an open prison to serve the rest of my sentence, which was a right result.

GREG FENTON: I think that halcyon period lasted from 1988 to 1991. Towards the end of Most Excellent [at The State in Manchester], the mood definitely changed, and it wasn't so much the change in the drugs as the change in the people coming into the clubs, which increased the violence. We knew who our friends and crowd were, and you started seeing people coming in who dressed differently and were definitely there for different reasons.

When The Haçienda closed temporarily in 1991, we were still running Glitter Baby. Most Excellent at The State was absolutely fine, then it moved to The Brickhouse, which was also fine, and then it moved to The Wiggly Worm, which was originally Peter Stringfellow's club in the Seventies. One night a gang came in, who I think were from Salford, and just started kicking off and belting people, which was horrible. Then one week some people were turned away on the door; they went away, came back shortly afterwards and ram-raided the door. They actually just drove a car into the door of the club. Looking back now that's obviously hard to believe, and it was shocking at the time, but it was another episode in what was becoming a catalogue of violence. It was a real shame, because here was this beautiful thing that a lot of people treasured and it changed their lives for the better, and then a few people ruined it. We were just young and wanted to have an amazing time and play amazing music.

You would hear horrible things weekly from people who worked at The Hacienda... it's not why I got into clubs. In 1991, when The Haçienda closed, that really felt like the end of something. I know some people like to say that the scally element in Manchester contributed this, that and the other to building the scene, and yes, some of them certainly did. But some of them were also hugely responsible for ruining it for everyone, because of the violence.

It was almost ironic for me that I came from Belfast and the Troubles there to all this trouble in Manchester. I think in Belfast you could, for the most part, get on with your own thing and nobody would bother you, even though there may have been things going on around you. In Manchester, in the end, you couldn't get away with your own thing. The kudos for some people, of being able to swan into a club and act however they wanted and do whatever they wanted, was too attractive for some people, and that ruined it for everyone. It's so sad. Even now I feel really sad just talking about it.

ANDREW BARKER: 808 State did a track with Björk so she spent a bit of time hanging out with us in Manchester while we were recording. We were in the Most Excellent that night when Salford ram-raided the door, which was mental... trying to drive a car through the doors of the club! I was sat inside with Björk and she couldn't believe it. She was like, "This city, Manchester, is *crazy!*"

★

Although The Haçienda remained open until 1997, for some, including some of the resident DJs, it was never quite the same after its initial closure. Although it was hardly the only club in Manchester that had suffered at the hands of increasing gang problems across the city. After the press had bandied around the term 'Madchester', a few now began to dub the city 'Gunchester'.

SASHA: Once the Shelley's residency in Stoke kicked off everything seemed to fall into place for me. A lot of people in the music industry, like A&R guys, used to travel up to go to The Haçienda, so when it closed down they used to come to Shelley's instead, and I was hanging out with them and I started getting offered remixes.

It all happened very quickly for me and I wasn't really prepared for it. I don't know if I was necessarily against celebrity DJ culture, I was just very, very shy and just wasn't prepared for what the fuck was going on. I was actually shy to the point of… well, I found it was quite crippling, to be honest. I was a wallflower. I didn't know how to deal with social situations at all. I was very, very insular, and it just really freaked me out. I'd walk into rooms and everyone would know my name and it did my nut in. It took me quite a while to get used to it because I didn't know how to read people back then. I was really young, and I wasn't prepared for it at all, and I certainly hadn't got into it for those reasons. I hadn't got into it thinking I want to be a star and I want to make a lot of money, so all of a sudden I was like, "What the fuck is happening to me?" It was all new. In the South, Oakey and Cox had already been making a name for themselves, but the way things exploded around me, I don't think that had happened before. I was the first DJ on the cover of *Mixmag**, and the whole thing freaked me out. It took me a good two or three years to accept what was happening to me and become comfortable with *me*. Somebody would come up and ask me for an autograph and I'd get pissed off with them because I just couldn't get my head around it.

---

* *Mixmag* was originally launched in 1982, a magazine aimed at DJs. With the advent of acid house it changed its focus to clubs and club culture. In 1991, they put Sasha on the cover and proclaimed him "the first DJ pin-up".

Interior shots of The Hacienda. June 1987.

Hacienda crowd through the smoke. CAMERA PRESS/IAN TILTON

Crowds on the dancefloor of The Hacienda, February 22, 1990. CAMERA PRESS/IAN TILTON

The Hacienda's main dancefloor, 1989. PETER J WALSH/PYMCA

Singer Shaun Ryder (left) of the Happy Mondays with Factory Records boss Tony Wilson at a window surrounded by posters for the band, 1989. KEVIN CUMMINS/GETTY IMAGES

Carl Cox, DJing, 1990s. ROB WATKINS/PYMCA

Mike Pickering (left) and Graeme Park in the DJ booth at the Hacienda. Manchester, 1990. DAVID SWINDELLS/PYMCA

DJ, producer and co-founder of Boys Own, Andrew Weatherall, 1990. JOHN MCMURTRIE /RENTA/PHOTOSHOT

Singer Shaun Ryder of the Happy Mondays climbs on the letter E from the 'Hotel' sign on the roof of the Hotel Subur Maritim, Sitges, Barcelona, during the filming of the video for 'Step On', March 1990. KEVIN CUMMINS/GETTY IMAGES

MR. C: I first met Colin Angus from The Shamen in 1988 at Clink Street, and then he used to come to The Dungeons when we moved there. I also used to see him at these great parties around Bethnal Green that were run by a black gang from the East End called The Run Tings Crew, because they used to 'run tings'.

Anyway, The Shamen had written this track called 'Move Any Mountain' and asked Paul Oakenfold to mix it. They told Paul they wanted a rapper on it, and Paul said, "Well, there's only two rappers on the scene really, there's E-Mix from Clink Street, and Mr. C." E-Mix was more of soulful vibe and I was more of an acid vibe, so Paul said to Angus, "You should really speak to Mr. C," and Angus said, "I don't know why I didn't think of that myself." So he got Charles Cosh, their manager, to approach me. I already knew Charles because he organised a couple of parties out in Stratford and I had DJed at them. So I said "Let me hear the demo."

I really liked the name of the band. I'd first came across the word 'shaman' in 1985 when I read Carlos Castaneda's *The Teachings Of Don Juan: A Yaqui Way Of Knowledge**, and it fascinated me, so I was already really introduced to shamanism. So I really like the name of the band and the way it was spelled differently, with a twist. The vibe was shamanic and the song was positive – it was about being able to move mountains with your own strength, with a subversive tone that was about taking acid. So I really liked the vibe of the song, even though it wasn't black music, which is where I come from. This was a white version of house music but I thought with my involvement it could go a long way, so I was up for being involved.

The name of the track then changed to 'Progen' because there was already a track out called 'Move Any Mountain', although it wasn't an acid house track. 'Progen' was big throughout 1990, and I was also the first person to be asked to remix it. About 20 different people went on

---

* First published in 1968, Carlos Castaneda's *The Teachings Of Don Juan: A Yaqui Way Of Knowledge* was his account of meeting the Yaqui Indian sorcerer Don Juan Matus and learning 'shamanism'. The authenticity of his books have been questioned by some critics.

to remix it, and they eventually put out a whole album of remixes of that one song, called *Progeny*.

I did a few gigs with the group at The Garage, but they already had a DJ called Sticker so there wasn't really a lot of space for me, and my sound was also more urban. They could only afford to pay me £50 to rap at the time and I was getting paid £150 to DJ, and that was my livelihood. I would DJ twice a week and that £300 would pay for my records and give my mum some rent; I come from a very poor family so I couldn't afford to give up DJing at that stage. So Colin used to rap on the tracks when they played live.

Then in 1991, they decided to re-release 'Move Any Mountain' and reshoot the video. We went to Tenerife to shoot the video and while we were there, both Colin and Will asked me to join the band fulltime. I said, "OK, if you're going to cut me in and pay me the money I will lose through not DJing, and let me get involved in production and songwriting, then count me in." Tragically, a week later Will was dead [Sinnott drowned off the coast of La Gomera, days after shooting the video]. At first it was like, "Look, this is over," and Colin said, "Nah, I'm not doing it anymore," because Will was his best mate, you know. I just told him, "Whatever you say, you're the guvnor." It really hit me hard and we were all in mourning. We went ahead with the rerelease of 'Progen/Move Any Mountain' because that's what Will would have wanted. Then we got an influx of mail from our fans that was relentless, saying things like, "Please keep the band going, The Shamen are the most important band there's been ever, there's never been a band before that talks about human evolution, politics, society and altered states of consciousness." So with the pressure from the fans, Colin decided to continue and asked me if I was up for it. I told him he had my full and unequivocal support. He then asked Plavka Lonich [the group's lead singer] if she wanted to continue and she said no, so we then moved on to record the *Boss Drum* album.

★

After the success of 'Loaded', Primal Scream then asked Andrew Weatherall to work on the production of the follow-up album. The album that became *Screamadelica* would, for many, become the defining acid house album. 'Loaded' was the first sign that the combination of the leather-clad Glaswegian rockers and Weatherall had mastered the marriage of acid house and rock'n'roll. But with *Screamadelica*, the band and Weatherall went much further. "'Loaded' taught us about rhythm and space," Bobby Gillespie later reflected. "We've always been good at harmony, but learning how to use a sampler gave us a whole new set of colours." Containing both soaring euphoric highs and melancholic come-down moments, *Screamadelica* was basically an ecstasy album made by people with impeccable record collections, and perfectly captured the mood of a new generation at the start of a new decade, acid house's *Sgt. Pepper's Lonely Hearts Club Band*.

ANDREW WEATHERALL: Even though 'Loaded' had been a big record, neither myself or the band had anything to lose – it was just one single. I think that's what helped [*Screamadelica*] become a great album. There was no PowerPoint demonstration at the beginning of the recording where we planned it all out. They just said, "We've got these songs, we've recorded them as a band and here you go." We didn't sit down and think, "Right, we're forging the future here." It was more, "Ok, we've got a bit of money now, we can afford to go into a slightly better studio." As great as Bark Studio in Walthamstow was, I think they thought if we can make a record like that in a little studio like Bark, imagine what we might be able to do in a slightly big studio, with more of this newfangled electronic equipment. That was it really. We went into Eden Studios in Chiswick, and I was a bit of a kid in a sweet shop really.

I'd been hanging out with the Scream a bit by that stage, and when they gave me a new track I kind of knew what they had been listening to, to come up with that track – "OK, that's a bit of that, a bit of that and a bit of that." So I then went and listened to those records I thought influenced the tracks. But I didn't have the musical or technical skills to accurately copy those records, which I think was a good thing. Some people accused it of being a record collector's kind of record, but it could have been a lot worse. If I was more technically adept at that time, it would have turned into a bit of a pastiche because I would have known how to copy those records more closely. As it was, I think it's an authentic approximation, and that's what makes it timeless and interesting; although it's very of the moment, it still resonates. It's a weird record. It's still sounds strangely modern, although there are certain sounds in it that date it a little bit. You could put your finger on it a little bit but then it would go somewhere else. If I had known how to get the snare sounding exactly like the records I was listening to, or the brass sounds, I don't think it would have been such a good record, personally speaking.

IRVINE WELSH, AUTHOR: I was at a really crap Christmas works do, an Edinburgh council works Christmas do, and this pal of mine said, "You've got to try this ecstasy." I hated the whole Christmas party thing so I thought I'd give it a go. After the party ended, we went on to Pure, which back then was UFO, Fiction and Brainstorm. Basically that night in Pure, I totally got it. It was a complete revelation and I just thought, "Fuck me, I could have done this two years ago." From that night I became a regular at Pure and a few of the other Edinburgh nights like Fever. I also used to go over to Glasgow for the Slam nights at The Arches, and Sub Club. Then I started going to The Haçienda and Back To Basics in Leeds. Then I became a regular at Sabresonic, Weatherall's club. I'd just go wherever there was a party and a club night happening. I just became obsessed with it, and lost in it for a few years.

★

Screamadelica reached number eight in the UK charts and won many accolades, including *Melody Maker*'s album of the year in 1991 and, in 1992, the first Mercury Music prize. It is widely accepted as a seminal album of the Nineties.

On a more commercial level, The Shamen and Mr. C were about to have their biggest hit, a track called 'Ebeneezer Goode', which was littered with thinly disguised drug references and was initially banned by the BBC.

MR. C: Colin was at a Synergy vs Decadence rave at the The Town & Country Club in Kentish Town [now known as The Forum]. Everybody was off their heads and this guy came up to Colin on the dance floor and put his hands on his shoulders and said, "Man, Es are good, Es are good." Colin started laughing, and I thought there's a song in there: "Es are good, Es are good... Es are... Ebeneezer... Ebeneezer Goode!" He said to me that night "Let's do a song called 'Ebeneezer Goode', about a Dickensian character. I want it to be a rap song." I said "OK, let's do it, but I want to do it in a cockney accent," which wasn't my normal accent – I wouldn't usually ham up a cockney accent.

I was under specific instructions from Colin to drop the 'h' in 'he' in every line. If you leave the 'h' in it's 'he' and it's about this guy, but if you take it away it's about ecstasy. So I wrote the verses then gave it to Colin, whose vocabulary is far greater than mine – he's a real intellect – and we sent them back and forth between us until we came up with the final draft. I knew as soon as we recorded the vocal we had a hit; I said to my friends, "This is going to be a number one hit."

It was a send-up of the rave community. It was a send-up of E culture, rather than a celebration of it. The Dickensian character of Ebeneezer Goode was a composite character of nine different people on the scene, including ravers, DJs, a lighting engineer, just a bunch of people who were complete lunatics on the scene. It had its warnings in there too like, "E's the kind of character that should never be abused, E's very much maligned and misunderstood." Of course people didn't get all that, they just got the chorus, "E's are good," and we became the evil acid house band promoting ecstasy. They didn't even get the verses – it's only years later after I explained about dropping the 'h' that most people get it. If you listen properly, it tells you from the first line, "There's a guy in the place, got a bitter sweet taste" – because E tastes bitter – "and E goes by the name of Ebeneezer Goode": that's telling you straight away that Ebeneezer Goode is ecstasy.

We did *Top Of The Pops* several times [in September 1992] and we always did the vocals live. Instead of rapping, "Has anyone got any salmon?" I said, "Has anyone got any underlay?" Next week I was on Radio 1 being interviewed by Mark Goodier, and he said, "Tell me about the drug references in 'Ebeneezer Goode'," and at first I said, "There's no drug references in 'Ebeneezer Goode'," denying it completely. Then

I said, "OK, 'Has anyone got any salmon?' means 'salmon and trout', which is mockney for snout or a cigarette, and 'Vera Lynn' means 'skins', so it's about making a spliff. 'Salmon' means nicotine, the government's drug, and hundreds of thousands of people are dying of lung cancer, so I apologise for promoting smoking, the government's drug." Then Mark Goodier said, "But on *Top Of The Pops* last week you said, 'Has anyone got any underlay?' What does that mean?" I said, "Oh, that's a rug reference." Hilarious. My finest moment.

It didn't surprise me when we went to number one Basically, from 1986 I knew I was going to be a house music pop star, as a rapper. I knew it. Everything I've done in my career has been based on meditation, creative visualisation and positive thinking, and I had mapped it all out. In 1986, I had actually had a vision of myself on *Top Of The Pops*. House music pop stars didn't exist in 1986, so I created this role. I wasn't hoping this would work out and I would become a house music pop star, I *knew* it was going to happen.

The kids these days have no idea who The Shamen are. You ask most kids in their early twenties these days, "Have you heard of The Shamen?" and they'd say, "No." They'd know The Prodigy, Underworld, The Chemical Brothers and all those bands we opened the door for, but if you ask them, "Have you heard of The Shamen?" they'll say, "No." But why should I care? It makes no difference to me. I've always reinvented myself, which is why I'm ahead of the game. My music is light years ahead of what's happening in the clubs now. What's happening in the clubs now is normal house music, my music is advanced.

IRVINE WELSH: My writing career starting taking off, and I was just spending most of my time in record shops. I started DJing and I was out in Ibiza for a couple of summers and was just completely obsessed with it. Eventually it got to the stage where it was taking over everything and I decided I had to either go right into it and give up on all the writing stuff, or just pull back, because it was just taking over. Especially when I started DJing, because when you're DJing you've got to be right on top of it, you've got to be playing records and listening to records all the time, and the writing was starting to suffer.

248

I think *Ecstasy* [Welsh's 1996 collection of three novellas] was one of my least favourite books because I wasn't giving it the kind of time I should have been doing. So it did take over, but the great thing about those days was I met so many fantastic people, and a lot of them are still close friends to this day. It was a great time for me. I'd been through punk, and been in a punk band and all that, so in a way acid house for me was like a second bite of the cherry. I'd gone from being this guy who kind of went out and got fucked up to living a kind of nine-to-five yuppie life with a mortgage and all that stuff. Acid house was like a second coming of craziness for me. It was also fascinating because all the things that punk was supposed to be about, acid house delivered.

That political side of hedonism was always interesting to me. Punk was like, "How do we kick the doors down and grab a piece of this, move all these old fuckers aside and take control a bit?", whereas acid house was more like, "Fuck all that, we don't want a part of any of it. We're going to go and do our own thing which is totally separate." Which was ultimately far more threatening to the establishment than if you were trying to join it or change it in some way.

★

While new people, like Welsh, were still discovering the scene, many of the early adopters felt a lot of the magic had already been lost.

MIKE PICKERING: It had all gone sour by this stage, but the very last straw for me was when The Haç was still open, and I had a knife pulled on me on The Haçienda's birthday. David Morales was playing that night and I remember him saying to me, "You've not got fed up of DJing have you... you'd never get fed up of DJing would you?" and I said, "Between you and me, there's a lot of trouble in there. A lot of gang trouble." I was still enjoying DJing all over the place, just not in the club I loved. Anyway, that night I was DJing upstairs and he was playing downstairs. I got a knife pulled on me by some little Salford kid. The top half of the DJ booth was open and he just took my beer, I said, "That's my beer," and he pulled a knife on me, so I just said, "You know what... have the fucking beer," and shut the door.

Meanwhile, someone had thrown a bottle downstairs that had smashed just behind David and the glass went over him and over the decks. I walked out and met him at the front door as he was walking out from downstairs, and I said, "I told you, didn't I?" and he just went, "Man, let's get the fuck out of here." We walked out of the front door of The Haçienda, and I never set foot in there again.

M People had taken off*, and I DJed at Renaissance a lot, and at Cream, but it was never the same for me. Imagine playing at a packed Wembley every week and then going to play at Stockport County.

Nothing could ever replace The Haçienda.

---

* Mike Pickering formed M People in 1990 with Paul Heard, Shovell and vocalist Heather Small. Their first album, *Northern Soul*, made their name, while their second album, *Elegant Slumming*, won the Mercury Music Prize. Their dance pop sound hit a chord with the record-buying public and they went on to have massive commercial success throughout the Nineties.

CHAPTER 11

The Legacy

"It changed a lot of people's lives for ever. It had a profound effect on anyone who experienced a night in a warehouse, a field, a basement or a club. It was an absolutely amazing experience for a whole generation."

Danny Rampling

PETER HOOK: Without Ian Curtis there would have been no Haçienda [the club was built with Joy Division/New Order/Factory's money], and without The Haçienda there would have been no Madchester. It changed the face of Manchester whether you like it or not. The whole indie music merging with dance music, the fashion, everything: it all came from The Haçienda. When I was in New Order I never took any notice of anniversaries. You were totally focused on New Order, so I never paid any notice to anything else. But since I split with them I've started taking more notice. I was talking to DJ Graeme Park and he said, "We've got to celebrate the 30th anniversary of The Haç because we're not going to be here for the 40th!" The people behind it, New Order manager Rob Gretton and Tony Wilson, aren't here, so

I decided to celebrate it.* I love everything we achieved. Tony Wilson, Rob Gretton, Ian Curtis, [producer] Martin Hannett – all these people should never be forgotten for what they did for Manchester. The rest of New Order should be proud, too, because without their investment this never would have happened. We lost a fortune but my accountant always tells me: "You'll never miss the millions you lost until you're skint," so it's a good incentive to keep working.

FIONA ALLEN: When Factory opened Dry Bar, what's now called the 'Northern Quarter' in Manchester didn't even exist – that part of town was the arse-end of nowhere at night but now it's the cultural heart of the city, and Dry Bar has been copied so many times.

I don't think hardly anyone appreciated the creative freedom Wilson and Factory gave people back then. If they've got any sense of perspective when they look back now, they must appreciate it. There was a massive scally movement in Manchester. I remember reading an interview with some minor member of a Factory band and they dismissed Wilson as a posh fucker, and I just thought, "You're just ignorant." Because he opened up a dead part of town, and a dead city as far as I'm concerned, and he made it the centre of the country, and the city is still trading off the back of that.

[He] took a chance on people and invested in them, personally and financially, when no one would have given them a chance. He made everyone believe they could do what they wanted to do. I don't know anybody else who would put up with the Happy Mondays, but he did, and great stuff came out of it.

MARK MOORE: I don't think kids nowadays quite get how revolutionary and countercultural it felt. It changed, and stopped being

---

* In 1999, Rob Gretton died at the age of 46 as a result of a heart attack. Tony Wilson developed renal cancer and, after a lengthy physical and financial battle (he was refused NHS funding for the drug Sitent) with the disease, he also died of a heart attack in 2007. The Union Flag on Manchester Town Hall was lowered to half mast upon news of his death. *24-Hour Party People* was a semi-autobiographical film based on Wilson's life, also documenting the rise of Factory Records.

about a holy sacrosanct where you knew you were going to go out and expand your consciousness and also have a fucking brilliant time. It became about just getting off your head, which was sad really. Originally we had viewed it as the spiritual sacrosanct, we were all going to go on a journey and we were going to have a fucking good time doing it, while we were being cosmic and spiritual about it. So I stopped talking drugs, and I would tell people in interviews, "Oh, I don't take drugs anymore," and they would all be like, "You *liar!*" and I'd say, "I *don't!*" Although admittedly that didn't last long.

The interesting kids today that I talk to seem to view the initial acid house explosion almost in the same mythical manner as we viewed the Sixties. I was talking to Adamski* recently and I said, "Isn't it funny at our age, being in this position where all these kids think we're cool?"

DAVE HASLAM: Breaking down social and musical barriers was an important part of what was achieved. In the late Eighties, courtesy of Thatcher, communities had been fragmented, ghettoised, marginalised; but on the Haçienda dance floor those divisions, that horrible selfishness, seemed to melt away. The best music revolutions have always been about synthesis – that's been the case ever since the birth of rock'n'roll; Elvis bringing together white country music and black rhythm & blues. We had that synthesis: influences, people, coming together.

DANNY RAMPLING: It changed a lot of people's lives for ever. The strength of the whole experience was more than just going to a club and listening to music. It changed a million mindsets. It had a profound effect on anyone who experienced a night in a warehouse, a field, a basement or a club. And people have enduring memories to this day, quite rightly so. It was an absolutely amazing experience for a whole generation. It completely deconstructed the way we were thinking back then. If you

---

* Adamski, aka Adam Timley, was an early British house producer who played at a lot of the early raves. His huge breakthrough hit, 'Killer', featured Seal on vocals (who went on to be a huge star in his own right) and spent four weeks at number one in May 1990.

look at youth culture now, it's just gang culture and violence and knives and just wasting that youthful energy. If only we could have it all again, because youth culture is screaming out for positive change. It really is.

NICKY HOLLOWAY: Sometimes you don't understand how important something is at the time, you only realise later. But acid house felt really important *while* it was happening. We all knew it was our Woodstock, our equivalent of the Sixties thing. We knew we were part of something that people would be talking about 25 years later, and here we are. It's amazing that most of the people who were part of the scene then are still making a living out of it now.

FIONA ALLEN: I remember the Hot nights [at the Hacienda] with the swimming pool were so absolutely incredible. It's so sad that something so creative and beautiful quickly got ruined and shut down because of the violence and greed of some people, and the situation between the gangs and the police.

To be honest, I had mixed emotions, even at the time. From being one long party it quickly changed and I found myself in situations I didn't want to be in, with people I didn't want to know, hearing about stuff I didn't want to know. It would be nice to remember the great bits without that awful downside, but I can't separate the two. When The Haçienda closed, they just had to shut it really, there was no option. It was such a shame. I just left town and moved to London.

ANDREW WEATHERALL: A lot of the people I met then are still working in the business, but that's the same as any burgeoning underground club scene: it attracts interesting and like-minded individuals who become your friends and colleagues later down the line. I love nightclubs and discos, but they're not *that* important to me – it's what happens afterwards. Being in a club is *so* of the moment – that's the only important, tangible moment, that second when you're hearing that record with those drugs coursing through your veins. The club or disco is so about the moment, which I love, but it's fleeting. To me it's more about who you meet and where you go *afterwards*. It's great when you're in a big crowd of people and the one thing you've got in common is you're in the same space, listening to the same music and you're on the same drugs, but what's more important to me is what have you got in common with those people when you're outside of that moment and that situation? That to me is what's always been more important. I went to clubs because I like to dress up and I like to meet like-minded people, but I want something outside of that. I don't live for the disco. The disco is a catalyst for me, it always was, even when I was a kid. It was just a catalyst or a manifestation of a much wider universe that I wanted to be involved in. That's what I've always thought, and I still think it to this day. I love clubbing and I love discos, but they're not that important. They are for those fleeting moments when you're on the dance floor, and those fleeting moments can turn into three or four hours, but for me they were always a catalyst or a manifestation of something much more interesting outside of that. What brings us all here? Why are we all on the same drug? Why are 200 people in a basement on a wet Thursday night? I love the fact that they're here, but I want to find out more about them. They're hearing me play music but I want to know about them, I want them to talk to me about books or art or something. That's when you find out who your friends are.

I think any club scene which has a new drug as a catalyst in its infancy is going to be creative. It's only when it gets abused… it's the same with any area of human life. Being the shaved, greedy chimpanzees we are, we want everything and we want it now. People become greedy for experience. The way I look at it, there's sacrament and hymn for religious people, or rock'n'roll or acid house and narcotics for secular people, but they're both manifestations of the same thing – the basic human desire to transcend yourself. We're no different. Whether it's religious or secular, you still have that same human desire. The problem is greed within that desire. Greed within religion leads to fundamentalism and all the social problems that brings, and greed within nightclubs and discos leads to addictions and all the social problems *that* brings. Both religion and secular celebration can be mind-expanding experiences, it's just the greed that can spoil things. Nightclubs, to me, are the flip side of the coin to people going to church on Sunday mornings.

That greed manifested itself quite quickly in acid house, and I was as greedy as anyone. I could see it manifested in myself. But that's the inherent tragedy of the human condition. It's that desire for exploration and ambition to push things forward which has taken us from flying 200 yards, 20 foot off the ground in 1903, to just over 60 years later flying someone to the moon. That brilliant human lust for experience and that urge to push things forward is the same human urge that has taken us from Molotov cocktails to the atomic bomb. It's that desire, lust and greed, which separates humans from the animals, but the human tragedy is the very thing that improves us will eventually destroy us.

BOY GEORGE: Acid house wasn't really political until the raves started and the police started clamping down on them, and people startling battling against the police. Then it became political because it felt like the authorities were trying to dictate what you should be doing. It was a really interesting, fascinating time. There was a real sense of excitement, of going to parties in the middle of nowhere that no one knew about. It's pretty impossible for a young kid to appreciate just how revolutionary it felt. You can get a flavour of what it felt like through the music, but if you weren't there it's hard to understand, just like it's hard for me to understand exactly what the psychedelic revolution felt like in the Sixties. But I think you have to be really careful not to come across as some old guy saying, "Oh, you've missed it all… back in the day," etc, etc.

I think dance music is still exciting, and probably as exciting now as it has been for a long time. There's lots of really great music being made. I've had my periods of cynicism, but at the moment it feels really exciting. When I first heard 'Lost In You' by Dusky, that to me feels like Soul II Soul. I'm a big black music fan, so when there's a lack of soul in the air that's when I start to get a bit worried: "Oh no, there's not enough soul around," but at the moment it feels like there has been a return to that. I'm told by those in the know that Radio 1 are obsessed with getting black artists on their playlist at the moment.

Obviously the internet now means everything gets swallowed up so quickly nowadays, particularly pop music and the charts, which have become even more disposable. But I think there's another life on the internet for things that are more quirky and interesting. There's so much music being made that some of it falls through the net and is waiting to be discovered. I've got friends all around the world now who send me tracks on a regular basis. If anything I think it's better than it's been for ages.

PAUL RUTHERFORD: The purity of the first explosion felt really intense. You could tell it was going to change music and it did change music, and it changed pop music. Its influence is really widely felt. The initial intensity was about three years long for me. But it made as much sense as punk to me, and I could definitely feel a shift in music, in the business and in culture.

Nothing has felt like that since to me, but I think part of that is because I'm a bit of an old twat, which I'm sure means my cultural antennae is slightly withered with age. But I do think everyone is too easily bought and sold nowadays; it's not about music anymore, it's about business.

MARTIN FRY, ABC: I remember Mark White [fellow member of ABC] looking at his record collection and saying, "I don't need any of this now, it's all about house music. I'm never going to listen to this stuff again." He was adamant about it and was going to chuck it all out. I said, "Wait a minute, what about Bowie?" and he said, "Forget Bowie. It's all about Ten City and Frankie Knuckles now." Which summed it up for me. For musicians like us, it was so radical.

I'd been going to The Haçienda since the day it opened, as I actually went to the opening night in May 1982. I was living in London and when acid house kicked off, I started drifting or gravitating back up there. Mike Pickering is a really old friend of mine and I used to drive up to The Haçienda some weeks on Wednesday for Hot and then Friday for Nude as well. Friday night in particular was incredible. Once I got friendly with people at Shoom, often a car full of us would drive up. It was a complete sea change, a whole new philosophy to going out. You were meeting different types of people in the clubs you hadn't come across before. I got really friendly with people at Shoom that I would never have met if it wasn't for acid house. Gay, straight, art students, terrace casuals, it didn't matter who you were. Anyone who made the effort to embrace it was welcome.

Shoom was the one for me though, really. I've still got a copy of the Shoom fanzine and a Shoom badge which says something like, 'It's started.' People used to make things for each other at Shoom and bring them each week, handmade things. It was really personal and friendly – I've never seen that at any other club, and it was absolutely sincere. You might think now that sounds ridiculous, "People bringing each other presents to a nightclub? *What?*" but it was very, very sincere. I think people had really had enough of what was going on in the outside world at that time. It was a youth movement. I was older than most people, I was in my late twenties, and it was definitely a youth movement.

DAVE HASLAM: There was a really naïve period of a few months where people were finding their feet, quite literally, and working out how to dance to this music. I suppose it's happening to a new generation in America now – they're working out how to rave, what to wear and how to dance.

JAZZY M: I think it was a two or three-year journey. It was a supernova explosion. Fuck me. I remember saying to people in 1988, "But it's not new! I've been playing it since '84, man!" But you know what, who cares really? I'm not sure how much the kids nowadays care. You try and tell them and most of them will be like, "Who? What? You're old, mate." I remember listening to my granddad or my uncles when I was young, telling me, "You don't know how good you've got it," and that was in the Seventies, when we didn't have it good at all, so they must have been Stone Age. Most of the kids don't get where it comes from. Even my own kids, my daughters who are 26 and 22, they grew up with me, and they don't even know the history really. They have an idea and they know I was a DJ, but if I sat them down and questioned them about what happened back in the day and how revolutionary it felt, they don't really know. But does our generation really know how revolutionary rock'n'roll felt when it first arrived in the Fifties? No, of course we don't.

We might love the music but there's no way we can appreciate just how revolutionary it felt. My youngest daughter's boyfriend, who is 21, is more interested in my history than she ever will be. Maybe it's a male thing, I don't know, but I've heard him say over dinner, "Jade, don't you know your dad is the godfather of house in the UK?" And she'll be like, "Yeah, I know, shut up." Even my own daughter!

There's definitely not been a revolution like it since. The internet has enhanced everything but it's also damaged everything. It's dismantled our ability to be individual. Everything is available at the click of a button, you don't need to create something yourself.

If I could go back with just one pound and invest it, knowing what I know now, I would be a millionaire, but that's only money. I have the richest feeling I could possibly ever have, which is the feeling of knowing you were part of something. That's something you can't buy. You'll never be able to buy that. Which is why I feel sorry for the following generations, that they haven't had anything as powerful. It's not because we lived through those days, it's because they lived through us. It was real, it *was* life, and without getting too deep, that's what's missing nowadays. The last thought on my mind at the time was what I was going to make out of this financially.

ANDREW WEATHERALL: Was it more important than punk or the Sixties? I don't know how you can compare, or make a league table. They were all right for their time. Music from the Fifties still resonates today, and there are plenty of people still listening to it, same with the Mods and the punks – they were all great catalysts that were right for their time and I'm not sure you can compare them because there were different social conditions. But they're all manifestations of that basic human need to transcend, which will never end. So I don't think you can put them in a league table of importance because they all have that basic human need behind them. The basic human needs are to reproduce, get shelter, eat food and also, I think, the need to transcend oneself. You don't put those in any order, you try and do them all at once, to stay alive.

We're still seeing the reverberations of acid house though, because the predominant pop sound is a dance/club-orientated sound, whether that's techno, dubstep or drum'n'bass, that's the sound across the world. But that's not just down to acid house. The biggest effect acid house had was not necessarily sociological but technological: dance music and electronic music is the biggest music in the world not because of acid house per se, but because acid spurred people on to make electronic music, which prompted people to make new drum machines and software. So it's more of a catalyst, if you like.

Punk rock was the first door opening; it was saying, "Anyone can do this." But you still had to go into a studio to make a record, so you still kind of had to have someone's permission. But with acid house all you needed was a drum machine and maybe a 303. You didn't have to ask anyone's permission to make music, to make art.

That led to the situation we are in now, where you can make and release music made on your laptop in your front room. Not even a laptop – you can now do it on a tablet. It's the ultimate punk rock dream come true. But there's also a bit of 'be careful what you wish for' because there's no quality control. Democratisation is great because everyone can do it, but on the other hand it's not great because everyone can do it. I'm sure if you went back and asked the old punks, they wouldn't be so keen on that situation. Punk rock opened the door and said anyone can do it, but acid house allowed everyone the *means* to go out and do it.

It changed a lot of people's lives for the good. Without acid house Terry Farley would still be a gas fitter and I'd still be a building site labourer or selling expensive slacks in the Shires. So it changed a lot of people's lives for the good, but it did change a lot of people's lives for the bad too. There are some people from back then that I still see out and about who are not in a good place, who I worry about. Any heady brew of hedonism, music and drugs is going to affect those who are heavily involved in it. I've managed to maintain a career – not a *career*, I hate that word, but maintain a job in it, while it destroyed other people. But such is the history of club culture since time immemorial. We think what we're doing is terribly modern, but this transcendence through drugs and music has been going on for hundreds of years. We can probably trace nightclubs as we know them back to the turn of the last century. The hedonism of the pre-First World War generation was probably as bad as anything we got up to. Every generation likes to think they're terribly modern and the first to do these things but believe me, they're not.

★

A year after Rob Gretton died, a memorial gig was organised at Manchester Ritz and I asked Tony Wilson and Peter Saville (designer of many Factory Record album sleeves) to discuss Rob's life and legacy in conversation. Saville suggested Rob and himself had taken advantage of a moment of cultural paralysis.

PETER SAVILLE, ART DIRECTOR/DESIGNER: So many people in 1976 saw an enormous change. With the establishment and youth culture there was a moment of paralysis, like those TV ads where everything around you is stationary. Lots of us stepped through to the other side at that point. Rob was one of them. He created a new life for himself as a band manager, and had to decide how to do it in this new world. Before that he'd had some tedious jobs in an office on Oxford Road.

★

The explosion of acid house was perhaps the last such moment of paralysis in British youth culture and that is one of its most enduring legacies. It was a brief period when a whole bunch of interlopers and renegades managed to slip through to the other side before the establishment, the authorities and the music industry caught up with them. As if the back door to what had previously been a private party had opened when no one was looking and a whole bunch of gatecrashers sneaked in. Once they were there, they set about changing the party from within.

ANDREW WEATHERALL: Part of me was scared at first at being identified as an interloper, but when you put it like that, it's a good thing. Sometimes gatecrashers are the ones who make the party happen. I've been at quite a few parties that were pretty fucking dull until the gatecrashers turned up, because they are the ones who generally turn up with the best drugs and the best women and a mixtape far better than whatever was already playing, and they go, "Fuck this, put *that* on."

We were never careerists. Careerists don't tend to come in the back door, they come in the front door with a bunch of flowers and an introductory note from a mutual Masonic acquaintance and are given a brief on the how the business works. We weren't like that. We came in the back door, like you say. So yeah, after 25 years I feel a lot prouder about being a gatecrasher.

SASHA: If you'd have told me back then that 25 years later people would still be talking about acid house, I wouldn't have been surprised because it did feel like a proper musical movement and a happening. But I would have been surprised if you'd told me I would still be making a career out of it. That would have shocked me. I never thought it was something that would last and be a lifelong career, I thought it was something that would be a laugh for a while and then I'd have to grow up and get a real job.

Maybe one day I will grow up.

Epilogue

It is a quarter of a century since acid house first exploded in the UK and its impact is more prevalent than ever. It has shaped British culture and influenced everything from fashion to film, television to interior design.* It redefined our fundamental notion of a night out, and it even changed the law** of the country.

But acid house didn't start out as anti-establishment. At first it was pro-hedonism, and if the establishment or authorities got in the way, ravers found increasingly ingenious ways of circumnavigating them. It only became anti-establishment when the establishment decided to use everything in its power to crush it. The scene was almost reluctantly politicised.

Rather, acid house was about the moment. It was a bubble of escapism from what, in contrast, seemed a mundane reality. Pre-internet, it was something that had to be experienced, and experienced collectively.

---

* Many bars in Manchester and further afield took their interior design lead from The Haçienda. Moreover, the prevalence of warehouse apartments in northern British cities, such as Manchester, can be at least in part attributed to the influence of acid house.

**The Criminal Justice and Public Orders Act, 1994.

As the acid house generation came of age, their Prime Minister told them "there is no such thing as society". 'Society' as an idea had been under attack for a decade, as Margaret Thatcher promoted her vision of a country of individuals with their own agendas. The fact that acid house culture proved her so wrong is perhaps what really concerned the government most. Authorities fear assembling masses, and they had never before seen a youth culture that could bring 30 or 40,000 people to a field in the middle of nowhere at short notice simply to dance.

Acid house had all the classic hallmarks of the youth revolutions that had gone before: the 'folk devil' causing moral panic similar to that ushered in by the punks, Mods and rockers. It also drew on all those cultures, sometimes quite directly – Tony Wilson, Rob Gretton and Alan Erasmus started Factory Records and later opened The Haçienda after seeing The Sex Pistols. But acid house was more egalitarian than any of those previous youth cultures. Student or gangster, gay or straight, black or white, young or middle-aged, hippie or football hooligan, car mechanic or chart-topping pop star: acid house did not discriminate.

Before acid house, a nightclub was the place revellers went to get drunk and, before the night was over, hopefully meet someone of the opposite sex. Or possibly fight someone of the same sex. Acid house, aided by the introduction of ecstasy, turned the nightclub into what it was supposed to be all along: a place to dance. Some have argued that ecstasy made the white man dance. But it made *everyone* dance. I don't think either of my parents ever took to the floor on their own in a nightclub – hardly any of their generation did. But the perfect storm of cutting-edge technology which brought music production to teenagers' bedrooms, a fresh genre of music and a new drug led a whole generation to lose its inhibitions on the dance floor.

Ecstasy also instigated another change: it's too simplistic to say that it (and acid house) cauterised the football violence festering like an open wound in English football at the time, but both were certainly major contributing factors. As the late, great Tony Wilson, co-founder of acid house beacon The Haçienda, said, "It's hard to fight someone you were hugging the night before."

But as with any hedonistic experience, some took it to the extreme. There was an innocence to the scene's first years which was inevitably lost. Ecstasy was always an integral part of the mix, but for a few the drug-taking engulfed everything else. The mood in the clubs changed as revellers graduated from ecstasy to cocaine, drawing the seedier aspects of drug culture on to the dance floor. Violence threatened to replace the love, stabbings replaced hugs.

While drug gangs smelled big money, the music industry smelled big business. Once acid house went overground, it is striking just how quickly it seeped into the mainstream, with the industry quick to capitalise. The scene hit the front pages of the tabloids and rapidly became part of the nation's psyche. By the mid Nineties it fed storylines in soap operas. While Thatcher's government had done everything in its power to clamp down on acid house during the late Eighties and beyond, when Tony Blair's New Labour party won the 1997 general election – bringing to an end 18 years of Tory government – it adopted D:Ream's 1994 rave anthem 'Things Can Only Get Better' as its victory song. Acid house parlance even seeped into the language. Royal Mail encouraged customers to post more letters with the ad campaign 'Get sorted' (slang for doing a drug deal). By the end of the Nineties, *Mixmag* declared, "Raving is as English as fish'n'chips."

When any youth culture is commercialised, it is always mourned by those who were there at the beginning. The tunnel-eyed drug dealer in *Withnail And I* moans, "They're selling hippy wigs in Woolworths, man. The greatest decade in the history of mankind is over…", just as many acid house innovators lamented when property developers turned their beloved Haçienda into a block of flats.

At the birth of acid house, the early DJs were renegades, outsiders. Now they're establishment figureheads. DJs have long played an integral part in pop history – Tom Wolfe referred to Murray The K* as "one of the new 'culture makers'" in his 1965 collection of essays,

---

* Murray Kaufman was an influential American DJ and music industry figure during the Fifties, Sixties and Seventies. He was the first DJ to welcome The Beatles to the USA and became firm friends with John, Paul, George and Ringo..

The Kandy-Kolored Tangerine-Flake Streamline Baby – but acid house turned them into superstars. The most successful DJs no longer just play records; they're producers, songwriters, label owners, entrepreneurs and recording artists in their own right. Paul Oakenfold, one of the earliest acid house converts and founder of Spectrum, started in a scruffy venue on Streatham High Street before graduating to touring with Madonna. He now has a residency in Las Vegas, which in previous times would have gone to the likes of Elton John or Dolly Parton.

But one thing has remained the same: meeting these ravers 25 years on, the sense of community is still strong. Many of the friendships struck on the dancefloor exist to this day, outliving some marriages and jobs. Acid house was such a departure from what had gone before, both musically and socially, that it felt like a clean slate. And for almost all who experienced it, the 'Second Summer Of Love' has since influenced their lives to varying degrees. Many ravers found a way to make a living out of the culture – not just the DJs and promoters, but graphic designers, fashion designers, or in some more illicit cases, drug dealers. Some have moved on. Some have struggled to move on. All still hold the moment dear. For many, the acid house peak is a high they'll never match. A few years after Manchester United won the unprecedented treble in 1999 – a high they have also since failed to replicate (and one they are unlikely to) – impassioned Reds hung a banner in Old Trafford that read, 'If I hadn't seen such riches I could live with being poor.' It's a sentiment with which those who experienced the euphoria of the initial acid rush can wholeheartedly empathise.

Many of those interviewed here bemoan the fact that there is no longer a gestation period allowing a scene to develop a real identity. Youth culture has become such a commodity that 'professional trendspotter' is now a career choice. Those promoters organising raves 25 years ago would have killed to have smartphones, Twitter and Facebook at their disposal. But if Shoom started tomorrow, it would be on YouTube the following morning and replaced with the 'Next Big Thing' a few days later. Youth cultures, and nightclubs in particular, are cyclical in their nature: a scene starts in a dirty basement or warehouse and evolves, ascending to the opulent superclubs, where the over-commercialisation in turn inspires a return to basics and a more intimate experience. Yet in the quarter-century since acid house drove a generation to the dancefloor, the UK has not seen an explosion of youth culture on the same scale, and it's possible we may never again.

Every generation of teenagers wants to believe their time has come, that they are living through exciting times. But that usually fades with age. Talking to the main protagonists of the acid house generation, the feeling towards what they experienced 25 years ago has only ever grown stronger.

Acknowledgements

Huge thanks to all of those who took the time to be interviewed for this book, or helped with research and/or tracking down the original protaganists, some of whom had disappeared to India or Thailand and had not been heard of for a long while.

Special thanks, as ever, to the late great Anthony Wilson. Plus Robert Leo Gretton, Alan Erasmus, Joy Division, New Order, Mike Pickering, Leroy Richardson and everyone else connected with Factory Records and The Haçienda. Paul Mason, Jon DaSilva, Graeme Park, Jon Drape, Bobby Langley, Billy Caldwell and Fiona Allen.

I owe a huge debt to those who have inspired, aided and abetted me, both over the years and in the research for this book, including all of the above, plus Shaun William Ryder, Arthur Baker, Irvine Welsh, Steve Geese, The Adg, John The Duck, Eric Barker, The Spinmasters ("shout going out"), Graham Massey and 808 State, Gerald Simpson, Chris Jam, Kermit, Chris and Anthony Donnelly, 'Kid' Batchelor, Mark Moore, Noel Watson, Greg Wilson, Cymon Eckel, Terry Farley, Andrew Weatherall, Steve Hall and everyone connected with *Boy's Own*, Trevor Fung, Alfredo, Danny Rampling, Bill Brewster, Jazzy M, Timna Rose, Nicky Holloway, Anton Le Pirate, Winston and Parrot, Luke Unabomber, Justin Unabomber, Moggsy and everyone connected with Electric Chair, Darren Greene, the Habits, Johnno, Paul Benney, Fiona Bowker and everyone connected with Bugged Out, Steve Smith, Chris York, Emma Warren, Darren Laws, Justin Robertson, Paul Mardles, Greg Fenton, Richard Hector-Jones, Jane Hector-Jones, Jeff Barrett, Robin Turner, John Niven, Moonboots, Jason Boardman, John McCready, Dave Haslam, Chris Sharratt, Rachel Newsome, Sarah Champion, Paul Flynn, Steve Tagger, Nick Cooper, Marcus Graham, Phil Griffin, Hana Borrowman, Andrea Ahimie and everyone connected with City Life, Bruce Mitchell, Suddi Raval, Ken Tappenden... and those who preferred their name to be kept out of print – you know who you are.

Thanks to Caspar Llewellyn-Smith and *Observer Music Monthly*. Interviewing some of the protagonists included here for an *OMM* feature on the 20th anniversary of acid house sowed the seed for this book.

Huge thanks to Matthew Hamilton at Aitken Alexander Associates and David Barraclough and Lucy Beevor at Omnibus Press.

Thanks to my mum and dad, the old ravers.

And finally to all those I've met on the dancefloor over the years. Keep the faith.

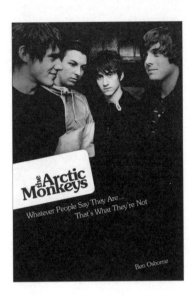

ARCTIC MONKEYS
What People Say They Are, They Are Not
by Ben Osborne

Coming ten years after the group's inception, *Whatever People Say They Are, They're Not* is the first comprehensive biography of Arctic Monkeys, the supreme British group of the internet age.

It's the story of a talented group of hip-hop loving school friends from Sheffield who entered the music scene just in time to become the first band to be propelled to stardom by online community groups. They qualified as the fastest-selling British group ever, with all four of their albums going straight to Number One.

Ben Osborne's biography charts the band's early years in the suburbs and their fast-track success as *Arctic Monkeys*. He identifies the sometimes low-profile people who helped shape the band's music and career — a career whose high spot to date has been a performance to an audience of over 27 million at the 2012 Olympics.

Ben Osborne is a writer, DJ, musician and founder of the Noise of Art art collective. He has presented an electronic music show on Xfm, was one of the original presenters on NME Radio and has written for The Guardian *and* The Times *amongst others titles. He is the author of* The A-Z of Club Culture, *a critically acclaimed book about electronic music.*

Available from **www.omnibuspress.com**

ISBN: 978.0.85712.859.1
Order No: OP54901

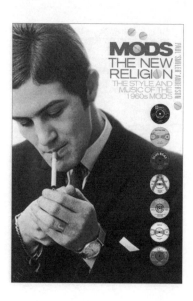

MODS
The New Religion
by Paul Anderson

Mod may have been born in the ballrooms and night clubs around London but it soon rampaged across the country like a speed-fuelled plague. Young kids found a passion for sharp clothes, music and dancing, although for some the pills, thrills and violence were much more important.

Now, at long last, the original Mod generation tell it exactly how it was, in their own words. First-hand accounts from top faces, scooterboys, DJs, promoters and musicians build up a vivid snapshot of what it was really like to be in with the in-crowd.

Packed with rare photographs, ephemera, art and graphics of the era and featuring interviews with Eddie Floyd, Martha Reeves, Ian McLagan, Chris Farlowe and many more, Paul Anderson's book really is the last word on all things MOD.

"Mods: The New Religion *is the book you need to know about the real Mod scene… and the nearest you can get to a Mod Bible.*" – Steve Ellis (Sixties Mod and Lead Vocalist of The Love Affair)

Available from **www.omnibuspress.com**

ISBN: 978.1.78038.549.5
Order No: OP54780

MORRISSEY & MARR
The Severed Alliance
by Johnny Rogan

Morrissey & Marr: The Severed Alliance is among the most successful – and controversial – rock biographies ever published. Having denounced the book and called for the death of its author Johnny Rogan, Morrissey later did a U-turn and cited it as evidence in the royalty-related court case brought by Smiths drummer Mike Joyce.

Now, 20 years after it was first published, Rogan has returned to his definitive Smiths biography to produce a completely revised edition based on new information and new interviews to add to the almost 100 initially conducted over a four-year period.

Widely acclaimed as one rock's leading writers, Johnny Rogan now brings yet more insight and analysis to his best-selling book that revealed, for the first time, the true and unsanitised story of The Smiths – the most important group of their generation.

Reviews of the original edition:

"A hugely readable and fascinating book... flawlessly informed. A superb achievement." ***** *Q* magazine.

"A major achievement" – *New Musical Express*

"A bloody marvellous book" – *Melody Maker*

"A page-turner of the first degree" – *The Sunday Telegraph*

"Personally I hope Johnny Rogan ends his days very soon in an M3 pile-up" –
Mor*rissey*

Available from **www.omnibuspress.com**

ISBN: 978.0.58712.128.8
Order No: OP54428

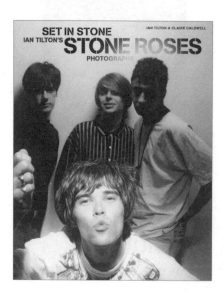

SET IN STONE
Ian Tilton's Stone Roses Photographs

Set In Stone is a brilliant photo record of the legendary Stone Roses who helped define the exuberant mood of the 'Madchester' movement in the late 1980s. They played some unforgettable concerts, recorded two albums and eventually split in 1996.

Photographer Ian Tilton knew them from the start and was along for the ride. His pictures document every key moment in the hectic first life of a band that eventually reunited at the end of 2011.

From their first TV appearance to the famous Spike Island gig, Tilton's photos caught the spirit of the band and the flavour of the times. The best of those vibrant pictures have been collected here and are presented along with comprehensive background notes to each photo session.

Ian Tilton is an award-winning theatrical photographer based in north-west England. He began his career in the Eighties taking photos of acts that included Guns N' Roses and Iggy Pop, as well as The Stone Roses. His famous shot of an exhausted and tearful Kurt Cobain was hailed by Q magazine as one of the six best rock photographs of all time.

Available from **www.omnibuspress.com**

ISBN: 978.0.85712.785.3
Order No: VO10549